FINDING YOUR
ROOTS

FINDING YOUR ROOTS

Easy-to-Do Genealogy and Family History

JANICE SCHULTZ

an imprint of the American Library Association

HURON STREET PRESS

CHICAGO · 2013

JANICE SCHULTZ retired in 2013 as the genealogy librarian/branch manager of the Midwest Genealogy Center of the Mid-Continent Public Library, where she worked for twenty-six years. Over the years, Ms. Schultz has served the American Library Association's Reference and User Services Division as the history section chair, the genealogy committee chair, and the local history chair. She is currently president of the Missouri State Genealogical Association. Ms. Schultz frequently teaches genealogy classes at the Midwest Genealogy Center and in the local community. She has lectured at genealogy conferences throughout the state, at the Missouri Library Association Conference, and at the American Library Association's annual conference. Some of her classes are available at www.mymcpl.org/genealogy/online-presentations.

Published by Huron Street Press, an imprint of ALA Publishing
Printed in the United States of America
17 16 15 14 13   5 4 3 2 1

Extensive effort has gone into ensuring the reliability of the information in this book; however, the publisher makes no warranty, express or implied, with respect to the material contained herein.

ISBNs: 978-1-937589-00-4 (paper); 978-1-937589-23-3 (PDF). For more information on digital formats, visit the ALA Store at alastore.ala.org and select eEditions.

Library of Congress Cataloging-in-Publication Data

Schultz, Janice Lindgren.
    Finding your roots : easy-to-do genealogy and family history / Janice
    Lindgren Schultz.
       pages cm
    Includes bibliographical references and index.
    ISBN 978-1-937589-00-4
     1. United States—Genealogy—Handbooks, manuals, etc. 2. Genealogy.
  I. Title.
  CS47.S38 2012
  929.1072'073—dc23   2012016804

Cover design by Karen Sheets de Gracia. Image © Iozas/Shutterstock, Inc.
Text design in Chapparal and Caecilia by Kimberly Thornton.

♾ This paper meets the requirements of ANSI/NISO Z39.48–1992 (Permanence of Paper).

contents

Perhaps you have a mysterious person in your family's background. Now is a great time to find out about that person—or any other unknowns in your lineage. When I began my genealogy research in 1987, it was all about microfilm, books, periodicals, and postage stamps. While the basics of genealogy research have not changed, the tools have. Today your genealogy is as close as your Internet connection. There is a plethora of material waiting for you—you just need to know where to find it. This book will help you discover the resources available and give you ideas on where to search.

In the book I refer frequently to Ancestry.com and Ancestry Library Edition. The Library Edition is a product of Ancestry.com that is available to users in libraries. If I refer simply to Ancestry or Ancestry.com I am referring to Ancestry Library Edition as well. Ancestry also owns Fold3 (formerly Footnote.com). Fold3 is available to both the library market and the general public. I also mention FamilySearch often. It is a web page of the Family History Library in Salt Lake City, Utah. The Family History Library is owned by the Church of Jesus Christ of Latter Day Saints (Mormon). I discuss many websites in depth throughout the book, but these come up more than others. I also mention many book titles. With only a few exceptions, the books I mention can be found in the stacks of my library and on the shelves of other genealogy organizations.

By profession I am a librarian, though my degree from the University of Missouri is in Information Science and Learning Technologies. Some feel *librarian* to be an archaic term, but I am proud to bear the moniker. For twenty-six years, I worked at the Midwest Genealogy Center of the Mid-Continent Public Library System, which has thirty branches in Jackson, Clay, and Platte counties in Missouri. Under the tutelage of my predecessor, Martha Henderson, I learned the basics of genealogy. She encouraged me to attend genealogy conferences, where I gained even more knowledge about this fascinating subject. Even now, as a volunteer, working through tough genealogy problems with patrons and working with my top-notch staff at the Midwest Genealogy Center provides challenges and opportunities for growth.

The administration and board of Mid-Continent Public Library were enormously supportive, facilitating my attendance at genealogy and professional conferences and my participation in committee work.

Another tremendous asset has been my association with other genealogy librarians around the country through my work in the History Section of the Reference and User Services Association of the American Library Association. I have learned a lot from each of them, and I know I can call on any of them with difficult genealogy questions.

This book owes its existence in part to Ray Wright's masterful *Genealogist's Handbook* (published by ALA Editions in 1995). I am indebted to Ray for recommending me to Michael Jeffers, publisher at ALA Editions. Readers familiar with *The Genealogist's Handbook* may find sections of chapter 1 reminiscent of that book's first chapter; these are all that remain of my early attempts at revision. I originally intended to update Ray's book, but what emerged from my work was something entirely my own.

This book will take you on a journey of genealogy from an American standpoint, beginning with the basics of genealogy in the United States and then delving into foreign research. I hope that you will both enjoy the pages to come and find the information you need to begin your own genealogy research. Genealogy is a fun and addicting hobby—enjoy the ride!

chapter one

Getting Started
Do You Know Who You Are?

IF YOU ARE READING THIS BOOK FOR THE FIRST TIME, YOU ARE EITHER new to genealogy (if so, welcome to the world of genealogical research!) or perhaps you want a refresher in genealogical research. Then again, you may be an avid genealogist devouring all you can read on the subject. Whatever the reason, I hope this book can be of help to you. Genealogy is more popular now than ever before. Since the 1970s, Americans have been trying to discover who they are. Not in the sense of physical or philosophical attributes, but, rather, in wanting to know their origins. The wealth of information on the Internet has made the pursuit easier, but the desire to begin the trek is varied. Your interest might stem from religious reasons. If you are in the oldest generation in your family, you may want to find the answers to questions everyone else in the family is asking. Now that many of the baby boomers are becoming the oldest generation, many are seeking some answers to such questions as: "What was Grandmother's maiden name?" or "What nationality are we?" When relatives start asking those questions, the desire for knowledge begins. When the desire for information coincides with added leisure time during retirement, genealogy becomes an active pursuit.

We are a nation of immigrants, and many of us are far removed from our immigrant ancestors and thus far removed from the names and stories of those ancestors. In the United States, the most recent burst of interest in family origins coincided with the bicentennial celebration of our nation's founding and with the publication of Alex Haley's *Roots*.[1] The subsequent presentation of *Roots* on network television in the form of a miniseries added to its impact. Libraries, archives, and historical and genealogical societies were amazed by the increasing number of researchers wanting to trace their family history. In 2010, Americans saw the first airing of *Who Do You Think You Are?*, a network television show that followed famous personalities in search of their ancestry. First aired in England by the BBC in 2004, *Who Do You Think You Are?* took Great Britain by storm. The show's popularity spawned similar broadcasts in other countries, including the United States. Henry Louis Gates Jr. also used celebrities in filming *Faces of America* on PBS. When genealogy hit prime time, another surge of interest hit libraries and archives as well as the Internet, and another generation of genealogists was born.

Who am I? Where did I come from? It is the search for the answers to these questions that helps us discover who we are. Somehow we feel our own identity is linked to that of our ancestors. When we are young, our identity is linked to the smaller world of our parents, grandparents, siblings, aunts, uncles, and cousins. Much of our security and even a sense of family pride depend on our relationships with these people. As we age, our world becomes wider. We learn that, in addition to our living relatives, we have family who are now long deceased. Curiosity about older generations is but an extension of our search for identity and security.

Learning about history also sensitizes us to family history. I recently visited the World War I museum in Kansas City, Missouri, and I began to wonder about my own family's participation in that war. We read about wars, economic hard times, epidemics, and other historical events and wonder how our family fits in. Sometimes answers come as we sit around picnic tables at family reunions or at weddings and funerals as we visit with relatives. As grandparents, aunts, uncles, and parents reminisce about the past, children begin to learn the folklore or legends of their family. However, in today's mobile and disjointed world, children often don't know their near kinfolk, let alone the identity of both of their parents. Often the answers to questions about ancestors' lives and roles come only through discovering those relatives in books and original records.

Learning about our ancestors helps us understand ourselves better. We discover inherited traits that affect our own personality or health. Knowing that our hair or eye color and many other traits were influenced by ancestors helps us recognize how firmly tied we are to past generations. This link to the past provides a measure of stability in a world filled with transient values and heroes. Our research may also benefit us by providing an early warning of health problems we or our children could inherit that might be avoided by taking timely precautions.

> The Surgeon General has created an online tool for recording family health history to share with one's relatives. Entitled *My Family Health Portrait*, the feature can be accessed at https://familyhistory.hhs.gov/fhh-web/home.action.

WHERE DO I BEGIN?

In this chapter you will learn the basics of beginning a genealogy project:

- Write down everything you already know (birth, death, and marriage information—also called vital records) about yourself, your parents, grandparents, and so on.
- Ask your family members for information about themselves or their parents, grandparents, and so on.
- Look for documents in your own home or in the possession of your relatives.
- Search out documents that tell more about your ancestors in books, in original records, and on web pages.

Genealogy, simply defined, is the study of one's family origins. More specifically, it is the history of a line of descent of a person, family, or group of ancestors. This history can also be called *ancestry*. In genealogy we seek to find ancestors. *Ancestors* are those family members who came before you. Your parents, grandparents, and great-grandparents are your ancestors. You are a descendant of those ancestors. A *descendant* is one who comes after someone else. Your children and grandchildren and great-grandchildren are your descendants. A record of your ancestors is called a *pedigree*.

As any genealogist will tell you, the quest to find your ancestors starts with yourself. You then go from the present to the past, recording the names of each generation on an ancestor (or pedigree) chart or into a genealogy software program. (Genealogy software programs are discussed later in this chapter.) Begin by identifying family members you already know. When using a printed chart (see figure 1.1), it is best to use a pencil to record the information.

1. Write your full name: first, middle, and last name (also called a *surname*). If you are a woman, record your maiden name as your surname. All the women in your pedigree will be recorded with their maiden names, and all surnames should always be recorded in all uppercase letters.
2. Write down the date and place of your birth and the date and place of your marriage (if appropriate).
3. Next write down the full name of your father. On a numbered pedigree chart you are number 1 and your father is number 2. Males from this point forward will be the even-numbered people on your chart. The females will be the odd-numbered individuals. Record the name of your father, his place and date of birth (if known), the date and place of his marriage to your mother (if a marriage occurred), and the date and place of his death (if appropriate).
4. Your mother will be next. She will be number 3 on your chart. Record her full maiden name. Again, write down the appropriate known information of her birth and death. You will note that on a printed pedigree chart, the date and place of marriage is not shown under the mother's name. It is recorded only under the father's name.
5. Continue to go back in time, recording the full name of each individual ancestor—first, middle, and last names. Record the

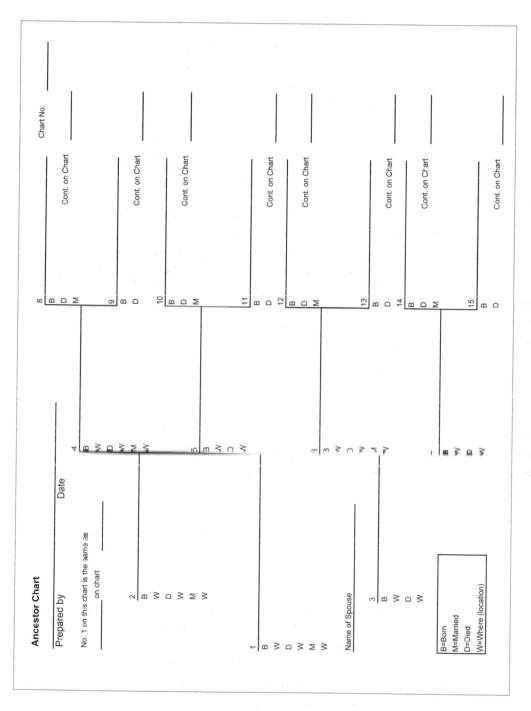

Figure 1.1 Sample ancestor chart

dates and places of births, deaths, and marriages, where known. The information you are lacking for individuals and the names of ancestors in past generations will soon be noticeable and will be the information you will seek in your genealogical research. (See the completed chart in figure 1.2.)

6. In a traditional pedigree, the names you will be recording are the names in your blood line. If you were adopted you can choose to record your adoptive family if that is most meaningful to you, but your biological family is your true pedigree.

Note the pedigree of Harry Truman in figure 1.2. Mr. Truman was born 8 May 1884. Genealogists often record the date European style—day, month, and year. Whatever style you choose in recording the information, make sure that you spell out the name of the month. Writing out the name of the month will eliminate confusion should you choose to write the date format differently than another person might read it. On a Swedish church record my grandfather's birth is recorded as 10-12-82. He was born on the 10th of December in 1882 (European style), not the 12th of October as some Americans might think. It could have caused a problem for me when I recorded the information into my pedigree, but because I already knew when he was born I was not confused. But you don't want to confuse others looking at your pedigree, so do them a favor and write out the name of the month. It is also important to include four digits for the year in which the event occurred. You will be looking for your ancestors' information in records from various centuries, so don't confuse the situation for others who might look at the information later.

Going back to figure 1.2, you will note that all of Harry Truman's vital information is recorded—birth, death, and marriage. His wife's name is included as "spouse," but her pedigree and vital information are not shown.

Harry Truman's father was John Anderson Truman, number 2 on the chart. His mother, Martha Ellen Young, is number 3. Harry's paternal grandfather, his father's father, is two times two, or number 4. His father's mother is two times two plus one, or number 5. Each person's father's number is double the number given that person on the chart, and the mother's number is doubled plus one. Should the researcher

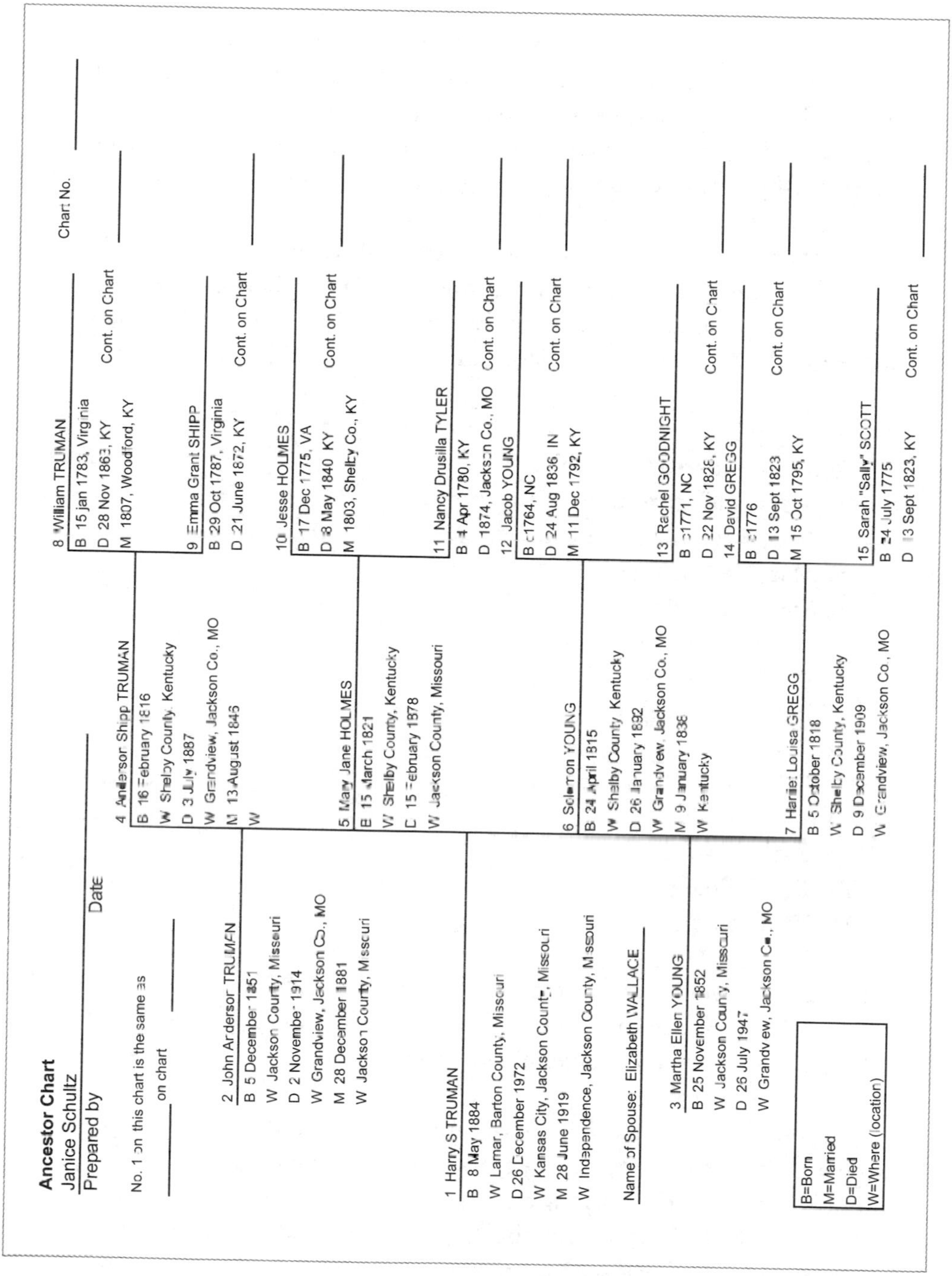

Ancestor Chart

Janice Schultz

Prepared by _____ Date _____

No. 1 on this chart is the same as _____ on chart _____

Name of Spouse: Elizabeth WALLACE

1 Harry S TRUMAN
B 8 May 1884
W Lamar, Barton County, Missouri
D 26 December 1972
W Kansas City, Jackson County, Missouri
M 28 June 1919
W Independence, Jackson County, Missouri

2 John Anderson TRUMAN
B 5 December 1851
W Jackson County, Missouri
D 2 November 1914
W Grandview, Jackson Co., MO
M 28 December 1881
W Jackson County, Missouri

3 Martha Ellen YOUNG
B 25 November 1852
W Jackson County, Missouri
D 26 July 1947
W Grandview, Jackson Co., MO

4 Anderson Shipp TRUMAN
B 16 February 1816
W Shelby County, Kentucky
D 3 July 1887
W Grandview, Jackson Co., MO
M 13 August 1845
W

5 Mary Jane HOLMES
B 15 March 1821
W Shelby County, Kentucky
D 15 February 1878
W Jackson County, Missouri

6 Solomon YOUNG
B 24 April 1815
W Shelby County, Kentucky
D 26 January 1892
W Grandview Jackson Co., MO
M 9 January 1838
W Kentucky

7 Harriet Louisa GREGG
B 5 October 1818
W Shelby County, Kentucky
D 9 December 1909
W Grandview, Jackson Co., MO

8 *William TRUMAN
B 15 Jan 1783, Virginia
D 28 Nov 1862, KY
M 1807, Woodford, KY
Cont. on Chart _____

9 Emma Grant SHIPP
B 29 Oct 1787, Virginia
D 21 June 1872, KY
Cont. on Chart _____

10 Jesse HOLMES
B 17 Dec 1775, VA
D 8 May 1840 KY
M 1803, Shelby Co., KY
Cont. on Chart _____

11 Nancy Drusilla TYLER
B 4 Apr 1780, KY
D 1874, Jackson Co., MO   Cont. on Chart _____

12 Jacob YOUNG
B c1764, NC
D 24 Aug 1836 IN
M 11 Dec 1792, KY
Cont. on Chart _____

13 Rachel GOODNIGHT
B c1771, NC
D 22 Nov 1826, KY
Cont. on Chart _____

14 David GREGG
B c1776
D 13 Sept 1823
M 15 Oct 1795, KY
Cont. on Chart _____

15 Sarah "Sally" SCOTT
B 24 July 1775
D 13 Sept 1823, KY
Cont. on Chart _____

Chart No. _____

Figure 1.2 Completed ancestor chart

7

decide to continue recording names in the Truman line after William Truman, number 8 on the chart, then another chart would be prepared with William Truman appearing on line 1 of the second chart. The first chart would be chart number 1 and the second would be chart number 2. At the top of the second chart, the researcher would write "No. 1 on this chart is the same as No. 8 on chart 1."

Another way to record the pedigree is on an Ahnentafel chart. *Ahnentafel* is the German word meaning "ancestor table." It is a very easy, basic way of organizing your family pedigree. In the Harry Truman example, the Ahnentafel would look like this:

1. Harry Truman
2. John Anderson Truman
3. Martha Ellen Young
4. Anderson Shipp Truman
5. Mary Jane Holmes
6. Solomon Young
7. Harriet Louisa Gregg
8. William Truman
9. Emma Grant Shipp
10. Jesse Holmes
11. Nancy Drusilla Tyler
12. Jacob Young
13. Rachel Goodnight
14. David Gregg
15. Sarah Scott

The numbers would continue for as many generations as there is information. You may see charts like this as you look at other people's genealogy. Knowing what those numbers mean will help you understand the information presented.

As you enter information into the ancestor chart, what you think you know may or may not be correct. I always use a pencil when entering information onto my working sheet to make changes easier. Whenever data for individuals is lacking, the discovery of the life events for those people becomes the research objective: Where and when were they born, and to whom and when were they married? What were their lives like? Who were their parents? By making the discovery of information

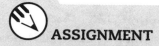

ASSIGNMENT

Fill in a blank pedigree chart with as much information as you already know. You may copy the blank pedigree chart found in this book (figure 1.1) or download a form from the Internet:

www.ancestry.com/trees/charts/ancchart.aspx
www.mymcpl.org/genealogy/family-history-forms

about a specific person your research goal, you define the scope of your efforts in terms of the time period and locality. This is where you will begin your search—wherever you see blanks in your pedigree.

GENEALOGY OR FAMILY HISTORY?

Because this book is designed for both the genealogist and the family historian, the terms *genealogy* and *family history* will often be used interchangeably. No parts of this book apply only to genealogists or to family historians. The main goal for any researcher should be to produce a family history that is based on sound genealogical research and that interprets ancestors' lives in terms most readers will understand. Even though both terms are used in this text, each has its own definition and its own field of study. However, we can serve our families best when we master the skills of both disciplines.

Genealogy, as it has already been defined, is the study of a person's lineage. As shown previously, we search out the names of parents, grandparents, and great-grandparents and list them on a chart. We then continue to search for the names of the children of each generation as well as the persons these children married. Because names are often repeated in each generation, dates and places of events help define each individual. A genealogy, in its truest sense, identifies ancestors or descendants by showing their names, event dates, event places, and relationships.

Family history, on the other hand, is a study of our ancestors' or descendants' lives. Once the family historian has reconstructed a family using names, dates, and places, he or she then searches for stories, artifacts, records, social history, and other information that describe the activities of family members. Family history explores how people interacted with other family and community members, how they earned a living, and what they believed. Family historians search for any resource that will permit them to reconstruct their ancestors' lives and the world in which they lived. Within a family history, our forebears become defined not only in terms of names, dates, and places but also by what they did during their lives. This book is for genealogists and family historians interested in learning about specific families. It focuses on how to find records about specific ancestors and use this information to extend lineages as well as to reconstruct forebears' lives.

Trying to define genealogy becomes increasingly complex in today's society. In July 2011, the *New York Times* printed an article entitled, "Who's on the Family Tree? Now It's Complicated."[2] The author points out the difficulty of defining relationships, family, and genealogy with children born via sperm donors, surrogate mothers, and same-sex partners as parents. "Some families now organize their family tree into two separate histories: genetic and emotional." In its truest sense, *genealogy* has been defined as tracing blood lines. Although that definition may not be always true today, in this book *genealogy* will be defined in its strictest sense.

BEYOND GENEALOGIES

Genealogists often become collectors of names. The sole pursuit of names of ancestors does little to acquaint us with those forebears and the world in which they lived. Knowing the facts of birth, marriage, and death seldom satisfies the drive to relate our lives to the experiences of our progenitors. That is where family history comes in: it is the study of how ancestors lived and their relationships with people and institutions. The pursuit of family history helps us completely understand the names on our pedigree as individuals. Compiling our genealogy is the first step in discovering the history of our family.

Until the late 1970s, few genealogies told the story of a family. Most consisted of traditional lineage and ancestor or descendant charts. During the past thirty-plus years, more and more books have used genealogies as frameworks upon which to stretch the fabric of individual and family lives or family history. These publications are devoted to describing, interpreting, and comparing ancestors' lives with those of their contemporaries and of their descendants—us.

Family historians find out about ancestors' lives from interviews, family records, and other documents that teach us how wars, financial depressions, racial unrest, strikes, riots, and elections changed or did not change the lives of our forebears. Knowing about our ancestors' health, the size and structure of their families, and how long they lived or from what they died will also help us understand them. Our ancestors were not passive observers; they were involved in the world around them—in local politics, in strikes against employers, and in controversies over religious or racial issues. Where did they stand and how did they act out their feelings? Answers to these questions will help us understand history from a personal perspective seldom presented in textbooks. To learn even more, we can compare our ancestors' lives to those of their neighbors and even to those of their contemporaries in other parts of the country. Like us, our progenitors were the products of their own place and time in history. We cannot relate to them unless we understand what life was like in their day.

RESOURCES FOR GENEALOGY AND FAMILY HISTORY RESEARCH

The Records

The major obstacle to finding ancestors is knowing where to look for records about their lives. Sometimes records can be found at home or with relatives. Often we need to search books and records preserved in libraries, archives, historical societies, or government offices. Many documents, both digitized copies of the original and transcribed records, can be found on the Internet. Wherever you look, the goal of your search will be an understanding of the places your ancestors lived and the roles of local institutions in their lives, as revealed through the records of your ancestors' interactions with these local agencies.

Generally speaking, you will search among three types of records to reconstruct your family's history: family records, the research results of others, and original records. These records may be found in someone's personal possession, in a records repository, in a research facility, or on the Internet. Each of these record types is explained in greater detail in subsequent chapters. In this chapter, the terms are introduced to help you better understand the process of re-creating your ancestors' lives.

Your research begins in the records you and other family members have. You should also conduct a survey to discover what other researchers have published or contributed to genealogical indexes, computer databases, or the Internet about your family. Finally, you fill in the remaining gaps in your family's story by using original records such as censuses and birth, marriage, or death records.

FAMILY RECORDS

Family records are the certificates, heirlooms, stories, and other bits of family history found in the homes and memories of relatives. They include the oral histories you gather by interviewing family members and their friends, neighbors, and coworkers. Although some people may have gaps in their memories of the past, much of what they tell you may be true. Oral records must be evaluated for accuracy as must any other sources you use.

PUBLISHED RECORDS

When researchers take information from original and oral records, evaluate and enhance it, and then publish it, we have another type of resource: published records. Some genealogists have taken all of the names and other personal data from vital records, cemetery records, and other original records and published them as research tools for others to use. *Apprentices of Virginia 1623–1800*[3] is an example of this type of resource. The author used original American and English records to identify about two thousand early apprentices in Virginia. Family histories and genealogies are also examples of published sources.

Such published research may have been contributed to genealogical or historical societies, libraries, or newsletters or periodicals or published in books. Although the term *research* evokes visions of dusty volumes on library shelves, it can also include the Internet, computer databases, card indexes, and pedigree and family chart files kept at local genealogical or historical societies and libraries. It is simply the research of other persons that has been made available to the public.

Genealogists also use many other types of published sources: family and local histories, biographies, newspapers, and genealogies are examples. These sources usually describe events that took place many years before the history or genealogy was written. They may be based on research in original sources but are a later interpretation of those sources. Some of these family histories, genealogies, or biographies may have been published as books or Internet pages while others may have remained in typescript or manuscript form.

ORIGINAL RECORDS

Documents created by public (government) or private agencies to describe your ancestors or their activities are considered *original records*. Birth certificates, marriage licenses, and wills probably come to mind as you think about original records. You will learn that churches, businesses, and clubs, as well as national and local government agencies, created many records that detail parts of your ancestors' lives.

Discovering the feelings and the life activities of ancestors requires innovative uses of well-known original sources such as birth, marriage, and death records, uses genealogists and family historians sometimes overlook. For example, popular sources such as birth records will help you determine child spacing and family size. Marriage records may help you calculate the ages of the bride and groom. Death records will generally tell you the cause of death. Less often used sources such as court records will inform you of trials or lawsuits that involved your family. Minutes of town or religious councils may name your ancestors as participants in local events. Even if your family is not mentioned, minutes will at least indicate what was going on in their community that may have touched your ancestors' lives.

Original records may be created at the time of an event or much later. Their purpose is the same no matter when they were created: to witness that an event took place and list those people involved. The birth and marriage records found at many county courts are examples of original sources. Sometimes an agency or institution will create a document that describes contemporary events as well as some that took place many years before the document was created. These are original records, too. For example, a driver's license lists a person's birth date but was created many years after the person's birth. A death certificate describes the date and place of death but contains information about the date and place of the deceased's birth or marriage. A census shows us where a family lived and who were in the household; it also may list the ages and birthplaces of these persons.

Reference Sources

Reference sources such as gazetteers, history books, and encyclopedias, both in print and online, are important in researching and writing a family history. These sources describe the places ancestors lived and what happened during their stay there. Reference books may also explain where to look for original records or other resources. For example, *The Handybook for Genealogists*[4] is a book you might use to learn more about the records created in the places your ancestors lived. To find the location of a town or village, use a gazetteer. To locate the nearest historical society, you might look in *Directory of Historical Societies and Agencies in the United States and Canada*.[5] The following chapters will help you identify reference books and published resources that will make the search for records easier and their interpretation more precise.

The Internet

The Internet is often the first place genealogists look today to find information. No longer do they have to find a repository for the information they are seeking. Finding information online has become easier and sources more plentiful. The Internet puts the world of knowledge at your fingertips. You can find transcriptions of records, digitized original records, compiled pedigrees, and numerous databases containing information. Search engines, such as Google, and RootsWeb (www.roots web.ancestry.com) are good starting points. Ancestry.com is an excellent database (although you must pay to use it) and contains the largest amount of data on the Web. Some libraries subscribe to Ancestry Library Edition, which allows library patrons to use the database free of charge.

The Internet has not changed the principles of sound genealogical research, however; evaluating the sources is the key to good documentation.

EVALUATING THE ACCURACY OF SOURCES

Regardless of the sources you consult, be critical of their accuracy. Were original sources prepared by eyewitnesses? Did the people interviewed have a chance to see the events they describe, or were they close to people who were eyewitnesses? Do published sources agree with what you know from doing research in original records or from reading the books of knowledgeable authors? Do you note a bias in any resource that might make it less accurate? Let's look at an example of this concept. John and Joe are driving separate cars. John is driving through an intersection, and Joe is turning left at the intersection but coming toward John in the opposite direction. John's car hits Joe's car. There are three witnesses to the accident. Nancy was in her car immediately behind Joe. Jim was just coming out of a coffee shop on the corner when the accident occurred. Melissa was standing at the corner talking on her cell phone. Joe and John both have first-hand knowledge of the event, but either's account may be biased. Nancy, Jim, and Melissa each saw the accident, but none saw it from the same perspective. Let's say a newspaper reporter interviews just one of the witnesses for a story. Will she be able to report it accurately? Can we rely on the newspaper article for complete and accurate information?

Any source may provide correct or incorrect information. Original sources created by eyewitnesses when the event occurred are preferred because they have a high probability of being accurate. Later sources should not be discounted, however, because they may be more accurate than some contemporary ones. Should you prefer the testimony of living witnesses over contemporary written sources? That depends on the accuracy of your informant's recollections. The key to success in using oral history is verification of testimony. People's memories only contain what they have observed, heard, or felt. Sometimes they have been given false information by others. On some occasions they may not have observed an event accurately, storing incorrect data in their memories. Then, too, there is always the danger that they have simply forgotten the facts, and attempts to recall them have created a less-than-accurate image of the past. In the previous scenario will Joe or John or any of the witnesses be able to relate an accurate account

family group record. Make it a practice to record the source of your information every time you record a name, event, or place. If you are using a computer program, there is ample space for sources and notes.

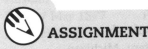

ASSIGNMENT

Fill in a blank family group sheet for a family unit in your ancestral line. You may copy the blank family group sheet found in this book (figure 1.3) or download a form from the Internet:

www.ancestry.com/trees/charts/ancchart.aspx
www.mymcpl.org/genealogy/family-history-forms

GENEALOGY SOFTWARE

The use of paper genealogy forms is waning among genealogists. It is much easier and often more convenient to use a genealogy software program for recording and organizing your family records. The following are just a few of the many genealogy software products available:

- **Family Tree Maker** is produced by Ancestry.com and is often available in bookstores and stores that specialize in computer software. It is updated frequently and is also available online through Amazon.com or Ancestry.com: www.familytreemaker.com.
- **Legacy Family Tree** is a free download and is updated one to two times per year: www.legacyfamilytree.com/Download.asp.
- **The Master Genealogist** is available online from Wholly Genes: www.whollygenes.com.
- **Roots Magic** is available for purchase online: www.rootsmagic.com.
- **PAF—Personal Ancestral File** is available as a free download from FamilySearch: https://familysearch.org/products (select Personal Ancestry File from the list).

All the genealogy software programs speak the same computer language—GEDCOM. This gives you the option to change to another software program if you choose to upgrade or if the first program you choose is not to your liking. It also allows you to share the information with other family members, no matter what program they might be using.

Putting data into one of the programs is fairly easy. Just enter a name and the dates and places of vital records into the software program. Then you can add a spouse, parents, and children to that person's record. Each person is linked to another person. The benefit of using software is the ability to generate a variety of reports from your data. You can easily create a pedigree or family group sheet according to the option selected. Many of the programs allow you to input photographs. Should you desire to create a genealogy book, most programs will format the data into simple sentences and can generate a table of contents and an index. Genealogy programs come and go, so it is best to look online for options when you are ready to make a decision on which to buy. Cyndi's List (www.cyndislist.com/software.htm) can help you find a software program that is right for you. Dick Eastman's blog, *Eastman's Online Genealogy Newsletter* (http://blog.eogn.com), often has reviews of genealogy software. Search his past newsletters for "software reviews" to find reviews of the latest programs. You can also search past newsletters for the name of a particular software program you may be considering. (Note: Dick Eastman's site does not support older versions of Internet Explorer. He suggests you upgrade to the latest version of the browser or make a switch to Firefox, Chrome, or Opera.)

Some families are finding that social networking sites that provide collaborative family trees are a good way to record their genealogy. The site you create is generally password protected to allow access only to those you invite to view the data. A collaborative site allows all family members to contribute names and dates, thus building the family tree much faster. The caveat, however, is that not all family members use accurate information sources. You can find links to collaborative sites at www.cyndislist.com/social-networking. (Cyndi's List, organized in categories, is a "must use" site for links to genealogy websites.)

ORAL HISTORY

We can gather information and stories about our family from other family members. Oral history is a process of collecting stories from living people about their own experiences or about their memories of people they have known. An interviewer will record the information of the person being interviewed by taking written notes or by making an audio or video recording. Start by choosing the subject of your interview. It is a good idea to interview all of your older family members while they are still alive—parents, grandparents, aunts, uncles, and so forth. You will also want to interview siblings and cousins.

Before the interview, formulate the central question or issue you wish to know about. Your goal may be to learn about your family's experiences during the Great Depression. Perhaps you want to interview everyone who knew your grandfather and record their stories about him. Maybe you would like to have the subject tell about his or her life experiences. Whatever your purpose or focus, try to stay on target and select your interview subjects accordingly. Make a list of questions to ask, but don't strictly adhere to them. Be flexible. Your interviewee may go off on a different track, but if you feel it is worthwhile, let the conversation continue. If the interview is not going where you would like, however, steer the interviewee back on course.

The knowledge living people have of ancestors and past events cannot be duplicated. Tidbits about people's habits, interests, physical traits—all of these can add a great deal of information to those names on our pedigree. Take the case of my husband's grandmother, Evelyn Meyers. She shared information about her grandparents, long ago deceased. She stated, "Grandpa was very small and dear. Grandma should have been a man—very large and meaner than dirt to grandpa. If he didn't mind her, she hit him over the head with an iron frying pan."[6] Now where else can you find that kind of information? Even though I never saw a photograph of her grandparents, with that description I can now picture them in my mind and I can imagine their personalities.

Next, determine the medium you will use—paper, audio, or video. If using audio or video equipment, practice using it before conducting interviews. Set up a quiet place in which to conduct the interview. Make sure the interviewee knows the purpose of the interview and understands that it is not a private conversation. If you are using audio or video equipment, begin your recording by stating who, when, and where you are interviewing and the intended content of the interview. If you are recording notes on paper, write down this information. Limit the length of time of the interview. You do not want to tire your interviewee with a lengthy session of more than an hour. After the interview, review your notes or listen to the interview and make sure you understand all that was said. If you have other questions, go back for another interview.

An example of oral histories in the making can be found at the Story-Corps website (http://storycorps.org). StoryCorps is an initiative to record the living history of America through a partnership of National Public Radio and the Library of Congress. Since 2003, this organization has been traveling the country and recording the oral histories of everyday people. Visit the StoryCorps website to read more about the project, hear the stories, and discover the project's list of Great Questions (http://storycorps.org/record-your-story/question-generator/). The Library of Congress also ahas a Veterans History Project (www.loc.gov/vets) that records the stories of American military veterans. Numerous websites give examples of oral history questions and guidelines for conducting oral history interviews. Because URLs constantly change, it is best to use a search engine to find these sites; use *oral history* as your search term.

Selected Books about Oral History

- Hart, Cynthia, and Lisa Samson. *The Oral History Workshop: Collect and Celebrate the Life Stories of Your Family and Friends.* New York: Workman, 2009.
- Nickerson, Janice C. *Saving Family Memories: A Step-by-Step Guide.* Toronto: Moorshead Magazines, 2009.
- Smith, M. J. Rutherford. *Colouring In the Leaves: Questions to Ask Family Members When Interviewing Them about Their Personal History.* Toronto: Ontario Genealogical Society, 2010.
- Sommer, Barbara W. *The Oral History Manual.* Lanham, MD: AltaMira Press, 2009.

FAMILY HEIRLOOMS

Treasures in your family's attic or family heirlooms can give you clues about your ancestors. The list is long, and not all can be mentioned here. Information about your family's history can be found in attics, basements, filing cabinets, home offices, or even historical societies. The following are just some of the sources for which you might look.

Family Bibles

Family Bibles often contain information on births, marriages, and deaths. The information found in these treasure troves needs to be analyzed carefully, however. If someone immediately went to the family Bible to record a death or birth, then the information is probably accurate. But if you notice that the recordings of many events that cover a period of years are in the same ink and in the same handwriting, that information may have been recorded years after the events took place. That information might not be accurate. Finding the owner of the family Bible can be an adventure in itself. My husband and I tried to track down such an heirloom after hearing a story about his great-grandfather's sister who supposedly took the Bible with her. We gave up the search when we found out her children and husband had predeceased her and there were no potential heirs. She was apparently not on speaking terms with the rest of the family, so we could only assume the item was lost to the family.

Diaries, Letters, and Memoirs

Diaries, letters, and memoirs can be excellent resources for discovering life events, migrations, relationships, church memberships, and glimpses of everyday life.

Diaries were often begun with a significant event in someone's life, such as starting out in a covered wagon on a journey to Oregon. What did he or she see along the way? What new sights, plant life, and animals were encountered along the trail? We have all heard of Anne Frank's *Diary of a Young Girl*. While in hiding from German forces during World War II, Anne Frank wrote in her diary of her fears and hopes and of her observations of the people around her. She gave the world a glimpse of life within the walls of that secret place and allowed us to sense what she was feeling. The diaries of our ancestors will most likely never be seen beyond one's own family, but they can be one of the most valuable and precious possessions we can discover.

The chances of finding the diary of one of your ancestors are slim as many of our ancestors were illiterate, but you might find a diary of someone who had similar experiences. Alexander Street Press, a book publisher and library database vendor, has developed a number of databases containing diaries of common individuals. These online products describe each diarist by age, sex, and location, and then allow you to read about his or her experiences, which can help you interpret the time in which your ancestor lived and the events she or he experienced. Several bibliographic publications, such as *American Diaries: An Annotated Bibliography of Published American Diaries and Journals,*[7] can help you find repositories that contain diaries.

We seem to have forgotten the impact of letters on lives of the past, but letter writing was the way that families stayed in touch when separated by miles. Everyday events were shared. Expressions of love flowed from the pages. Life's major mileposts were noted—births, deaths, and marriages. Here is a portion of a letter written by my grandfather, who immigrated to America when he was 18 years old, to his sister in Sweden on April 23, 1945:

Dear Sister!

I write some lines to let you now [sic] that we still are alive in spite of it is a long time ago I wrote. We all are well. Melvin, Alan, and Arvid are in the war but no one is in Europe. Alan and Arvid have been out nearly 2 years. Melvin went away after New Years Eve. Arvid wrote that he perhaps will bee [sic] back soon. I think he is ill. But he hasn't said anything himself. But Alan has told me. They have seen each other several times, but Alan is futher [sic] north now so they can't meet more. I don't remember if I mentioned that Norma has a boy. He is more than 2 years. Melvin also has a boy but his [sic] only 8 months.

Thanks to a grandson of that sister, the letter made its way back to me. My grandfather never returned to Sweden after immigrating, but letters and photographs were frequently shared across the ocean.

tain times during your ancestors' lives. It can help you determine factors that influenced their lives and events in which they might have been involved. I like *The Almanac of American History*[8] for giving a brief description of each year of American history from precolonial days through 2003. The years contained in the book are in chronological order beginning in the 1500s and continue through 2003. National and international events as well as wars, inventions, disasters, names of elected individuals, and other interesting facts are found for each year. Combining the timeline of your ancestor and a timeline of historic events really helps you envision your ancestor in history. As you can see below, as we add historic events into the timeline, we see what else is happening in the world around our ancestor. This context can be helpful if you later decide to convert your research into a book.

Sylvester McGeorge Timeline [including historic events]

1826 Born, Ohio—Fiftiethth anniversary of the Declaration of Independence

1852 Married, Cass County, Michigan—Completion of the Michigan Southern Railway

1853 Son born, Cass County, Michigan—Franklin Pierce inaugurated as the fourteenth president of the United States

A TRIP TO THE LIBRARY

Your local public library is a good place to start researching your family history. Libraries usually have historical and other records for their local communities. But be aware that genealogy is a specialty field in which only some library staff members have developed an expertise. The good news is there is usually someone on staff who loves genealogical research and will be happy to help you. It is best to call ahead and make sure someone is available to help you get started and show you around the collection.

Many public libraries have formed partnerships with their local genealogical society and maintain a genealogy section or room in the building. The genealogical society members then contribute time to helping genealogists who come into the library. Some genealogical

(🕐) GENEALOGY: TWENTY MINUTES A DAY

Begin your genealogical adventure by writing down what you already know about your family and putting it on a pedigree chart and a family unit chart. Look it over carefully to see what you are missing. Is there anyone in your family to whom you can write, e-mail, or phone to find out more information? Compose a letter or an e-mail or write down a list of questions you want to ask. It is a great way to become reacquainted with family members with whom you have lost touch. Start searching the Internet for clues. Some useful websites follow this section.

societies have a separate library building. The USGenWeb Project maintains a great website for finding what records and libraries are available in a county. Go to http://usgenweb.org/states/index.shtml, select a state, and then select a county to find resources for that area.

Many libraries in the United States specialize in genealogical research. The largest one is the Family History Library in Salt Lake City, Utah. Although it is a private library, all are welcome to do research there free of charge. See the website at https://familysearch.org to find out about the library and its Family History Centers—small branches of the library in local communities. The Library of Congress, the National Archives, and the DAR (Daughters of the American Revolution) Library, all in Washington, D.C., are excellent places to research your family. *Family Tree Magazine* in 2009 compiled a list of "Nine Genealogy Libraries to Visit Before You Die." Check out that list at www.familytreemagazine .com/article/9-libraries.

Historical societies, university libraries, and special libraries are other facilities in which you might find genealogical information. Historical societies have the mission to preserve history in the town, county, or state in which they are located. The history of a community incorporates the history of those who lived and worked there as well. You might find information about your family in one of those facilities. You will certainly have a better appreciation for the area in which they lived by researching the local history. University libraries are also repositories for the archival papers of alumnae. This treasure trove of paperwork might be worthwhile to you in your research. Special libraries are corporate, business, and medical libraries, among others, and are usually housed within a corporation, business, or research hospital. Although their collections are not of prime genealogical research value, you might find just what you need in one of those libraries. The *American Library Directory*[9] is an excellent reference book for determining the location of libraries and discovering the subject areas they collect. The directory is available in most public libraries.

THE INTERNET

Will you find all your genealogy on the Internet? At this time the answer is no. There may come a time when all information is digital and available on the Web, but until then the Internet is only one of the tools you will use in researching your family. Here is a reminder of the websites discussed in this chapter:

- *Eastman's Online Genealogy Newsletter*: http://blog.eogn.com
- Family History Library: https://familysearch.org
- Family Tree Maker genealogy program: www.familytreemaker .com
- Genealogy forms: www.ancestry.com/trees/charts/ancchart .aspx, www.mymcpl.org/genealogy/family-history-forms
- General searches: search engines such as Google; RootsWeb: www.rootsweb.ancestry.com
- Legacy Family Tree genealogy program: www.legacyfamilytree .com/Download.asp
- Links to genealogy websites: www.cyndislist.com
- The Master Genealogist genealogy program: www.whollygenes .com
- "Nine Genealogy Libraries to Visit Before You Die": www.family treemagazine.com/article/9-libraries
- Oral history information: http://storycorps.org, www.loc.gov/vets
- PAF—Personal Ancestral File genealogy program: https://family search.org/products (select Personal Ancestry File from the list)

- Roots Magic genealogy program: www.rootsmagic.com
- The Surgeon General's *My Family Health Portrait*: https://familyhistory.hhs.gov/fhh-web/home.action
- USGenWeb Project: http://usgenweb.org/states/index.shtml

...

Our journey into the past begins with discovering what we already know, charting our pedigree, and forming our ancestors into family units. Then we discover what others might know and what documents they might have in their possession. Then, creating a timeline of your ancestors puts them in historical perspective. You've started the trek—now it's time for the research!

NOTES

1. Alex Haley, *Roots* (New York: Doubleday, 1976).

2. Laura M. Holston, "Who's on the Family Tree? Now It's Complicated," *New York Times*, July 5, 2011, A-1.

3. Harold B. Gill, *Apprentices of Virginia 1623–1800* (Salt Lake City, UT: Ancestry, 1989).

4. *The Handybook for Genealogists*, 11th ed. (Baltimore: Genealogical Publishing, 2006).

5. *Directory of Historical Societies and Agencies in the United States and Canada* (Madison, WI: American Association for State and Local History, biennial).

6. Evelyn Meyers, oral history interview by Janice Schultz, March 1983.

7. Laura Arskey et al., *American Diaries: An Annotated Bibliography of Published American Diaries and Journals* (Detroit, MI: Gale Research, 1983–1987).

8. Arthur M. Schlesinger Jr., *The Almanac of American History* (New York: Barnes and Noble Books, 2004).

9. *American Library Directory: A Classified List of Libraries in the United States and Canada, with Personnel and Statistical Data* (New York: R. R. Bowker, annual).

chapter two

The First Steps in Finding Records

IN CHAPTER 1 YOU STARTED ON THE QUEST FOR KNOWLEDGE ABOUT YOUR family. I hope you have taken the time to put what you already know onto a pedigree chart and family unit charts. We discussed the types of records you will be seeking to find out more information about your ancestors. Now we will discuss the important documents that are most sought after by genealogists—vital records and census records.

VITAL RECORDS

Vital records are an important element in genealogical research. Specifically these are birth and death records, but marriage records often are considered part of this category. Those new to genealogy are often surprised to find that not everyone in their lineage has a vital record. We assume that because we have a birth certificate for ourselves, death certificates for our grandparents, and a marriage certificate for our parents, everyone at all times had those events documented by a record-keeping parent of that person. You will rarely find these records on the Internet, even in the form of an index.

Before state-held records, births were recorded in county or, in some eastern states, city courthouses and are obtainable there. The *Handybook* or the *Red Book* will tell you when counties were keeping records and if the records still exist. Be aware that doctors and midwives reported births to the record keeper. If no doctor or midwife was present at the birth, there is not likely to be a record. Births were recorded in a book by the county clerk—one line per birth. Birth certificates were unnecessary in those days. You didn't have to prove who you were. Sometimes pre-twentieth-century birth records can be found on the Internet in a digital form, in an index, or in a transcribed copy.

The names found on a birth record, such as the name of the father, are usually provided by the mother. (See figure 2.3.) Will the information on the birth record be accurate? On a birth certificate, the information provided about the date, time, and place of birth, the weight and length of the child, and the doctor's name should be accurate. The mother's name will most likely be accurate, and the information she provides about herself—her age and place of birth—will be as accurate as she wishes it to be. The information about the father will be as accurate as the information she knows or wishes to share. In some states, if the parents are not married at the time of the birth and if the father does not give written consent for being legally responsible for the child, his name will not be listed on the birth certificate.

Figure 2.3 A birth record for my grandmother, Alma Israelson, in Houghton County, Michigan. Her name is on the left with her birth month, December, and day, the 29th. The year is not shown here but is at the beginning of the entries for the year. Her parents' names are on the right, Israel and Mary Israelson, along with their places of birth, which in both cases was Norway. Israel's occupation as a miner is also given. From FamilySearch (https://familysearch.org). Digital image from microfilm 2320575, digital folder number 4207019, image number 156.

Death Records

A death record, at a minimum, will tell you the name of the deceased and the cause of death. As with birth records, modern death records will be found in each state's department of health. These records generally began at the same time as birth records for a particular locale. A twentieth- or twenty-first-century death record will be written in the form of a certificate—an official document issued by a government entity that declares the date, location, and cause of a person's death.

A good starting place for finding death records on the Internet is www.deathindexes.com.

The right side of the certificate will show the information provided by the attending physician. The left side will have information provided by an informant. The informant can be anyone—parent, child, sibling, or even the landlady—who is present at the time and who can provide the information. You will find the complete name of the deceased, the date of death, the cause of death, and his or her age at the time of death. You may also discover the person's place of birth and occupation, the name of his or her spouse, and the names of his or her parents, including the mother's maiden name. The parents' place of birth is also listed—and is as accurate as the knowledge of the informant. Look at this information with a critical eye. It may be right—but it could also be wrong. My grandmother was the informant for her father's death certificate, but she did not state the correct names of his parents. (See figure 2.4.) She wasn't even close to being correct. My supposition as to why she provided the wrong information is this: My great-grandfather was born in Norway. He immigrated to the United States in 1863 or 1864, but his parents never left Norway. My grandmother never traveled to Norway and never met her grandparents. Either she did not know their correct names, or in the sorrow she felt at the time she did not remember their names correctly. I discovered the true names of his parents by obtaining the information from a relative still living in Norway.

Today most states automate their records. The electronic records are usually abbreviated death certificates giving the name of the deceased, cause of death, and place of burial. All of the other names and information found on the long form will be absent. Make sure when requesting a death certificate that you ask for a copy of the original death certificate. Some of these records can be found on the Internet, depending on the laws of the state and when the records become public. Online you

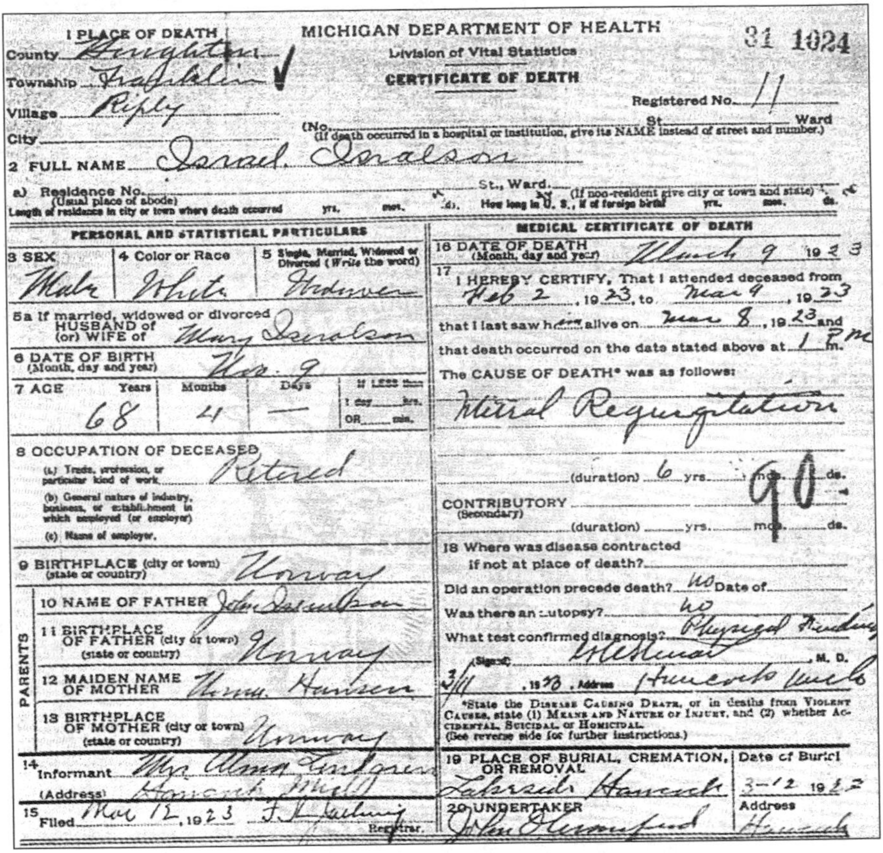

1 PLACE OF DEATH
County Houghton
Township Franklin
Village Ripley
City

MICHIGAN DEPARTMENT OF HEALTH
Division of Vital Statistics
CERTIFICATE OF DEATH

31 1024

Registered No. 11

(No. ____ St. ____ Ward
(If death occurred in a hospital or institution, give its NAME instead of street and number.)

2 FULL NAME Israel Israelson

a) Residence No. ____ St., Ward. ____ (If non-resident give city or town and state)
(Usual place of abode)
Length of residence in city or town where death occurred yrs. mos. ds. How long in U. S., if of foreign birth yrs. mos. ds.

PERSONAL AND STATISTICAL PARTICULARS

3 SEX Male
4 Color or Race White
5 Single, Married, Widowed or Divorced (Write the word) Widower
5a If married, widowed or divorced HUSBAND of (or) WIFE of Mary Israelson
6 DATE OF BIRTH (Month, day and year) Nov. 9
7 AGE Years 68 Months 4 Days —
If LESS than 1 day ____ hrs. OR ____ min.
8 OCCUPATION OF DECEASED
(a) Trade, profession, or particular kind of work Retired
(b) General nature of industry, business, or establishment in which employed (or employer)
(c) Name of employer.
9 BIRTHPLACE (city or town) (state or country) Norway

PARENTS
10 NAME OF FATHER John Israelson
11 BIRTHPLACE OF FATHER (city or town) (state or country) Norway
12 MAIDEN NAME OF MOTHER Anna Hansen
13 BIRTHPLACE OF MOTHER (city or town) (state or country) Norway
14 Informant Mrs Alma Lindgren
(Address) Hancock Mich
15 Filed Mar 12, 1923 F. H. Jarling Registrar.

MEDICAL CERTIFICATE OF DEATH
16 DATE OF DEATH (Month, day and year) March 9 1923
17 I HEREBY CERTIFY, That I attended deceased from Feb 2, 1923, to Mar 9, 1923
that I last saw h__ alive on Mar 8, 1923 and
that death occurred on the date stated above at 1 P.M.
The CAUSE OF DEATH* was as follows:
Mitral Regurgitation
(duration) 6 yrs. ____ mos. ____ ds.
CONTRIBUTORY (Secondary)
(duration) ____ yrs. ____ mos. ____ ds.
90
18 Where was disease contracted if not at place of death?
Did an operation precede death? no Date of
Was there an autopsy? no
What test confirmed diagnosis? Physical Finding
(Signed) ____ M. D.
3/11, 1923 Address Hancock Mich
*State the DISEASE CAUSING DEATH, or in deaths from VIOLENT CAUSES, state (1) MEANS AND NATURE OF INJURY, and (2) whether ACCIDENTAL, SUICIDAL, or HOMICIDAL.
(See reverse side for further instructions.)
19 PLACE OF BURIAL, CREMATION, OR REMOVAL Lakeside Hancock
Date of Burial 3-12 1923
20 UNDERTAKER John Hermanfield
Address Hancock

Figure 2.4 This death certificate is for my great-grandfather, Israel Israelson. From Michigan Department of Health, State Death Registers, Office of Vital Records.

might find an index to the death certificates, transcriptions, or even digitized copies.

Nineteenth-century and prior death records will be found in death record books in the courthouse—one line per person. The main reason counties kept these records was to have readily available information for causes of death in the area. You will only find the name of the deceased, his or her age, and the cause of death on one line of the death record book in the courthouse. Only attending physicians reported deaths to the county officials. If no physician was present, there will be no death record. Families did not have to provide proof of a death as we do today. Now we provide a copy of a death certificate to the Social Security Administration, the insurance company, the bank, and all other interested parties. Many of these older death records can be found on the Internet in one form or another—indexes, transcriptions, or digitized copies.

Marriage Records

Marriage records tell us the names of the bride and groom. They are the best place to find the maiden name of the bride and thus have a name with which to trace her family. Marriage records are seldom found at the state level. They are usually county or town records and are recorded from the date of formation of the county. There are several types of records you could encounter: marriage records, certificates, applications, returns, and bonds.

Marriage records are found in bound volumes in the courthouse in the county where the marriage occurred. Each record shows the name of the groom, the maiden name of the bride, the name of the officiating minister or the person who presided over the marriage, and sometimes the name of the church or the names of the witnesses or both. You might find letters after the name of the person presiding over the ceremony. "JP" means the person was a justice of the peace. "MG" stands for "minister of the gospel." (See figure 2.5.)

Figure 2.5 This document shows the marriage of Harry Truman and Elizabeth Wallace in Independence, Missouri, in 1919. They were married at Trinity Church. From Jackson County, Missouri, recorder of deeds: http://records.jacksongov.org/ search.asp?cabinet=marriage.

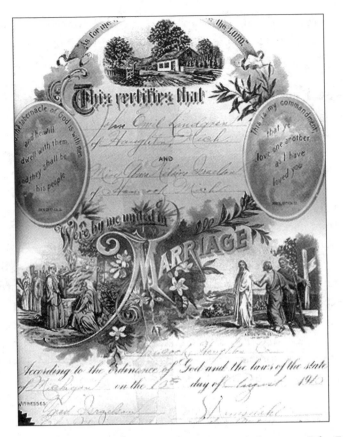

Figure 2.6 This marriage certificate was given to my grandparents, John Emil Lindgren and Alma Nilsina Israelson, by the minister of the church in which they were married. From author's personal papers.

A marriage certificate is the official record of marriage given to the bride and groom. A copy is also filed in the county courthouse. A marriage certificate might also be provided by the church in which the marriage occurred. You often find these in family papers. Marriage certificates are generally a later type of document—twentieth or twenty-first century. You will often find the full name of the bride and groom, date of application, date of marriage, name of the minister or the justice of the peace, and religious affiliation of the minister. You may also discover the names of the witnesses. A marriage certificate might also be given to the bride and groom by the church in which they were married. (See figure 2.6.)

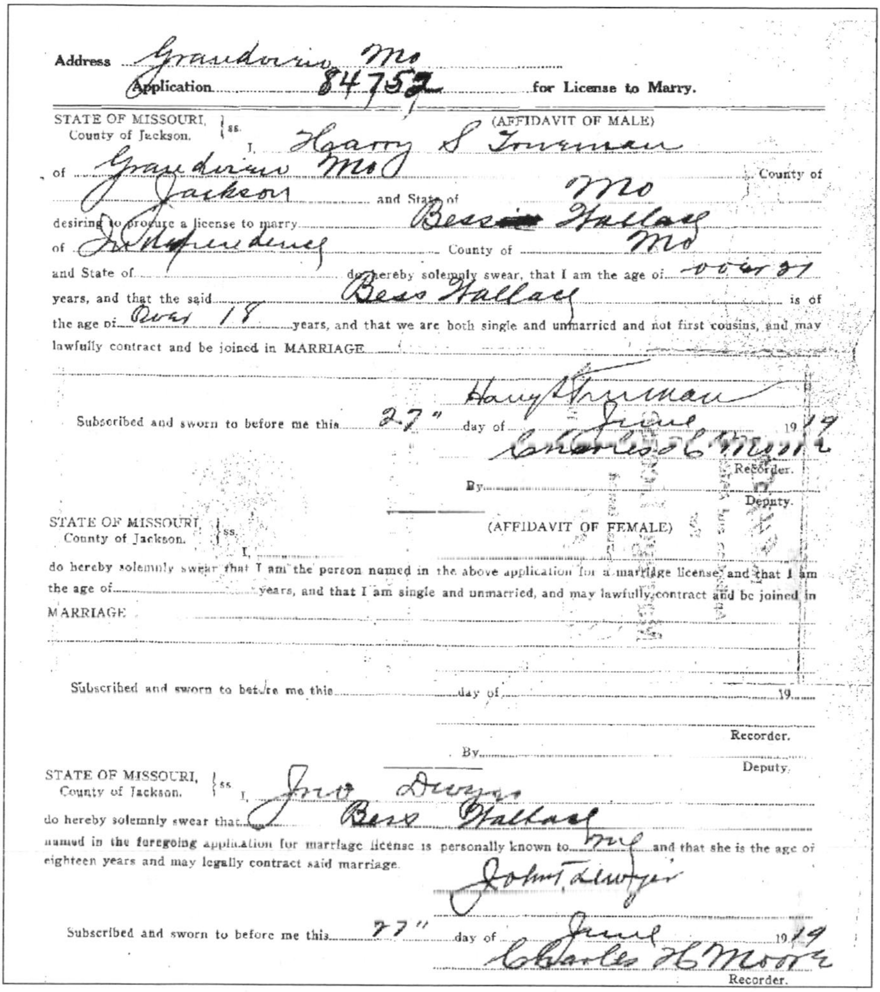

Figure 2.7 *This marriage application shows Harry S Truman of Grandview, Missouri, applying for a license to marry Bess Wallace of Independence, Missouri. From Jackson County, Missouri, recorder of deeds: http://records.jacksongov.org/ search.asp?cabinet=marriage.*

A marriage application is the document created when the bride and groom apply for a marriage license. Again, this is usually a later document—twentieth or twenty-first century—and the information found will vary from state to state. Marriage applications, like licenses and certificates, are county or town documents. The laws apply at the state level, but the records are generally kept and administered at the local level. The

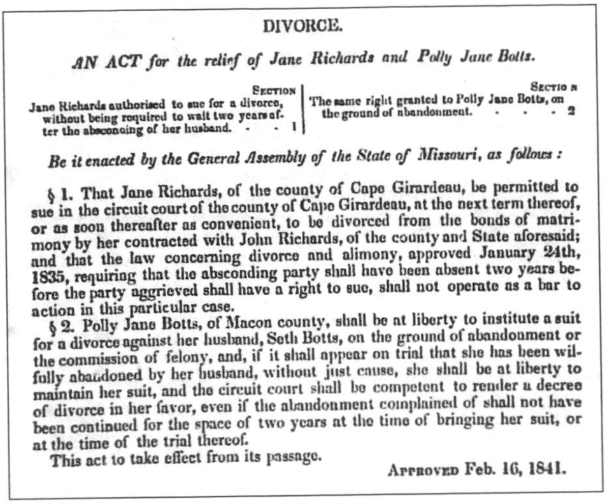

DIVORCE.

AN ACT for the relief of Jane Richards and Polly Jane Botts.

SECTION	SECTION
Jane Richards authorised to sue for a divorce, without being required to wait two years after the absconding of her husband. - - 1	The same right granted to Polly Jane Botts, on the ground of abandonment. - - - - 2

Be it enacted by the General Assembly of the State of Missouri, as follows:

§ 1. That Jane Richards, of the county of Cape Girardeau, be permitted to sue in the circuit court of the county of Cape Girardeau, at the next term thereof, or as soon thereafter as convenient, to be divorced from the bonds of matrimony by her contracted with John Richards, of the county and State aforesaid; and that the law concerning divorce and alimony, approved January 24th, 1835, requiring that the absconding party shall have been absent two years before the party aggrieved shall have a right to sue, shall not operate as a bar to action in this particular case.

§ 2. Polly Jane Botts, of Macon county, shall be at liberty to institute a suit for a divorce against her husband, Seth Botts, on the ground of abandonment or the commission of felony, and, if it shall appear on trial that she has been wilfully abandoned by her husband, without just cause, she shall be at liberty to maintain her suit, and the circuit court shall be competent to render a decree of divorce in her favor, even if the abandonment complained of shall not have been continued for the space of two years at the time of bringing her suit, or at the time of the trial thereof.

This act to take effect from its passage.

APPROVED Feb. 16, 1841.

Figure 2.9 This document shows two divorce records granted by the Missouri General Assembly in 1841. From Missouri 11th General Assembly, Laws, 1st Session 1841.

Vital records are important documents to find as you discover your ancestry. When available, they uniquely identify an individual and provide clues to names, dates, and locations of significant events. Uniformity in records was slow in coming, so the information you find will be varied. It is important to remember that the data found, even though it is on an "official" document, can be wrong—sometimes by transcription error, sometimes by ignorance, and sometimes by the desire of an informant to hide the truth. As with all documents, analyze them carefully. You have started another step in your quest to find your ancestry, and vital records can help you reach your goal.

THE INTERNET

Finding out which vital records are available can be as easy as browsing the Internet. Here are some websites to try.

- Death indexes online: www.deathindexes.com
- Marriage records online: www.idreamof.com/marriage.html
- Vital records: http://vitalrec.com, www.vitalchek.com

GENEALOGY: TWENTY MINUTES A DAY

Look at your pedigree chart and your family group sheets and note any missing dates and places of events. If you know the location of the event, check the Internet, the **Red Book, The Handybook for Genealogists,** or the **International Vital Records Handbook,** or all of these, as noted earlier in this chapter. Is the missing data available to pursue? Which record keeper has that information? Begin accessing those records to find out more about those ancestors. If the location is unknown, check census records to determine where those ancestors were living at the time of a specific event or if any hint is given about those locations. More information on census records follows.

CENSUS RECORDS

Federal census records are the backbone of genealogy. We might not be able to find a book about our family, a vital record, or a family member who has the information we are seeking, but a census record will list your family every ten years, and there you will find clues to your ancestral heritage. The records are useful for learning about your family members and the environment in which they lived.

The US census began in 1790 for the purpose of deciding congressional representation. A census has been taken every ten years since that time listing varying amounts of information, depending on the data Congress wanted collected. Census records are private for seventy-two years. When genealogists wanted access to the 1910 census, Congress passed a "privacy act" to allow limited access (Title 44, US Code). The law says that census records will be released seventy-two years after the official census date. Seventy-two years was the life expectancy at the time the law was enacted. This privacy of the census allows individuals to freely give the information sought without worrying about those who might see that data.

In taking a census, the enumerator (the person collecting the data) went from door to door (though the method has changed with more recent census takings) in the district assigned to him—an enumeration district. If the enumerator was in a large city with city blocks, he would

Effective Census Dates

The data collected each census year reflected the information for each individual on the effective census date—his or her age and who was in the household. Children born between the effective date and the date the enumerator came to the door were not to be counted; however, sometimes they were. The effective census dates were:

August 2, 1790	June 1, 1850	April 15, 1910
August 4, 1800	June 1, 1860	January 1, 1920
August 6, 1810	June 1, 1870	April 1, 1930
August 7, 1820	June 1, 1880	April 1, 1940
June 1, 1830	June 1, 1890	
June 1, 1840	June 1, 1900	

go around the block, staying on the same side of the street. When he was back at his starting point, he would go across the street and again go around the block. In a rural community he would travel up one side of the road and then down the other. Every family on a census page is a neighbor to the family listed above or below on the census form. However, if the neighbor lived across the street, the information could be several pages away.

It is important to know the questions asked in a particular census year to understand what information you can glean. A good website for finding out what questions were asked is that of the Minnesota Population Center at the University of Minnesota, http://usa.ipums.org/usa/voliii/tEnumForm.shtml. Basically, the more recent the census the more information you will find. The older the census, the less you will find. Let's start at the beginning.

Census Population Schedules 1790–1840

The earliest census schedules did not list every person by name. Only the head of the household was listed by name. All other people were simply counted—the total number of people, male and female, in an age category.

1790

The 1790 census was a basic enumeration of the taxpayers residing in a current US state. The enumeration of eleven states is extant:

Connecticut, Maine, Maryland, Massachusetts, New Hampshire, New York, North Carolina, Pennsylvania, Rhode Island, South Carolina, and Vermont. A preprinted form was not used—the enumerator created his own. The only names shown on this form are the name of the head of each household. Following each person's name are the numbers of free white males 16 years and older, free white males under the age of 16, free white females, slaves, and other persons in that house. In figure 2.10, the first individual listed is Charles Hatch. His household includes one male over the age of 16, two males under 16, one female, and nine slaves.

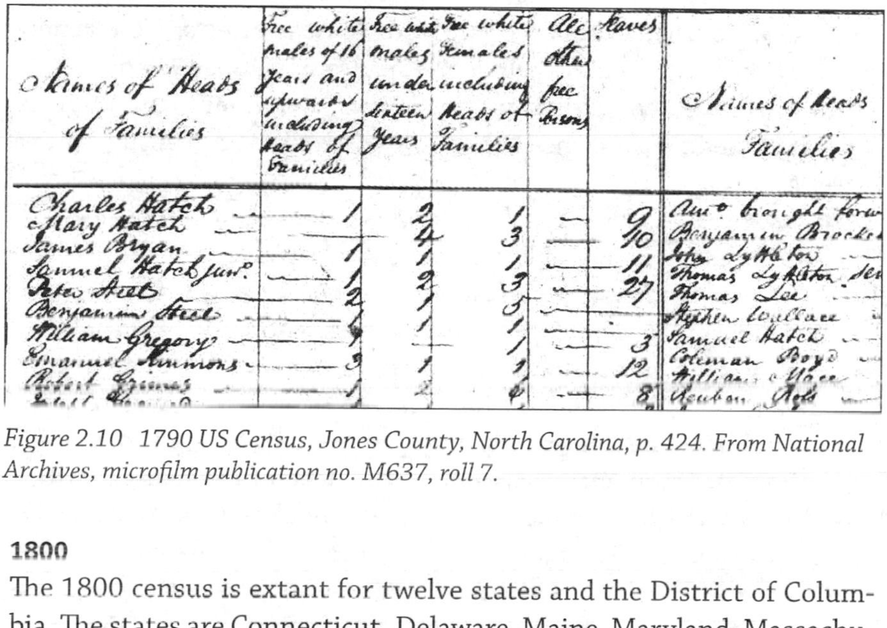

Names of Heads of Families	Free white males of 16 Years and upwards including Heads of Families	Free white males under sixteen Years	Free white Females including Heads of Families	All other free Persons	Slaves	Names of Heads of Families
Charles Hatch	1	2	1	—	9	Am^t brought forw
Mary Hatch	—	4	3	—	10	Benjamin Brocke[illegible]
James Bryan	1	1	1	—	11	John Lyttleton
Samuel Hatch Junr	1	2	3	—	27	Thomas Lyttleton Sen
Peter Steel	2	1	5	—		Thomas Lee
Benjamin Steel	1	1	1	—		Stephen Wallace
William Gregory	1	—	1	—	3	Samuel Hatch
Emanuel Simmons	3	1	1	—	12	Coleman Boyd
Robert Grimes	1	2	4	—	8	William Wallace
[illegible]						Reuben Ross

Figure 2.10 1790 US Census, Jones County, North Carolina, p. 424. From National Archives, microfilm publication no. M637, roll 7.

1800

The 1800 census is extant for twelve states and the District of Columbia. The states are Connecticut, Delaware, Maine, Maryland, Massachusetts, New Hampshire, New York, North Carolina, Pennsylvania, Rhode Island, South Carolina, and Vermont. Again, only the name of the head of the house is listed, and there was no preprinted form for the enumerator to use. The numbers of free white males and females are listed in the following age categories: 0 to 10, 10 and under 16, 16 and under 26, 26 and under 45, and 45 years and older. Also included are the numbers of free persons other than Indians not taxed and the number of slaves. The first individual on the schedule shown in figure 2.11 is David Anthony. His household includes one male under the age of 10, one male between the ages of 16 and 26, one male between the ages of 26 and 45, three females under the age of 10, one female between the ages of 10 and 16, and one female between the ages of 26 and 45.

Figure 2.11 *1800 US Census, Somerset County, Pennsylvania, p. 538. From National Archives, microfilm publication no. M32, roll 43.*

1810

The 1810 census is extant for sixteen states: Connecticut, Delaware, Kentucky, Louisiana, Maine, Maryland, Massachusetts, New Hampshire, New York, North Carolina, Pennsylvania, Rhode Island, South Carolina, Tennessee (Rutherford County only), Vermont, and Virginia. The categories are the same as those found on the 1800 census.

1820

The 1820 census is available for twenty-two states and the District of Columbia: Connecticut, Delaware, Georgia, Illinois, Indiana, Kentucky, Louisiana, Maine, Maryland, Massachusetts, Michigan, Mississippi, New Hampshire, New York, North Carolina, Ohio, Pennsylvania, Rhode Island, South Carolina, Tennessee, Vermont, and Virginia. You can virtually see the country expanding as more states are added to the enumeration. Again, only the name of the head of the house is listed. Numbers of free white males and females are shown in the same age categories as in the 1800 and 1810 censuses. Slaves are shown, male and female, in almost the same age categories. In addition, numbers of free white males between the ages of 16 and 18 are shown. Note that males in this age category are listed twice, once as 16 to 18 and again in the 16 to 26 age category. The purpose of the extra age category was to show how many men were of the right age for military duty. Also shown are numbers of foreigners not naturalized, persons engaged in agriculture, persons engaged in manufacturing, and all other persons except Indians who were not taxed. The census in figure 2.12 shows Samuel Brooks on the first line. His household includes one male child under the age of 10, one male between the ages of 16 and 26 (but not between the ages of 16 and 18), one male age 45 or older, two females under the age of 10, five females ages 10 to 16, three females ages 16 to 26, and one female age 45 or older. On the right-hand side of the schedule we see the number of slaves. It appears there are two male slaves between the ages of 14 and 26.

Figure 2.12 *1820 US Census, Fauquier County, Virginia, p. 130. From National Archives, microfilm publication no. M33, roll 136.*

1830

The 1830 census is the first that uniformly used a preprinted form. Twenty-eight states plus the District of Columbia are extant. The age categories are greatly expanded in this census enumeration. They include free white males and females in five-year age groups to age 20 and ten-year age groups from 20 to 100. Slaves are recorded in the following age categories, male and female: Under 10, 10 to under 24, 24 to under 36, 36 to under 55, 55 to under 100, and over 100 years of age. Free "colored" persons are recorded in the same age categories as slaves, both male and female. Numbers of aliens/foreigners not naturalized, deaf and dumb persons (in age categories), and blind people are also recorded. The census schedule in figure 2.13 shows Jesse Noland on the first line. His household includes one male age 15 to 20, two males ages 20 to 30, one male age 50 to 60, one female age 15 to 20, one female age 20 to 30, and one female age 50 to 60.

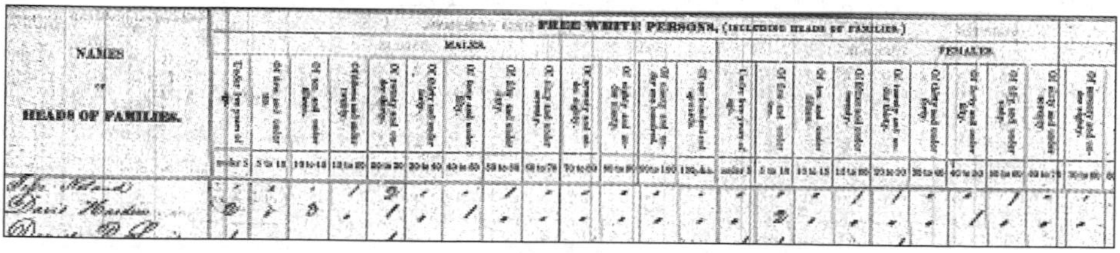

Figure 2.13 *1830 US Census, Jackson County, Missouri, p. 301. From National Archives, microfilm publication no. M19, roll 73.*

1840

The 1840 census is available for twenty-nine states and the District of Columbia. Age categories are the same as in the 1830 census, but much more information was desired by the government with this schedule including numbers of persons involved in the following: mining; agriculture; commerce; manufacture and trade; navigation of the ocean; navigation of canals, lakes, and rivers; and learned professional engineers. Military service in the form of pension holders was recorded as well. Those who were pensioners for Revolutionary or military services were recorded by name and age (see figure 2.14). Information about schools was also recorded. Universities or colleges, academies and grammar schools, primary and common schools with their numbers of students at public charge were shown. Finally, the numbers of those deaf and dumb, blind, and insane were given.

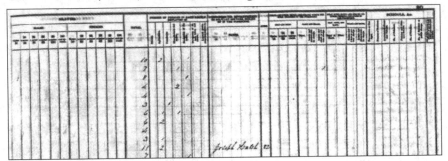

Figure 2.14 Pensioner Joseph Hatch, age 82, is listed in the 1840 US Census, Barnstable County, Massachusetts, p. 90. From National Archives, microfilm publication no. M704, roll 173.

HOW TO USE EARLY CENSUS RECORDS

Using these early census records can be frustrating. It's hard to determine your particular ancestor when only the name of the head of the house is listed. But if you use these early census enumerations as clues, they can help narrow your search when trying to determine the parents of an ancestor. Look back at the 1830 Jackson County, Missouri, census record example (figure 2.13). The Jesse Noland household has four males between the ages of 15 and 60 and three females between the ages of 15 and 60. If you were trying to find the father of a male between the ages of 15 and 20 with the last name of Noland living in Missouri, then you would have a possibility in Jesse Noland. However, you should also look at every male with the surname Noland living in

Missouri in that same year. Rule out anyone who did not have a male child in the correct age category. Those who remain will be those for whom you will want to do further research and find other documents that might list the names of children, such as a will or a church record. This research will give you first names of possible fathers and possible counties in which to search.

Census Population Schedules 1850 and Beyond

Beginning in 1850, census records list all people by name. The amount of information you can glean increases each year.

1850–1870

The 1850, 1860, and 1870 censuses contain basically the same information. For the first time all free persons in each household were listed by name. Enslaved persons were not listed by name in the 1850 and 1860 enumerations. The 1870 census marked the first time those who were former slaves were listed by name. Relationships were not given in these census records, so be very careful in your assumptions. Just because everyone in the household has the same last name does not mean that the first person listed is the father of each child, nor can you assume that the second person listed is the mother. In the example in figure 2.15, we see Josiah Finley, age 46. Julia Ann, listed under him, is 26 years old. Is Julia Ann a wife or a daughter? If she is Josiah's wife, is she his first or second wife? There is a Judson F. who seems to be 14 years old. Then there are two younger children—William, age 6, and Harriet H., age 9 months (9/12 equals 9 months). We could possibly conclude that Judson is the product of a first marriage, considering that Julia would have been only 12 years old at the time of Judson's birth, and William and Harriet are the children of Josiah and Julia Ann. But we can't jump to conclusions. More research will have to be done to determine the relationships here.

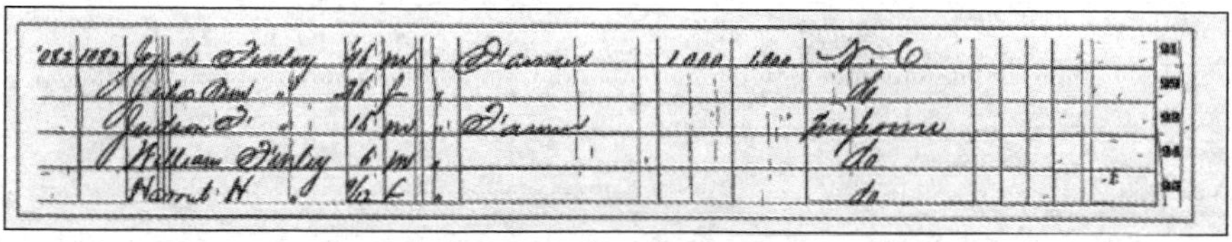

Figure 2.15 The Josiah Finley family is listed in the 1860 US Census, Clay County, Missouri, p. 993. From National Archives, microfilm publication no. M653, roll 614.

In addition to each person's name, the record shows his or her age, sex, color, occupation, place of birth, value of real estate owned (1860 and 1870 also show value of personal property), and whether the person can read and write. Also given is whether each individual is deaf and dumb, blind, insane, or idiotic. Supplemental slave schedules were also taken and are on separate microfilm rolls. Names of the slaves were not shown—only the owner's name and the slave's age, sex, and color (black or mulatto), whether fugitive from the state, the number manumitted, and whether deaf, dumb, or idiotic.

Do you see the places of birth of each person in the tenth column from the left in figure 2.15? Josiah was born in "N.C." meaning North Carolina. Julia Ann was born in "do." This is an abbreviation of *ditto*. Julia was also born in North Carolina. Judson's place of birth was Missouri. How can I tell that? It comes with lots of practice. In nineteenth-century writing, look for the long S especially when it occurs as a double S. It will look like "fs."

1880

For the first time the 1880 census shows not just everyone in the household but also how they are related to the head of the house. Possible relationships are wife, son, daughter, adopted son/daughter, stepson/daughter, mother/father/brother/sister-in-law, boarder, servant, and inmate. Other, more obscure relationships are also possible. Other information can also be found: the name of the street and house number (in cities), color, sex, age (as of June 1, 1880), month of birth if born within the census year, marital status, occupation, number of months unemployed during the census year, health (blind, deaf and dumb,

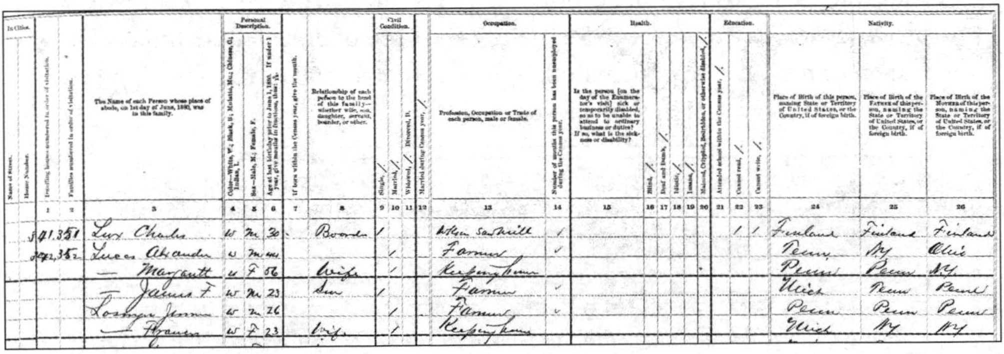

1	2	3	4	5	6	8	9	10	13	14	22	23	24	25	26
341	351	Lux Charles	W	M	30	Boarder	/		Works sawmill	/	/	/	Finland	Finland	Finland
342	352	Lucas Alexander	W	M	44			/	Farmer	✓			Penn	NY	Ohio
		— Margarett	W	F	56	Wife		/	Keeping house				Penn	Penn	NY
		— James F	W	M	23	Son	/		Farmer	✓			Mich	Penn	Penn
		Losinger Jerome	W	M	26			/	Farmer	✓			Penn	Penn	Penn
		— Frances	W	F	23	Wife		/	Keeping house				Mich	NY	NY

Figure 2.16 1880 US Census, Montcalm County, Michigan, p. 327. From National Archives, microfilm publication no. T9, roll 327.

insane, etc.), whether attended school during the census year, ability to read and write, and place of birth of each person and his or her parents. (See figure 2.16.)

1890

The 1890 census is extant for only about 1 percent of the enumerations. In 1921, a fire occurred in the Washington, D.C., building that

Figure 2.17 1890 US Census, Severe, Perry County, Alabama, p. 436. From Family History Library Film 0926497, roll M407_1, E.D. 78. Ancestry.com and the Church of Jesus Christ of Latter Day Saints, 1890 United States Federal Census Fragment [online database] (Provo, UT: Ancestry.com Operations, 2009).

contained the census schedules. Many schedules were partially destroyed, and others had smoke and water damage. Because of mold, the latter were destroyed about ten years later by Congress. This was the only census that had each family listed on a separate census sheet. (See figure 2.17, p. 55.)

1900

The 1900 census records the name of every person and his or her relationship to the head of the house. The unique element of this census is that the month and year of birth of every person are recorded along with each person's age. This is the only census to do so. The rest of the data found on these census schedules is similar to that of the 1880 census with the addition of the citizenship status of all foreign-born persons and their year of immigration. Under citizenship status you will find the abbreviations "al," which stands for *alien* (no effort has been made toward citizenship), "pa," which stands for *papers* (first or second papers have been filed in pursuit of citizenship), and "na," which stands for *naturalized*. Also recorded is ownership of the home (owned or rented), whether a house or a farm, and whether free or mortgaged. Figure 2.18 shows the place of birth of the individual (Norway in both cases), place of birth of the father (the first example shows Sweden and the second shows Norway), the place of birth of the mother (again, Sweden and Norway), year of immigration (1873), number of years in the country (27 years), and citizenship status (the first person is naturalized and the status of the second person in unknown).

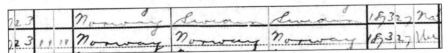

Figure 2.18 1900 US Census, Houghton County, Michigan, p. 269. From National Archives, microfilm publication no. T623, roll 715.

1910 AND 1920

The 1910 and 1920 census schedules are very similar to the 1900 census except the month and year of birth are not given. In addition to names and ages of each person in the household, we find the number of years each person has been married, the number of children each woman has borne, and the number of those children who are still living. The state or country in which each person was born plus the language spoken are given. Each person was asked his or her trade or occupation, the nature of the industry or business, whether the person was an employee, an employer, or working on his or her own account (self-employed), and, if an employee, whether the person was out of work during the year. Other questions concerned literacy, school attendance, whether the family's home was owned or rented and, if owned, whether mortgaged, whether it was a farm or house, and whether individuals were blind or deaf and dumb. On the 1910 schedule was a question on military service—whether a survivor of the Union or Confederate Army or Navy. Additionally in 1910 there was a special Indian Schedule that included the tribe of the Indian, tribe of father, tribe of mother, blood quantum, and marriage information. This schedule was to be used for Indians living on reservations or in tribal groups and in certain counties containing a significant number of Indians.

1930

The 1930 census, again, is very similar to the census schedules of 1900, 1910, and 1920. One difference, however, is that in this census, rather than finding the number of years married, we find the person's age at his or her first marriage. Often the number of times married is indicated by "M2" or "M3" when someone is in his or her second or third marriage. Remember, the age given is the age at the individual's first marriage. This census also gives the value of the person's home, if a veteran, what year he served, and a supplemental schedule for Indians on and off the reservation.

1940

The 1940 census was released on April 2, 2012. The questions asked on that census were address (if in a city), whether the home was owned or rented, value of the home if owned or the monthly rental amount if rented, whether the family lived on a farm, name of each person in residence on April 1, 1940, his or her relationship to the head of the house, sex, color or race, age at last birthday, marital status, education (highest grade of school attended), place of birth and, if foreign born, citizenship status and the country in which the person's birthplace was situated on January 1, 1937. Additionally, each person's residence on April 1, 1935, was sought—the name of the city, town, or village and state (or territory or foreign country), and whether on a farm. For persons 14 years and older, there was a question concerning employment. Congress was interested in whether people were working and, if they were working, whether it was for pay or profit or government support work (such as the WPA and CCC). Individuals who were seeking work indicated the number of hours they were employed or the duration of their unemployment, their occupation, whether they had their own business, and whether they received an income of $50 or more from sources other than wages or salary. Two persons from each page were selected to give additional information: place of birth of the person's father and mother and languages spoken.

· · ·

When you are looking at census records, you may find your ancestors in several different counties in the same state during their lifetime—but they never moved! County boundaries changed during the development of almost every state. Knowing what each county looked like during a census year—the county boundaries—is imperative. The *Map Guide to the U.S. Federal Censuses, 1790–1920*[4] will help you see the changes in boundaries from year to year. These maps have been reproduced on HeritageQuest. HeritageQuest is a subscription database available in many libraries across the country. The database has digital census images that can be searched by name or browsed by locality and year. As you browse census records (look for the Browse tab), you will see the option to view the state map (after you have selected the year and state you wish to browse).

Nonpopulation Schedules

In addition to the population schedules, nonpopulation schedules are extant for the years 1850 through 1880. Schedules after 1880 were destroyed after the statistics were gathered. The nonpopulation schedules are mortality, agricultural, manufacturing, and social statistics.

Mortality schedules give the names of persons who died in the twelve months prior to the census date. For instance, the 1860 mortality schedule includes persons who died from June 1, 1859, to May 31, 1860. Unfortunately these schedules do not show everyone who died within the ten years since the previous census. But since many states or counties were not keeping a record of deaths during the available years, it may be the only record of death for those individuals. For each person the following information is found: name, age, sex, marital status, state or country of birth, month of death, occupation, cause of death, and the length of the final illness. (See figure 2.19.)

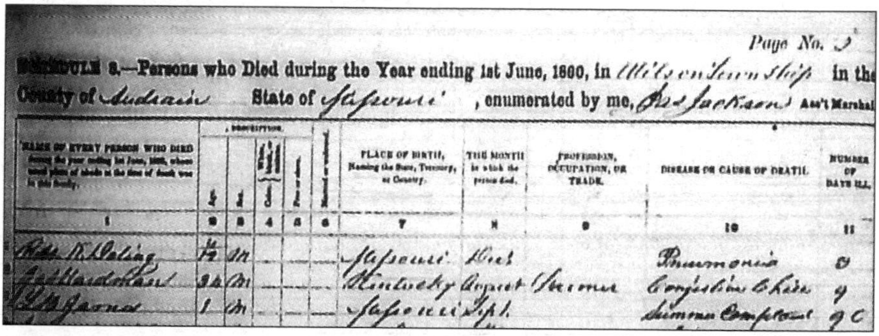
Page No. 3
SCHEDULE 3.—Persons who Died during the Year ending 1st June, 1860, in ... in the County of ... State of ... , enumerated by me, ... Ass't Marshal

Figure 2.19 Death records. From Missouri Mortality Schedule, 1860, Adair County, p. 3. Photographed by American Micro for the State Historical Society of Missouri.

Agricultural schedules record the following information for each farm: name of owner or manager; number of improved and unimproved acres; and the cash value of the farm, farming machinery, livestock, animals slaughtered during the past year, and "homemade manufactures." The schedules also indicate the number of animals owned by the farmer and the amount of crops grown during the preceding year. The 1880 schedules provide additional details, such as the amount of acreage used for each kind of crop, the number of poultry, and the number of eggs produced. Please be aware that not every farm was included in these schedules. Some census years limited the size of agricultural farm reported. If your ancestor is shown on a census with the occupation of "farmer" and significant real estate value is shown, then you will want to look at the agricultural schedules for that county. These schedules will give you a unique glimpse of your ancestor's life. (See figure 2.20.)

Manufacturing/Industry schedules are available for census years 1810, 1820, and 1850 through 1880. The 1810 data was not shown on separate schedules but was recorded as annotations on the population schedules. Because Congress did not designate what data was to be collected, the results vary within the schedules. In 1820, 1850, 1860, 1870, and 1880, you will find the name of the manufacturer doing business over $500, the type of business or product, the amount of

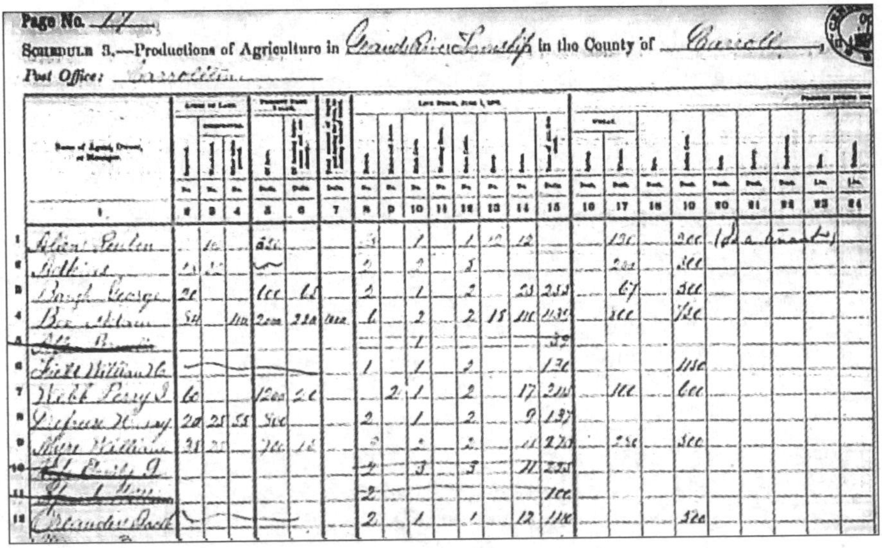
Page No.
Schedule 3.—Productions of Agriculture in Grand River Township in the County of Carroll
Post Office:

Figure 2.20 On this 1870 agricultural schedule, we see Reuben Allen on line 1. He had sixteen acres of improved land with the cash value of $350. He owned three horses, one milch cow, one "other cattle," twelve sheep, and twelve swine. During the year ending June 1 he produced 130 bushels of winter wheat and 200 bushels of Indian corn. From 1870 Agriculture Census, Carroll County, Missouri. Filmed by the State Historical Society of Missouri.

capital invested, quantities and types of products, and the number of men and women employed (see figure 2.21). Even though you may not find your ancestor's name on these schedules, you will be able to identify the businesses in your ancestor's community. If the census shows your ancestor's occupation as a worker in a linen mill, the manufacturing schedule could help you identify the place of his or her employment.

Social statistics schedules provide information about your ancestor's community. From 1850 through 1880, these schedules indicate the value of real estate; annual taxes paid; the number of schools, teachers, and pupils; the number and types of libraries and the number of volumes they had; the name, type, and circulation of newspapers; church denominations; the number of people each church could seat and the value of the property; the number of paupers and the cost of supporting them; the number of criminals convicted and in prison; and the average wages paid to farmhands, day laborers, carpenters, and female domestics. The information on these schedules is statistical only. You

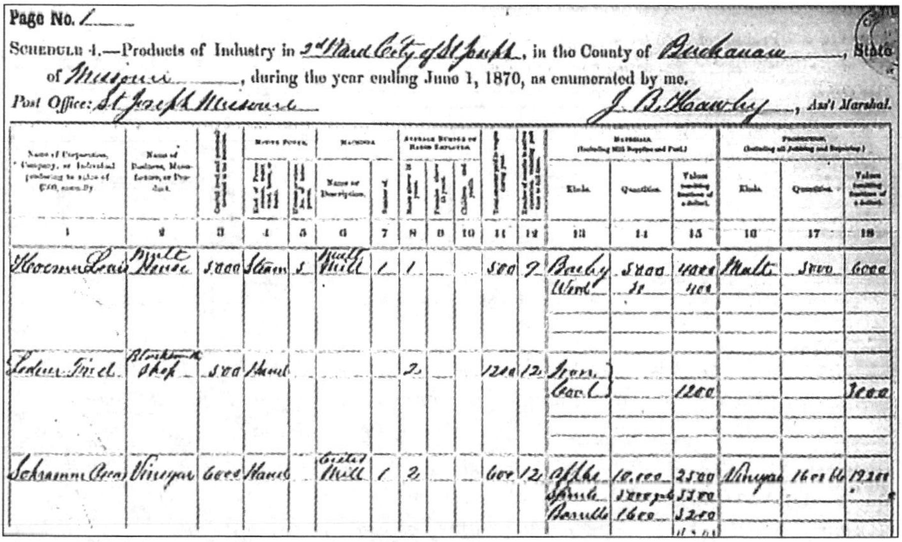

Page No. 1

SCHEDULE 4.—Products of Industry in 2d Ward City of St Joseph, in the County of Buchanan, State of Missouri, during the year ending June 1, 1870, as enumerated by me.

Post Office: St Joseph Missouri

J. B. Hawley, Ass't Marshal.

1	2	3	4	5	6	7	8	9	10	11	12	13	14	15	16	17	18
Hoevner Louis	Malt House	5000	Steam	5	Malt Mill	1	1			500	9	Barley Wood	5400 50	4000 400	Malt	5000	6000
Leder Fried.	Blacksmith Shop	500	Hand				2			1200	12	Iron, Coal		1200			3000
Schramm [illegible]	Vinegar	6000	Hand		Cider Mill	1	2			600	12	Apples Spirits Barrels	10,000 5000 gal 1600	2500 5500 3200	Vinegar	1600 bbls	19200

Figure 2.21 Line 1 of this 1870 industry schedule shows Louis Hoevner, who owned a malt house. The columns ask for the following: name of corporation or individual producing to the value of $500 annually; name of the business, manufacture, or product; amount of capital (real and personal) invested; type of power used and if steam or water; number of horsepower; name or description of machines; and number of machines. Information extends to the next page, which asks for average number of hands by age category; total dollar amount of wages paid; number of months in operation; kinds, quantities, and values of materials used; and kinds, quantities, and value of production. From 1870 Industry Census, Buchanan County, Missouri. Filmed by the State Historical Society of Missouri.

---

will not find your ancestor's name. But again, the economic and social life in your ancestor's community gives you a unique glimpse into that community. In 1880 you will also find the DDD schedules (Delinquent, Defective, and Dependent). These schedules record the names of delinquent, defective, and dependent (deaf and dumb, blind, criminal, indigent, etc.) individuals in the community. This is indeed a unique source. (See figure 2.22.)

States often took censuses in off-census years. Some, like the state of Kansas, were very regular. They took a census on the five years between federal censuses, beginning with the territorial census in 1855 and every ten years after. Other states did state enumerations more randomly. Excellent coverage of this topic is found in *State Census Records* by Ann

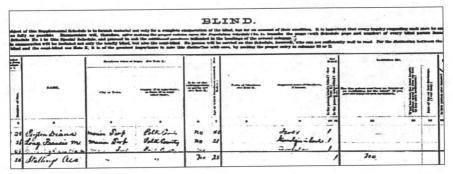

Figure 2.22 This 1880 DDD schedule shows those who were blind in Polk County, Missouri. The columns indicate name, city or town, county, and whether the person is self-supporting (yes/no). Also indicated are the form of blindness, cause of blindness, whether totally blind or semi-blind, whether ever in an institution for the blind, and whether also insane, idiotic, or deaf and dumb. From Missouri Historical Society, Census Books of St. Louis, Missouri. Filmed by Central Microfilm Service, 2121 Olive St., St. Louis, Missouri.

Lainhart.[5] Many state census records are found on Ancestry.com. I do not have a federal census in which my grandfather and his father are together in the same household. The two of them together on a census schedule would help prove a relationship I did not have otherwise. But the state census gave me that option. Michigan had an 1884 and 1894 state census. My grandfather and his father were shown together on the 1894 state census, which helped cement that relationship.

Population and nonpopulation census schedules are two of the best sources of information for genealogists. They were not intended to be significant genealogical sources when they were created, but with the limited availability of vital records, these schedules are a gold mine of information for family historians. William Dollarhide gives an excellent overview of all census years in his aptly named book, *The Census Book.*[6] For most researchers who are getting started, census records can jump-start their research and take them back to unknown ancestors quite rapidly. These records are definitely worth using.

THE INTERNET

Researchers have historically used census records on microfilm to find their ancestors, but today most people access census records through

🕐 GENEALOGY: TWENTY MINUTES A DAY

Look at your pedigree chart. For each person on your chart, your goal should be to try to find all of the available census records on which he or she was recorded. The more documents you find, the better able you are to compare the data. You might find on one census record that your great-grandfather was born in New York while another record might indicate the birthplace as Pennsylvania. On another census record you might find your ancestor listed as 26 years old but ten years later that same person could be listed as 34 years old. Census records can be found on microfilm at large genealogy libraries and the National Archives branches. Census records are also online and can be easily searched.

Internet databases where the records are digitized in their entirety. Two of the most popular subscription databases for census research are Ancestry.com (or Ancestry Library Edition, available in many libraries) and HeritageQuest, which is available through library subscriptions only.

Some census images are available free from FamilySearch (https://familysearch.org) and the USGenWeb Census Project (www.us-census .org). Printable extraction forms are available through Ancestry.com (www.ancestry.com/charts/census.aspx) and FamilySearch (https://familysearch.org/learn/wiki/en/United_States_Census_Forms).

NOTES

1. Alice Eichholz, ed., *Red Book: American State, County and Town Sources*, 3rd ed. (Salt Lake City, UT: Ancestry, 2004).

2. *The Handybook for Genealogists*, 11th ed. (Baltimore: Genealogical Publishing, 2006).

3. Thomas J. Kemp, *International Vital Records Handbook*, 5th ed. (Baltimore: Genealogical Publishing, 2009).

4. William Thorndale and William Dollarhide, *Map Guide to the U.S. Federal Censuses, 1790–1920* (Baltimore: Genealogical Publishing, 1997).

5. Ann S. Lainhart, *State Census Records* (Baltimore: Genealogical Publishing, 1992).

6. William Dollarhide, *The Census Book: A Genealogist's Guide to Federal Census Facts, Schedules and Indexes; With Master Extraction Forms for Federal Census Schedules, 1790–1930* (Bountiful, UT: HeritageQuest, 1999).

chapter three

Federal, State, and Local Government Records

COURTS HAVE PLAYED AN IMPORTANT PART IN THE LIVES OF OUR ANCES-
tors. The courts were established to keep the law, to hear cases, and to
conduct the business of the government. Your ancestors probably had
some dealings with a court during their lifetime. In looking at the types
of courts, you may need to think back to your high school civics class.
Do you remember your textbook mentioning the different branches of
government? The purpose of this chapter is not to delve into the specif-
ics of the courts system but merely to talk about the court records that
you can find.

There are several types of government jurisdictions: federal courts,
state courts, county courts, and town and township halls. Each conducts business, and each has a place where that business is conducted.
The country is divided into eighty-nine federal court districts within
the fifty states and one district in Puerto Rico. Each state is divided into
court districts within the state. Counties usually have one jurisdiction
that is the county seat—the city or town within the county where the

courthouse is located. In some states, towns or townships play a significant part in record keeping. The important thing to remember when looking for government records, in whatever jurisdiction or level, is that each is responsible for unique records. You will sometimes hear of a court being referred to as a *court of record*. This term describes a court that is required by law to keep a record of its proceedings.

The types of courts you might find within a courthouse are appellate courts or courts of appeals, circuit courts, criminal courts, family or juvenile courts, municipal courts, and probate courts. Appellate courts occur on the federal and state levels. These courts listen to appeals from lower courts. They are also called courts of appeals. Circuit courts are movable courts. The judge can and does move his or her court from place to place for a specific time to conduct business for the court. In a sense the judge is "riding the circuit." A family court is one that deals with domestic disputes, especially those regarding children. A juvenile court deals specifically with cases that involve children under the age of 18, such as adoption. Municipal courts handle misdemeanors and civil lawsuits involving less money than those cases heard in higher courts. In some states they only handle disputes and violations dealing with the city or local municipality, such as traffic citations. Probate courts have jurisdiction over wills and the administration of estates, including guardianships.

Look at the area in which your ancestor lived and the time frame in which she or he lived there. If your ancestor lived in an area long enough to conduct business, such as pay taxes, buy a house, record a marriage, or apply for a business license, then you can find information in the local jurisdiction. Sometimes we don't find any trace of an ancestor within a community. Those are usually the folks who were "passing through." They lived in a community for such a short time that they left no imprint in the area. But what if your ancestor was in an area for a long time and no record is in the courthouse? Courthouse fires are responsible for the loss of many important documents. Those fires could have occurred as a result of a lightning strike, faulty wiring, or burning during the Civil War. Counties with a loss of records due to fire are called "burned counties." When records are no longer at a courthouse because they have been destroyed, check other jurisdictions to see if copies or similar records are on file.

Courthouse fires are not the only reason for a loss or lack of records in a courthouse. First, there had to be a law requiring that the information be collected. If there was no law for births and deaths to be recorded, then that information is not available. Sometimes there was noncompliance with the law, and no one recorded the information. Improper storage of documents is yet another reason, such as storing the records in an attic where mice or climate conditions could cause their destruction. Security in courthouses has not always been what it is today, and documents have, as a result, "walked away." You also need to know when a county was formed. Your ancestor may have lived in the same home for his or her entire lifetime, but when new counties were formed from other counties, those living in the newly formed jurisdiction were suddenly living in a new county. The parent county, which usually continued to exist on a smaller scale, still held the records from its earliest existence. The new county will only have records from the date of its formation. The *Handybook* or *Red Book* can help you determine when a county was formed and from what parent county or counties.

Cases are divided into two categories—civil and criminal. Civil cases arise when there is a dispute between two or more people, legal entities, or corporations and may involve property damage, libel, divorce, personal injury, or breach of contract. Criminal cases comprise crimes or offenses committed against individuals or the state, including murder, theft, arson, or treason. Serious crimes are called *felonies*, and minor crimes are called *misdemeanors*. Courthouses are also where day-to-day business is recorded—births, marriages, deaths, and deeds, to name a few. One of the first things that comes to mind when we think of recorded documents is the vital records of birth and death. These documents were discussed at some length in chapter 2.

The records found in the courthouse are bound in books. You will find bond books, which are used by sheriffs and justices of the peace. In these you will find bail bonds and executor bonds. You will also find the docket book or court calendar. You could think of this as a table of contents to or a calendar of the proceedings of the court. In these books you will find lists of names of the plaintiffs (those who file a complaint) and defendants (those required to answer the complaint), the case file numbers, brief descriptions of the actions, lists of documents brought to the court, and the date of the hearing. These are kept in chronological order and may be found as separate docket books or order books. Often there are separate dockets for civil and criminal cases.

You can also find minute books in the courthouse. In these books are the minutes or notes taken by the clerk of the court—in other words, the daily record of the court. Proceedings are listed and include a brief account of all actions, names of the plaintiffs and defendants, brief descriptions of each case, and summaries of actions taken. These lists are in chronological order and are part of the court record. Fee books are also part of the court record. These books list fees ordered and collected.

The court record includes the minutes, pleadings (the cause for action by the plaintiff), documents filed (which can include evidence, correspondence, and petitions), orders (requiring a person to do or cease doing an act), and rulings (decisions by the court). Many times there are too many documents filed to be kept in a court record. In such cases, packets, folders, or bundles are created with all the pertaining documents. The packets are given the same number as the court record and usually put into storage. Such packets and bundles can be difficult to find unless you locate a friendly court worker who can tell you where they are. You will also find miscellaneous papers in storage. These are documents and papers that were not filed. There may also be "loose papers" somewhere in the courthouse, often in storage, in a basement, or in an attic. Loose papers are those documents that are related to a case but may never have been recorded in the minute books. Authors Gary Toms and Bill Gann used loose papers in researching their book *Widows' Dowers of Washington County, Tennessee, 1803–1899*.[1] They found rich documentation in papers housed at the Archives of Appalachia that had never before been used by researchers. Toms and Gann "recognized that the detailed information contained in these accounts would be of value to family history researchers, since full accounts did not occur in the recorded volumes in the courthouse in Jonesborough. These volumes ordinarily contain only a brief, abstracted entry for dowers."[2] Going beyond the easily found documents in a courthouse or archive is often needed.

WILLS AND PROBATE

Probate is the legal process of administering an individual's property or estate after death. *Webster's Third New International Dictionary,*

Unabridged (hereafter *Webster's*) says that *probate* is "the action or process of proving before a competent judicial officer or tribunal that a document offered for official recognition and registration as the last will and testament of a deceased person is genuine." The *last will and testament* is the record of a person's wishes as to the dispersal of her or his estate. The *probate record*, the entire group of papers generated in the probate process, can be found in a county courthouse. If an individual leaves a will, his or her estate is called *testate*. Think of this condition as someone leaving a "testament" or statement prior to his or her death. The types of wills are *attested wills*, which are prepared in writing and witnessed, *holographic wills*, which are written by hand by the person leaving the will, and *nuncupative wills*, which are dictated and written by someone else. In a will an *executor* is usually named. This is the person who will carry out the wishes stated in the will. If an individual does not leave a will, his estate is *intestate*, meaning he did not leave a testament as to the dispersal of his property. Intestate estates require a court process and ruling to divide the estate among the heirs. An administrator is appointed by the court to carry out the proceedings in the case. The probate court is under the jurisdiction of the state.

The probate process—settling the estate—has many steps during which probate packets are created. Documents, as they are recorded in court, are placed in a folder or folders. Notes are written on the outside of the folder (packet) to indicate items as they are placed inside. The documents inside the packets are the originals. There may be more than one packet if the estate is large or if a large number of documents have been created. The first step in the process occurs when the principal heir or the executor petitions the court for authority to begin the probate process. The executor is formally approved by the court at this time. In an intestate proceeding the court appoints the administrator. This person is often a relative. Bonds are posted or filed to protect the heirs, the executor or administrator, and the court with the amount posted equal to the assets of the estate. The bondsmen are usually relatives and friends and can be heirs. The bond is a binding agreement that the amount equal to the bond will be paid if certain acts are not done in the required manner. An inventory is taken in an intestate estate or in a testate estate if the will does not say "all" or "the remainder of my estate" is going to one specified individual. A disinterested party, not an heir, conducts the inventory. The inventory is filed within ninety days and often recorded in the will book.

The will is then "proven"—the witnesses of the will testify that they saw the individual sign the will, that he was in sound mental condition to do so, and he did it of his own free will. The will is recorded in the will book, and the proceedings are recorded in the court minute books. All heirs are then notified and are present at the reading of the will. The administrator or executor then petitions the court to sell the property as listed in the inventory. If minor children are involved, the petition could include an order to pay for their care while the estate is being settled. Property could also be petitioned to be sold if the heirs need money to pay expenses while the estate is being settled. The estate is advertised for sale, usually in the local newspaper. A record of the sale will be recorded in the court minute book. The list of buyers is recorded in the probate packet or will book. Low sale prices may indicate a family relationship. A guardian is appointed to provide legal assistance to minor children, those incapacitated, or those of low mental acumen. A guardian may be appointed even if one of the parents is still living.

When the settlement is near, a notice of the pending probate is publicized for three weeks in a local newspaper or posted in a public area (see figure 3.1). Any real estate will be divided at this time. A plat or drawing of the land is submitted to the court. If the property was to be sold and the money divided among the heirs, the final sale is presented. A final accounting is rendered by the executor or administrator and all other property is divided and the case is closed. Each heir will sign a receipt for property or cash received. The executor or administrator is released from her or his obligations. Guardians are released from their obligations only after minor children have reached the age of maturity.

When looking for probate records, look in docket books, minute books, will books, newspapers, and probate packets. The will is the most interesting of all the documents in the probate record. Here is where you will find information about family members and relationships. One interesting will I found in my research was for William E. Schultz. William had been married two times and had children from both marriages. The first marriage resulted in the birth of two sons. When William's first marriage dissolved, one son stayed with him and one went to live with his

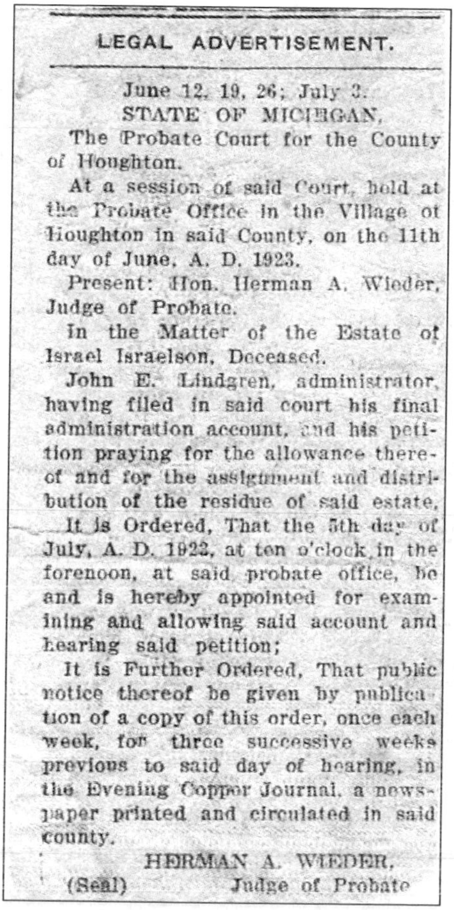

LEGAL ADVERTISEMENT.

June 12, 19, 26; July 3.
STATE OF MICHIGAN.
The Probate Court for the County of Houghton.

At a session of said Court, held at the Probate Office in the Village of Houghton in said County, on the 11th day of June, A. D. 1923.

Present: Hon. Herman A. Wieder, Judge of Probate.

In the Matter of the Estate of Israel Israelson, Deceased.

John E. Lindgren, administrator, having filed in said court his final administration account, and his petition praying for the allowance thereof and for the assignment and distribution of the residue of said estate,

It is Ordered, That the 5th day of July, A. D. 1923, at ten o'clock in the forenoon, at said probate office, be and is hereby appointed for examining and allowing said account and hearing said petition;

It is Further Ordered, That public notice thereof be given by publication of a copy of this order, once each week, for three successive weeks previous to said day of hearing, in the Evening Copper Journal, a newspaper printed and circulated in said county.

HERMAN A. WIEDER,
(Seal)   Judge of Probate

Figure 3.1 *This notice of pending probate was most likely published in the Houghton, Michigan,* Evening Copper Journal *in June 1923. The clipping was found in papers belonging to my aunt.*

ex-wife. His second marriage resulted in one daughter. William's will divided his property equally among his current wife, his daughter, and the son that had lived with him. The son who had lived with William's ex-wife was given five dollars. There is no indication why this was so, but I believe William did not want that son to inherit. He was given a negligible amount in the will to show to all that he was not accidentally "forgotten." (See figures 3.2, 3.3, and 3.4.)

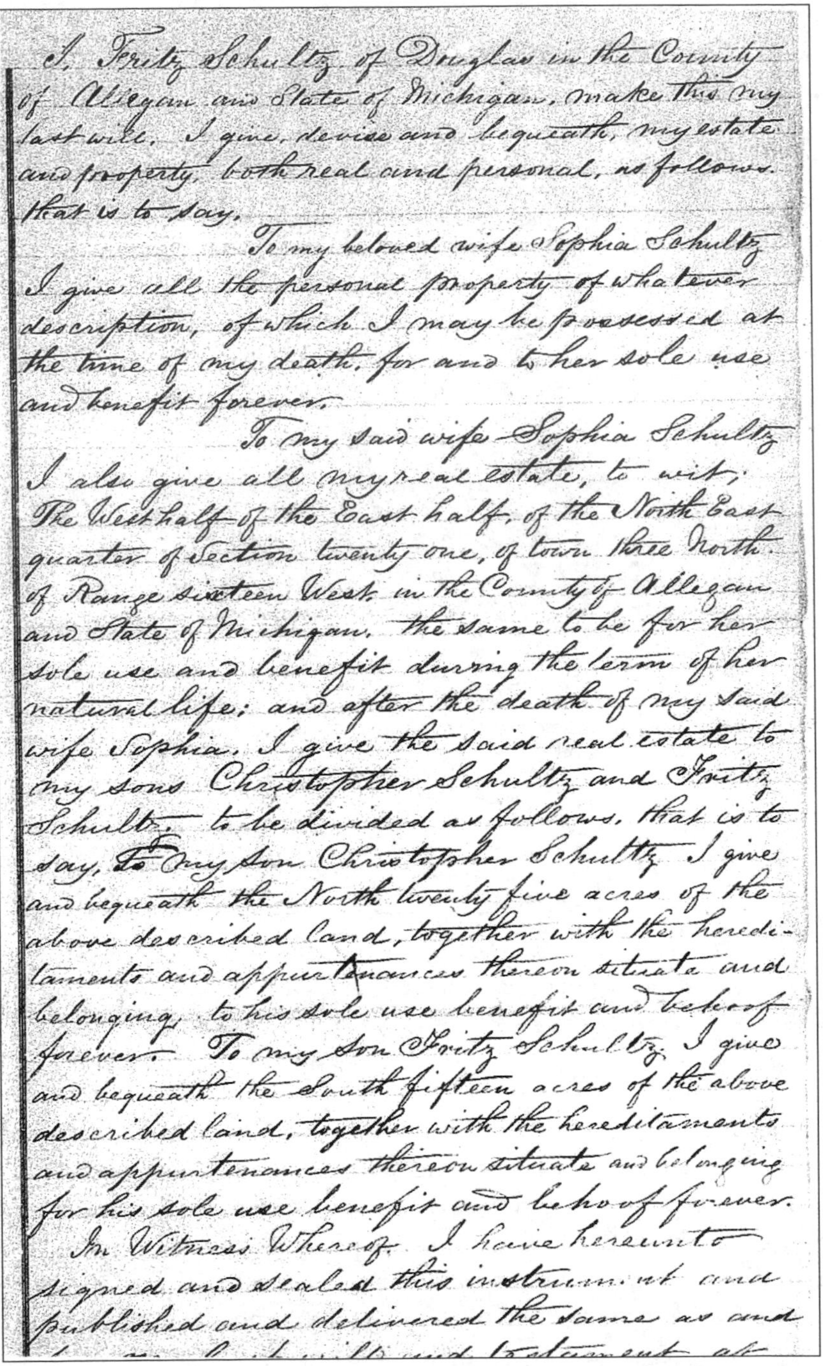

I, Fritz Schultz of Douglas in the County of Allegan and State of Michigan, make this my last will. I give, devise and bequeath, my estate and property, both real and personal, as follows. that is to say.

To my beloved wife Sophia Schultz I give all the personal property of whatever description, of which I may be possessed at the time of my death. for and to her sole use and benefit forever.

To my said wife Sophia Schultz I also give all my real estate, to wit; The West half of the East half, of the North East quarter of Section twenty one, of town three North. of Range sixteen West in the County of Allegan and State of Michigan. the same to be for her sole use and benefit during the term of her natural life; and after the death of my said wife Sophia. I give the said real estate to my sons Christopher Schultz and Fritz Schultz to be divided as follows. that is to say, to my son Christopher Schultz I give and bequeath the North twenty five acres of the above described land, together with the heredi- taments and appurtenances thereon situate and belonging, to his sole use benefit and behoof forever. To my son Fritz Schultz I give and bequeath the South fifteen acres of the above described land, together with the hereditaments and appurtenances thereon situate and belonging for his sole use benefit and behoof forever. In Witness Whereof I have hereunto signed and sealed this instrument and published and delivered the same as and

Figure 3.2 The will of Fritz Schultz names his wife and sons. From probate files at the Allegan County, Michigan, courthouse.

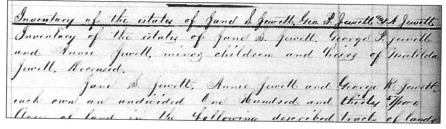

Figure 3.3 *This inventory from the estate of Matilda Jewett names her minor children. From "Inventory of the estate of Jane S. Jewett, George F. Jewett, and Annie Jewett, minor children and heirs of Matilda Jewett, Deceased," Jackson County [Missouri] Inventories, Appraisements, Sale Bills, v. B, 1866–1870. Filmed by Genealogical Society of Utah. Missouri State Archives film C3236, p. 6.*

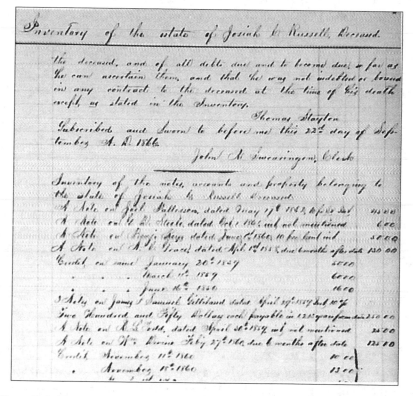

Figure 3.4 *This inventory of the estate of Josiah G. Russell lists the names of persons for whom he held notes. Inventories are a good way to find the names of individuals with whom a person associated, sometimes including the names of family members. From Jackson County [Missouri] Inventories, Appraisements, Sale Bills, v. B, 1866–1870. Filmed by Genealogical Society of Utah. Missouri State Archives film C3236, p. 7.*

LAND AND DEED RECORDS

Our ancestors often came to this country to have the ability to buy land. In many European countries, land was held by barons or landed gentry. Our ancestors left the eastern shore of the United States for the same reason—there was not enough land to be divided by all of the children. Individuals had several options in obtaining land: they could buy land from another individual, they could homestead, or they could receive the land as bounty land.

The United States has two types of land record keeping. Most but not all of the states east of the Mississippi River are called "state land" states. These states had land holdings when they were colonies or were formed from those states, and they took possession of those lands after the Revolutionary War. They are Connecticut, Delaware, Georgia, Kentucky, Maine, Maryland, Massachusetts, New Hampshire, New Jersey, New York, North Carolina, Pennsylvania, Rhode Island, South Carolina, Tennessee, Vermont, Virginia, and West Virginia. Hawaii and Texas are also state land states. In these twenty states, land is measured by metes and bounds. *Mete* means to "assign by measure," and *bound* is defined as "the external or limiting line of an object, space, or area . . . usually used in plural" (all definitions in this paragraph are from *Webster's*). The land was measured first by the degrees in distance using a compass and then in distance by using various units. The distance could be determined by using a *chain* ("a measuring instrument that consists of 100 links joined together by rings and is used in surveying"). This method would count the number of chains between two points. You probably have seen the use of chains in measuring football yardage. It is the same concept. Another measurement unit was a rod. A *rod* is "a unit of length equal to 5½ yards or 16½ feet." *Pole* was another measuring term meaning "a unit of length varying from one locality to another; *especially*: one measuring 16½ feet." Another term, used by the British, was *perch*, meaning "any of various units of measure (as 24¾ cubic feet representing a pile 1 rod long by 1 foot by 1½ feet, or 16½ cubic feet, or 25 cubic feet) for stonework." The land measurement would therefore give the number of degrees in a direction (north, south, east, west, northeast, southeast, northwest, or southwest) and the number of chains, rods, poles, or perches. Land measurements would often include a physical landmark such as a tree, watercourse, or fence. Because it usually

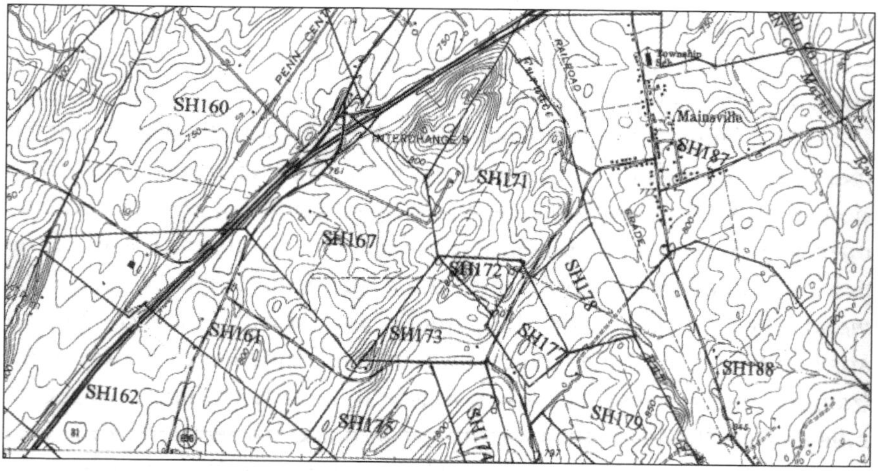

Figure 3.5 This metes and bounds plat has been drawn over a 1973 topographical map. From First Families of Cumberland County [PA], vol. 1: Shippensburg [with accompanying map] by Hayes R. Eschenmann (Carlisle, PA: Cumberland County Historical Society, 2005). You can see that the individual plats are not square. They are in varying degrees north, south, east, and west. The map accompanies a book containing the names and dates of the first surveys. Tract SH161 was surveyed in 1775 "on warrant to David Porter dated 18 Feb 1775" (Eschenmann. First Families, p. 32). Surrounding land was owned by James Dunn (SH162), David Foglesanger (SH175), John Maclay (SH173), and Benjamin Blyth (SH167).

included these physical attributes, the plat of land was seldom square. (See figure 3.5.)

When the colonies were first established, they had no western boundaries. Their lands went west without an end, except perhaps by the Pacific Ocean. By 1802, land owned by state land states outside their current borders was given to the US government. This territory was the basis for "federal land" states. The remaining thirty states are federal land states. Those states are, in alphabetical order, Alabama, Alaska, Arizona, Arkansas, California, Colorado, Florida, Idaho, Illinois, Indiana, Iowa, Kansas, Louisiana, Michigan, Minnesota, Mississippi, Missouri, Montana, Nebraska, Nevada, New Mexico, North Dakota, Ohio, Oklahoma, Oregon, South Dakota, Utah, Washington, Wisconsin, and Wyoming. When the US government was newly established, the country was land rich and cash poor. Land, known as bounty land, was given to veterans of the Revolutionary War as compensation for service in lieu of a cash payment. Other land was given later as bounty land for

They are the narrative of the survey and contain a detailed description of the survey procedure and process, including a list of the individuals who participated in the survey.

Land Entry Case Files

Public domain lands, those owned by the federal government, were either given away or sold at various times and in various ways in the early history of our country. The most common land dispersal laws were the Cash Sale Act of 1820 (also called the Cash Act or the Land Act), the Preemption Act of 1841, and the Homestead Act of 1862. To determine if land was granted by or purchased from the federal government, use the Bureau of Land Management (BLM) website to search for land patents (www.glorecords.blm.gov). A *land patent* is a legal document transferring ownership of land from the federal government to an individual. To receive the patent generally required living on the land for a set period of time as well as making improvements to the land. (See figure 3.8.)

The amount of land in question depended upon the act that was in effect. You can search the BLM website by name. You can also add the state and county into the search box, if you wish. If you find a record of the patent, you will be able to see the legal land description, the act involved, and a digitized copy of the land patent. You will then have the needed information to request the file, for a fee, from the National Archives. You can order online or request NATF Form 84 at www.archives .gov/contact/inquire-form.html. Look for the "Federal Land Entry Files" link.

The Cash Sale Act of 1820 provided for a cash purchase of land at $1.25 per acre. The records found in the case files show the name of the purchaser, the legal description of the land, the date of sale, and the receipt of payment. The Preemption Act of 1841 allowed those already living on federal land, called *squatters*, to purchase up to 160 acres before the land was offered for sale to the general public. Squatters were required to be a head of house, over the age of 21, a citizen of the United States or one intending to become naturalized, and a resident of the claimed land for at least 14 months.[4] The records in the land entry case files include the name of the purchaser, the legal description of the claim, the date of sale, statements from witnesses and the

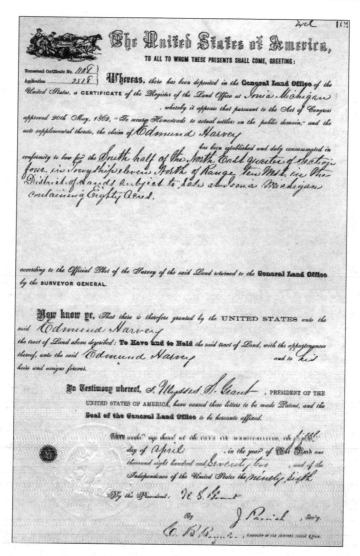

Figure 3.8 The image shows a land patent for land in Michigan received by Edmund Harvey. This copy was obtained from the Bureau of Land Management, but copies may now be printed from the BLM website (www.glorecords.blm.gov). The legal description as found on the website is as follows:

Accession	Names	Date	Doc #	State	Meridian	Twp-Rng	Aliquots	Sec. #	County
MI3000 __.109	HARVEY, EDMUND	4/5/ 1872	1108	MI	Michigan-Toledo Strip	011N-010W	S½NE½	4	Mont-calm

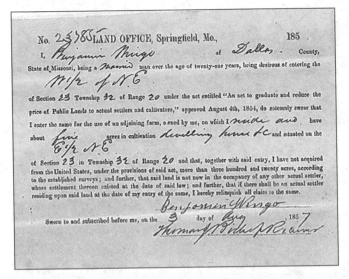

Figure 3.9 Part of the land entry case file of Benjamin Wingo, 1857. This file is under the Homestead Act of 1854. From National Archives, Online Public Access Database (http://research.archives.gov/description/300283).

claimant that the purchaser had established residence prior to making an application for purchase, a description of any structures on the land, and a statement of how the land was currently being used (see figure 3.9). Other homestead laws were enacted in the 1840s and 1850s.

The land entry case files for the Homestead Act of 1862 give the name of the purchaser, the application for the homestead, notice of intent to make the purchase, the marital status and number of children of the claimant, post office, a description of the house and any other buildings, a description of the crops grown, statements from witnesses testifying to the claimant's compliance with the act, a statement by the claimant as to the intended or current use of the property, receipts for fees paid, a copy of the final certificate, and proof of citizenship or intent to be naturalized. A description of where the declaration of intent was filed as well as any updated status of citizenship can be found in the papers.

Generally, five years had to elapse between the initial application and the awarding of the patent. Further information about the homestead acts can be found in *The Basic Researcher's Guide to Homesteads and Other Federal Land Records* by James C. Barsi.[5]

Deed Records

Buying land from another individual involves a transfer of the property deed. A *property deed* is the legal instrument in the transfer of real property. These records will be in a county courthouse. There are often two indexes to the deed records. One is an index of sellers and is called the grantor or direct index. The other index is of buyers and is called the grantee or indirect index. If you are tracing the ownership of a piece of land, which is called the *chain of title*, indexes are very important. You should work backward from one deed to the next to determine who conveyed the right of possession to whom. This is called a title search. Sometimes the indexes are available online.

In each deed record you will find the names of the buyer(s) and seller(s), relationships of individuals, the value of the land, the description of the property, and the date of the transaction. The deed, unless it is a modern one, will be handwritten. The first words in the deed will say "this indenture," meaning a legal contract. When people look at deeds for the first time, they are often confused by the term *indenture*. They may think that someone is offering himself (or herself) as an indentured servant. This is not the case. The date of the sale is given next. Later the deed is sent to the court to "prove" the sale. The parties involved are then named. The deed may say, "John and Jane Doe, husband and wife" or "John Doe and his wife Jane." The names of the buyer(s) and seller(s) are listed. The dollar amount of the sale is listed, the seller acknowledges he has been paid, and the basic property description is given. It is important to identify the property with as much detail as necessary to ensure the sale of the correct tract of land. You may see the term *heirs and assigns*. This term concerns the buyer: "to John Smith and his heirs and assigns." This means that the property can be inherited or sold at a future time. The seller then claims that he or she holds a valid title, and the deed is dated again. Each party then signs the agreement. You may find a release of spousal rights. A "dower release" means the wife has agreed to the sale of the property. A "release of courtesy rights" means the husband has agreed to the sale. There is an excellent form on the Internet that you can use when transcribing deeds: http://dohistory .org/on_your_own/toolkit/deeds_form.html.

There are two major types of deeds: warranty and quit claim. *Warranty deeds* assure that the seller holds the title and can legally sell the property. (See figure 3.10.) *Quit claim deeds* relinquish all rights held by the grantor to the grantee. There is no guarantee that the grantor is the sole owner. Therefore the grantor is only relinquishing his rights to what is his at the time of the sale. A quit claim deed does not promise title and, thus, offers no warranty. These deeds are often used to transfer property between family members as a gift. You will very seldom see a quit claim deed between nonrelated buyers and sellers. A quit claim deed is also used in divorce to transfer property from one spouse to the other, wherein the spouse who receives the marital home in the settlement is given a quit claim deed by the other spouse relinquishing his or her rights to the property. Deeds of trust will also be found in a courthouse. They convey property to a trustee and are often used to secure a promissory note or mortgage. A deed of trust specifies the collateral for the loan and gives the lender the right to seize and sell the collateral should the borrower fail to repay. In some localities you will also find deeds of adoption among the land deeds.

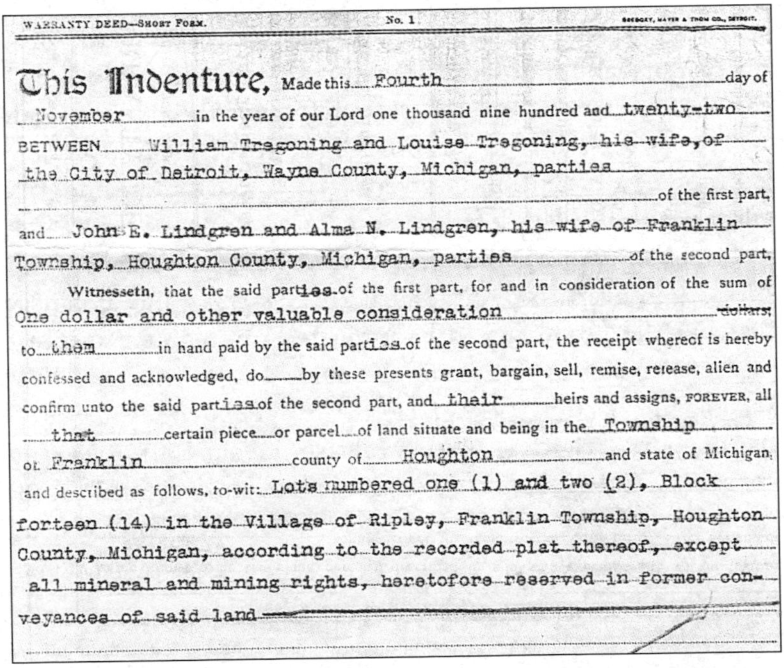
WARRANTY DEED—SHORT FORM. No. 1

This Indenture, Made this Fourth day of November in the year of our Lord one thousand nine hundred and twenty-two BETWEEN William Tregoning and Louise Tregoning, his wife, of the City of Detroit, Wayne County, Michigan, parties of the first part, and John E. Lindgren and Alma N. Lindgren, his wife of Franklin Township, Houghton County, Michigan, parties of the second part,

Witnesseth, that the said parties of the first part, for and in consideration of the sum of One dollar and other valuable consideration dollars, to them in hand paid by the said parties of the second part, the receipt whereof is hereby confessed and acknowledged, do by these presents grant, bargain, sell, remise, release, alien and confirm unto the said parties of the second part, and their heirs and assigns, FOREVER, all that certain piece or parcel of land situate and being in the Township of Franklin county of Houghton and state of Michigan, and described as follows, to-wit: Lots numbered one (1) and two (2), Block forteen (14) in the Village of Ripley, Franklin Township, Houghton County, Michigan, according to the recorded plat thereof, except all mineral and mining rights, heretofore reserved in former conveyances of said land

Figure 3.10 Warranty deed. From papers belonging to Alan I. Lindgren.

TAX RECORDS

You may be thinking, "Tax records!?" Yes, tax records can be used in genealogical research. Your ancestors paid taxes, and the records can give a glimpse of life in their time. Some tax records from earlier times still exist, but the availability varies from state to state and from county to county. Many of them have been filmed by the Family History Library. In tax records from colonial times, you might find the word *tithable*. Tithables are like taxes, but they were levied to help pay for the parish minister and were levied on all adult males.

Yearly tax assessments can help you determine age. Poll taxes were levied on all adult males beginning at age 16 or 18 or 21, depending on the locality. You may have to do a little research on the laws of the area in which you are researching, but once you know the age of majority in that area you can determine someone's approximate birth year by when he first appears on the records. For instance if a man first shows up on a poll tax record in 1821 and the age of majority is 16, you can assume he was born about 1805.

Property or real estate taxes and personal property taxes were (and are) levied on owners of real estate or personal property. Tax records can be used in place of missing land or census records. You can trace a man (and therefore his family) in a county year by year. In figure 3.11 we see a property tax record for Calloway County, Kentucky, in 1831. All the people on the list were property owners or owners of personal property. The community was a farming community. The right-hand page shows the crops and livestock subject to taxes. Only a portion of that page is showing on the image.

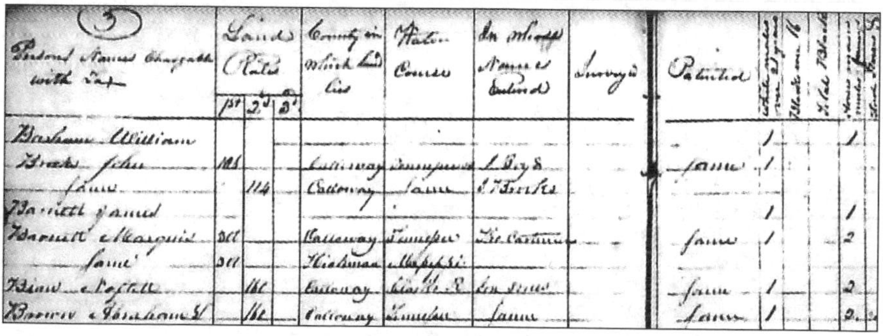

Figure 3.11 Property tax record. From Kentucky Tax Books, Calloway County, 1831, reel 54.

Our ancestors also paid income taxes. In 1862, the US Congress established an income tax to help pay for the Civil War, and it remained in force for about ten years. Cynthia G. Fox explains this rather unpopular tax in her article, "Income Tax Records of the Civil War Years."[6]

NATURALIZATION RECORDS

Naturalization is the legal process of obtaining citizenship. Naturalization records are the papers created when a foreign-born individual seeks citizenship in the United States. (See figure 3.12.) During colonial times people on this continent were either British citizens or aliens born outside the British Empire. Each colony had its own methods of naturalizing aliens for British citizenship. Those naturalization records can be found as legislative acts in the colonial papers of the colony in question. The first naturalization law in the United States was created in 1790. Before 1906 citizenship could be sought from any court of record. As described earlier, a court of record is any court that is required to keep records. This means that your ancestors could have been naturalized

Figure 3.12 Certificate of naturalization for Israel Israelson Lonbom as found in my family papers.

in a federal, state, or county courthouse and in any court within that courthouse. It also means that the hunt for those naturalization papers may be difficult.

The Naturalization Process

The process of obtaining citizenship can require many steps. In our ancestors' day, the years of residence required to complete the process ranged from two to fourteen, depending on the law in effect. Not all alien residents were naturalized, but they could begin the process shortly after arriving in this country or they could wait many years before starting the process. At some time after arriving in the country, usually a minimum of one year, an individual could declare his or her declaration of intent to become a citizen. (See figure 3.13.) The 1790 naturalization law required a residency of at least one year in the state in which the individual resided and a total of two years in the country. No declaration of intent was required, but the individual had to show proof of good moral character. Married women and underage children obtained derivative citizenship from the head of the household.

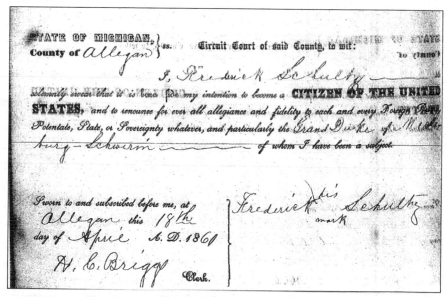

Figure 3.13 Declaration of intention of Frederick Schultz, April 18, 1860, Michigan, Circuit Court (Allegan County). From Index to Naturalizations 1850–1955, Declarations, v. 1–4, no. 1–100, 9346, 1850–1914. Filmed by the Genealogical Society of Utah, 1955. Film no. 1994145.

Derivative citizenship means that naturalization has been acquired from another person's naturalization. If you are looking for the naturalization of someone who came into this country as a child and you can't find a record of naturalization, his or her citizenship may have been given through the father.

In 1795, a total of five years' residency was required for naturalization. A declaration of intent was required, but it could only be filed after three years of residency. Derivative naturalization was still practiced, but single women over the age of 21 could apply for citizenship in their own right. In 1798, a more stringent law was enacted requiring a total of fourteen years of residency in the United States before citizenship was granted. However, legislation in 1802 reinstated the five-year requirement. Aliens were required to register with the court upon arriving in the country, and three years of residency were required before filing a declaration of intent. This became the naturalization code of the nineteenth century, with many revisions over the years.

No matter which law was in effect at the time your ancestor sought citizenship, a record of the paperwork was kept on file in the courthouse where the papers were filed, and a copy was given to the individual. As many as three steps were often required to obtain citizenship. In addition to the declaration of intent, there was an application for citizenship and an oath of allegiance. Each step could occur in a different courthouse and in a different court of record. Each time, a copy of the paperwork was kept in that court, and a copy was given to the individual. When the oath of allegiance was given, the new citizen received a certificate stating he or she was a citizen of the United States.

Citizenship could also be given to a group of individuals at the same time. People living in territories acquired by the United States were granted citizenship en masse. When land holdings were involved, property titles were verified and land claims were filed. Records of the land actions can be found in the *American State Papers*. These papers were early legislative and executive documents of Congress from 1789 to 1838. The *American State Papers* can be found online through the American Memory Project at the Library of Congress's website (http://memory.loc.gov/ammem/amlaw/lwsplink.html). Territories for which Congress provided group naturalizations are Louisiana (1803); Florida, Mississippi, and Alabama (1819); Alaska (1867); Hawaii (1900); Puerto Rico (1917); and the US Virgin Islands (1927).

A legislative act in 1862 allowed aliens serving as Union soldiers in the Civil War and honorably discharged to gain citizenship without declaring an intention to be naturalized. This act was intended to encourage alien support for the Union cause during the Civil War. Instead of the normal first papers, military discharges were filed in the courts. In 1894, the act was extended to aliens serving in the Navy or Marine Corps. In 1918, Congress passed a law allowing any alien who had been in service in any branch of the armed forces for three or more years to file a petition for naturalization without proof of the five-year residency requirement.

The year 1906 was pivotal in naturalization history. Prior to 1906, there were no standard forms for naturalization. Courts were supposed to record each alien's name, his or her native country, and the date of naturalization, but the information gathered by each court often varied from place to place. The exact town of birth was rarely provided. In 1906, responsibility for naturalization shifted from clerks of the court to the newly established Bureau of Immigration and Naturalization, later called the Immigration and Naturalization Service (INS). Courts were ordered to use standard forms, and any court of record could still be the facilitator of naturalizations.

The standard forms established in 1906 were the declaration of intent, the petition for naturalization, and the certificate of naturalization. Duplicate copies were to be forwarded to the bureau. A two-year residency was required before filing a declaration of intent. A total of five years fulfilled the requirements for naturalization. Derivative naturalization was still practiced.

Naturalization and Genealogy Research

The US Citizenship and Immigration Services (USCIS) has a genealogy program for genealogists who wish to obtain copies of post-1892 immigration records and copies of naturalization records between 1906 and 1956. The website is www.uscis.gov/portal/site/uscis. When you enter the site, look for the side bar and click on Genealogy. The records searched are the C-files, which are naturalization certificates from 1906 to 1956; alien registration forms (Form AR-2) from 1940 to 1944; alien files (A-files) from 1944 to 1951; visa files from 1924 to 1944 and visa records from 1944 to 1951 as found in the A-files; registry files from 1929 to 1944; and registry records from 1944 to 1951. C-files contain at least one application form (a declaration of intent or a petition for naturalization or both) and a duplicate certificate of naturalization or certificate of citizenship. The AR-2 files were completed by all aliens age 14 or older.

How can you determine when and where someone was naturalized? Begin with census records. The 1900, 1910, 1920, and 1930 census records give the year of immigration and citizenship status. If the person had begun the process but was not yet naturalized, the indication will be "pa" on the census. If the person had gone through all of the steps and was naturalized, the indication will be "na." The indication will be "al" if your ancestor was still an alien resident at the time the census was taken. Use your ancestor's location on all census records to begin your search of naturalization records. Search the courthouses in those areas. If there is no federal courthouse in the county in which your ancestor lived, he or she was most likely naturalized in the county courthouse. If your ancestor was living in a large city where there was a federal courthouse, check federal naturalizations at the National Archives field branch that covers that state. To find the list of NARA (National Archives and Records Administration) facilities, go to www.archives .gov/locations. If you find your ancestor in several different counties or states, or both, on census records, search all of those locations.

...

Family histories, county histories, family records, and family tradition are other good sources for discovering naturalization status, location, and date. Federal land records can also give clues to naturalization. To purchase land from the federal government, your immigrant ancestor must have obtained his or her citizenship before the end of the process in order to receive the land patent. The individual could start the naturalization process at any time after arriving in the United States. There was no set time to begin or end the process and no requirement that the person obtain citizenship if he or she did not want to buy land.

If you are going to visit a courthouse to look for any type of records, make sure you call ahead or check the website for open hours and for days on which the offices are closed. Courthouses are not closed only for federal holidays. In Missouri, for example, courts are closed on Harry Truman's birthday, May 8. Each state or municipality will have

GENEALOGY: TWENTY MINUTES A DAY

Review your pedigree and family unit charts. Create a timeline by year for your ancestor, indicating the locations of residence. What courthouses were within a logical distance? Depending on the era, consider the time it would take to travel there by horseback or by horse and carriage or by car. Where was your ancestor living when he or she died? Check the indexes for wills or probate records. These may be on microfilm, online, in a book in a library, or in the courthouse. Review census records. Did your ancestor own land? (Look for the value of real estate on the 1850–1870 census schedules and, using the 1900–1940 schedules, note whether the home was rented or owned.) Check the Bureau of Land Management website and the grantor/grantee indexes at the courthouse.

similar special holidays. Also ask for information about parking, the cost of making copies, and whether there are particular "research days" for genealogists. I made the mistake of not calling ahead when I went to visit a courthouse to look for marriage records. In my defense, I did not think I would have the time on this particular family vacation, but when the opportunity arose I jumped at the chance to do some research. When I arrived at the courthouse the clerk kindly told me that Tuesdays, Wednesdays, and Thursdays were days on which genealogists were welcome. Mondays and Fridays were particularly busy days for the office staff, and they didn't have time to help genealogists on those days. I was there on a Friday. It would have been an opportunity lost except the clerk took pity on me and allowed me into the vault to look at the marriage records. What a break for me! Don't expect all visits to turn out so well, however. Another unfortunate experience occurred when my husband and I were looking for probate records in a courthouse. We drove to the courthouse and discovered there was no free parking. After digging in my husband's pockets and my purse, we found enough coins to last us for an hour's visit. We walked up to the courthouse only to find that we had to go through security gates, with a long line of people ahead of us. We finally got to the appropriate office in the courthouse only to be told the older probate records had been moved to an offsite location "last week." We had to return to our car and drive three miles to the offsite location where, luckily, there was free parking. Don't make my mistakes. Make sure you call ahead before you visit the courthouse.

THE INTERNET

Many resources for researching court records are available on the Internet. Here is a reminder of the websites discussed in this chapter.

- Bureau of Land Management: www.glorecords.blm.gov (federal land patents, cadastral surveys, and land status records)
- Cyndi's List: www.cyndislist.com/us (select a state to find records)
- Deed transcription form: http://dohistory.org/on_your_own/toolkit/deeds_form.html
- National Archives and Records Administration (NARA): www.archives.gov/contact/inquire-form.html (to order land records), www.archives.gov/locations (to locate facilities)
- US Citizenship and Immigration Services: www.uscis.gov/portal/site/uscis
- USGenWeb Project: http://usgenweb.org. This is a free site with content derived from volunteer user input. Organization is by state and county. Each state and county page is maintained by a volunteer coordinator. The content varies by page, depending on the work of the coordinator. Each site may have transcriptions of courthouse records or indexes to records.
- You will also be able to find some records discussed in this chapter on Ancestry.com, Fold3 (military records), FamilySearch, and GenealogyBank.com (personal subscriptions are available at www.genealogybank.com/gbnk/ or check your public library for library access).

• • •

Visiting a courthouse can be a rewarding experience. Looking for your ancestors in books or finding information about them on the Internet is great, but holding an original document in your hands is an exciting moment. Knowing your ancestor was in that building and walked those halls can make him or her seem more real. Don't limit your research to secondary experiences. Spend some time traveling and creating a visual picture of the area in which your ancestors lived. You won't be sorry.

NOTES

1. Gary R. Toms and William R. Gann, *Widows' Dowers of Washington County, Tennessee, 1803–1899* (Milford, OH: Little Miami Publishing, 2004).

2. Ibid., preface.

3. www.glorecords.blm.gov/default.aspx

4. www.minnesotalegalhistoryproject.org/assets/Microsoft%20Word%20-%20Preemption%20Act%20of%201841.pdf

5. James C. Barsi, *The Basic Researcher's Guide to Homesteads and Other Federal Land Records* (Colorado Springs, CO: Nuthatch Grove Press, 1994).

6. Cynthia G. Fox, "Income Tax Records of the Civil War Years," *Prologue* 18, no. 4 (Winter 1986), www.archives.gov/publications/prologue/1986/winter/civil-war-tax-records.html.

chapter four

Military, Church, and Cemetery Records

MILITARY RECORDS

Very few of our ancestors have escaped military service during their lifetime and have served through selective service, military conflict, or war. Our nation has been involved in warfare throughout its existence, including events that occurred before we were a country. Knowledge of history, military history, and military operations is essential to effectively use military records. To understand the conflicts, a short US history lesson is needed, but all will not be discussed here. The Internet Archive has digitized *Alphabetical List of Battles: 1754–1900*.[1] It can be viewed free online at www.archive.org/details/alphabeticallist00stra. It can also be viewed on HeritageQuest.

Many of the early conflicts involved Native American tribes. Early settlers tried to take up residence on land in which Native tribes were well established and land that the tribes considered theirs alone. Indian wars occurred in the colonies of Virginia, Connecticut, Massachusetts, Rhode Island, New York, the Carolinas, Florida, and Georgia, and in territorial land now known as Michigan and Ohio. Each of these conflicts was named, with the longest and most well-known being the French and Indian War, also known as the Seven Years' War, which lasted from 1754 to 1763. It took place in the northern colonies and Canada and was a result of border conflicts between British and French colonists.

The American Revolutionary War lasted from 1775 to 1783. It was a long war and resulted in America's independence. On the American side, counties and towns maintained local militias to defend themselves against Indian attacks. These units eventually made up the bulk of the Continental Army. Some units only fought within the borders of their own colonies while others fought under the command of General George Washington. Each colony was requested to provide a given number of men for the Continental Army. A navy was also formed at the beginning of the war. Many men (and a few women) fought for the right to become a country. Many others gave patriotic service in other ways that may have included hay for horses, food for the troops, and the making of cannonballs and other ammunition. Each man provided his own uniform and rifle.

Several minor conflicts occurred after the Revolution until the War of 1812, which was our next major battle. This war was not as popular as the Revolution, and many Americans today know little about it. Fewer records are available for this conflict and less written material. The War of 1812 began, in part, as a result of the British navy's practice of seizing American ships and impounding American crews to supplement its need for additional men. It was not America's finest hour. Washington, D.C., was lost for a time to British forces and burned. A planned invasion of Canada failed. And America's biggest success, the Battle of New Orleans, was fought after the peace treaty had been signed.

After the War of 1812, Indian wars continued until 1858. During this time the Native American tribes east of the Mississippi River were forcibly removed to lands in the west using military personnel. The War of Texas Independence between Mexico and the territory of Texas was fought in 1836 with the Mexican War following several years after from 1846 to 1848. As a result of the Mexican War, the United States gained land in California, Texas, and New Mexico with the Rio Grande River established as the border between Texas and Mexico.

The biggest and bloodiest battle on our shores to date has been the American Civil War, also known as the War of Northern Aggression, the War Between the States, or the War of the Rebellion, among other names, covering the years 1861 to 1865. The cause of the war or why people fought varies depending on one's view. Some feel the war was fought for states' rights. Others feel it was the war to abolish slavery. The Confederate Congress enacted a conscription law in 1862 when it became apparent that volunteer forces alone would not fill the need for soldiers. The United States passed a similar law in March 1863. However, if a man paid $300, he could become exempt from service, or he could pay someone directly to fulfill his duty for him. The Civil War was complicated and often pitted brother against brother. Record access is good because both sides kept many records. However, more records survive for the North than for the South.

After the Civil War came more Indian wars. These were fought in areas now known as the states of North and South Dakota, Montana, New Mexico, California, and Idaho.

In 1898 a very short and not well-known war took place—the Spanish-American War. Fighting lasted from February to August and took place in Cuba and the Philippine Islands. The peace treaty, the Treaty of Paris, was signed on December 10, 1898. As a result of the peace treaty, Cuba gained its independence. The United States was granted Puerto Rico and Guam as territories and obtained the Philippine Islands for $20 million. The Philippine Insurrection followed the Spanish-American War and lasted many years longer, from 1899 to 1902, though the fighting was mostly sporadic. The United States had supported the Philippines in fighting the Spanish during the Spanish-American War, but when the United States did not give the nation its independence, the Philippine government went to battle. In 1902 the Philippine Islands were granted self-governance.

The war to end all wars, now known as World War I, was fought from 1915 to 1918. The United States entered the war in 1917. Many lives were lost in Europe through fighting, disease, and gassing. An assassination in Serbia began a ripple effect that resulted in the Triple Entente of England, France, and Russia declaring war against the Triple Alliance of Germany, Austria-Hungary, and Italy. Before the war's end, many nations had become involved. The United States stayed neutral for much of the war but declared war on Germany on April 6, 1917. The US forces gave a timely and needed boost to the Allied forces, allowing them a victory. In May of that year, Congress created the Selective

Service System requiring eligible males to register for potential military service. The World War I draft registrations have been declassified and have been filmed by the National Archives. They are available on Ancestry.com and Ancestry Library Edition. All draft boards closed following the war.

World War I did not end all wars, as people had hoped. What followed were World War II, the Korean War, the Vietnam War, and today's many and continued conflicts. Most of the records for conflicts after World War II are still classified documents and are unavailable for research.

The Records and Where to Find Them

All US military records are federal government records. As they become declassified the records become the property of the National Archives and Records Administration (NARA). Some of the declassified records have been microfilmed. Microfilmed records are easily accessible in the Washington, D.C., branch of the National Archives and at many of its field branches. To determine if the microfilm is available at a field branch near you, check the microfilm catalog online. Go to www.archives.gov/research/start/online-tools.html and select Go to Microfilm Catalog. Various public and research libraries across the nation have purchased National Archives microfilm. Contact your local library for information on its holdings. Many, if not all, of the microfilms have been digitized. You can find some of the digitized records on Ancestry.com and Ancestry Library Edition as well as on Fold3 (www.fold3.com). Some extracted or indexed military records are on the National Archives' Access to Archival Databases site (AAD; http://aad.archives.gov/aad), and some digitized copies are on the Archives' Online Public Access site (www.archives.gov/research/search). Other military records are still textual records (paper format). These records are slowly being digitized by Fold3. Nondigital records for wars prior to World War I can be viewed at the National Archives in Washington, D.C., or can be ordered from the agency (www.archives.gov/veterans). Records beginning with World War I are at the National Personnel Records Center in St. Louis, Missouri. They can be ordered through the NARA's eVetRecs System (www.archives.gov/veterans/military-service-records). Declassified records are available for viewing at the St. Louis facility, but an appointment must be scheduled in advance (see www.archives.gov/st-louis/military-personnel/visitors-and-researchers.html).

Many types of military records and related records have been created over time, some microfilmed and some not. They include service records, pension records, military histories, claim records, letters and diaries, other government documents, and state adjutant general's reports. The principal types of records, and those used most frequently, are indexes to records, compiled service records, and pension and bounty land records. An excellent guide to lists of the varied types of records is *U.S. Military Records* by James C. Neagles.[2] Consulting the National Archives catalog is also a good way to discover the myriad of records. Service records include muster rolls, enlistment records, rosters, discharges, prisoner lists, records of burial, oaths of allegiance, and payroll records. Pension records include a record of payment, proof of military service, and, in the case of a widow, proof of marriage. Military histories can be regimental histories written by someone within the regiment or by a military historian. Military histories may be privately printed or may be found within a county, state, or town history. Claim records are claims against the US government for personal or property damage. Letters to and from a soldier or personal diaries are frequently found in repositories within records sets. Other government documents are those printed and published by the Government Printing Office (GPO). State adjutant general's records are those that were collected and compiled by the person holding that office within a state. Older records are usually found in a state repository. The most frequently used records from the major military conflicts are discussed in the following paragraphs.

REVOLUTIONARY WAR
Records for the Revolutionary War have been microfilmed, and many are available online. The records were microfilmed by NARA, and many libraries have copies of them. Two of the best commercial sources for searching soldiers' records are Ancestry.com (and Ancestry Library Edition) and Fold3. The first records to search are the compiled service records. These are records that have been "compiled" for each soldier in the Continental Army or in state troops. As various muster lists, rolls, and reports were searched, records relating to individual soldiers were written on separate abstract cards. The cards for each soldier were compiled in a packet, like a paper envelope, and eventually microfilmed. Finding a soldier's compiled service record for Revolutionary War

service means he gave military service to the new nation. The service records will give very little, if any, personal data on the soldier. They will not give his age and will not state the names of members of his family. If there is more than one soldier with your ancestor's name, it may be difficult to determine which one is your ancestor.

If your ancestor received a pension or bounty land, you may be able to find additional information about him and his family. He could receive a pension for a disability incurred during service. This is called an invalid pension. Service pensions were also given. The longer the veteran lived after the war the greater the possibility that he received a service pension. The earliest service pensions were given to officers who remained in service until the end of the war. By 1832, anyone serving two full years could receive a pension. Widows, assuming they lived long enough, were also given pensions. The first widows' pensions were awarded to widows and orphans of officers in 1780. Eventually, as with service pensions, widows of all service personnel were offered pensions. The widows' pensions always give more information than other pensions. Not only did the widow have to prove that her husband served, she also had to prove they were married. The proof of marriage could have been a notarized statement of witnesses indicating knowledge of the marital union or a page torn from the family Bible. Bounty land was another option soldiers and widows were allowed. The military bounty land was an option for free land in the official bounty land area. Some of these bounty land awards were given by states. Others were given by the US government. The Military District of Ohio, land now known as the state of Ohio, contained the bulk of the land that was awarded.

Selected Books about Revolutionary War Research and Bounty Land

- Bockstruck, Lloyd de Witt. *Revolutionary War Pensions: Awarded by State Governments 1775-1874, the General and Federal Governments Prior to 1814, and by Private Acts of Congress to 1905*. Baltimore: Genealogical Publishing, 2011.
- Bockstruck, Lloyd de Witt. *Bounty and Donation Land Grants in British Colonial America*. Baltimore: Genealogical Publishing, 2007.

WAR OF 1812

Some records of the War of 1812 have been filmed, but there are no complete records of service. An index to the compiled service records has been microfilmed by the National Archives and is also on Ancestry .com and Ancestry Library Edition. Compiled service records for all soldiers have not been filmed. This is a very difficult war to research due to the lack of complete microfilmed or digitized records. The practice of giving pensions and bounty land for military service continued with the War of 1812. The longer a soldier or his widow lived after the war, the more likely he was to receive remuneration. By 1814, however, bounty land was frequently promised immediately upon enlisting for military service as it was becoming more difficult to raise troops. Bounty land for War of 1812 service was available in Arkansas, Illinois, Louisiana, Michigan, and Missouri. Pension and bounty land acts were enacted at various times, and therefore not all soldiers who received payment or land are found on all microfilms or lists. For instance, National Archives film series M858 contains War of 1812 Bounty Land Warrants for the years 1815–1858. Virgil White's *Index to War of 1812 Pension Files*[3] contains the names of the veterans or their widows receiving remuneration as a result of the pension acts of 1871 and 1878. The War of 1812 pension files are being digitized by Fold3 in conjunction with the Federation of Genealogical Societies (FGS) and Ancestry.com. The FGS is spearheading a fund-raising campaign to enable the digitization of the records, and Ancestry.com is matching dollar for dollar the funds raised. Fold3 has promised that the records will be searchable without cost on its site. The project should be completed by the end of the bicentennial of the war (2015).

Another source for information about Revolutionary War and War of 1812 soldiers is the Draper Papers. Also called the Draper Manuscripts, this is a collection of papers written and gathered by Lyman Copeland Draper (1815–1891). Draper was a military historian who developed a great interest in the Revolutionary War during his childhood. His grandfather, along with fellow Revolutionary War veterans, spent hours talking about their memories of the war and declared that it was the New England patriots alone who won the war. Draper spent most of his adult years either visiting or writing to veterans, writing to family members and acquaintances of veterans, and visiting courthouses trying to grasp a fuller picture of those early military events and those involved in the conflicts. Along the way he also developed an interest in the War of 1812 and the Indian wars. The original papers are housed at the Wisconsin Historical Society, but they have been microfilmed. Many libraries have copies of the films, including the Family History Library, which makes them available for loan.

The papers are difficult to use because there is no every-name index to them, but they are a very valuable source for serious scholars of those early wars. The *Guide to the Draper Manuscripts*[4] is invaluable when using the films. Very few of the papers are original, but there are many copies of documents and many letters that were sent to Draper. Muster rolls are interspersed throughout the papers. (See figure 4.1.) The papers are divided into 491 volumes in fifty sections. One of the volumes contains copies of court documents that were used as sworn testimonies that a soldier had served in the Revolutionary War. For example, in 1832 in the Spartanburgh District of South Carolina, John Collins, age 78, appeared before the judge of Common Pleas. His statement said, "I

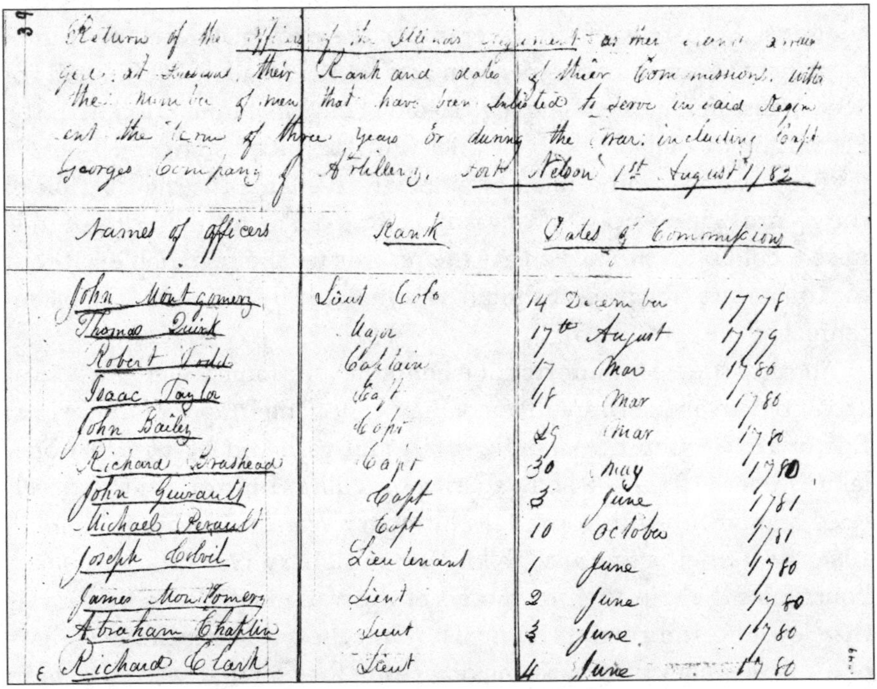
39

Return of the Officers of the Illinois Regiment as they stand arranged at present, their Rank and dates of their Commissions, with the number of men that have been Inlisted to serve in said Regiment the term of three years or during the War: including Capt Georges Company of Artillery. Fort Nelson 1st August 1782

Names of officers	Rank	Dates of Commissions	
John Montgomery	Lieut Colo	14 December	1778
Thomas Quirk	Major	17th August	1779
Robert Todd	Captain	17 Mar	1780
Isaac Taylor	Capt	18 Mar	1780
John Bailey	Capt	29 Mar	1780
Richard Brashead	Capt	30 May	1780
John Girault	Capt	3 June	1781
Michael Perrault	Capt	10 October	1781
Joseph Calvit	Lieutenant	1 June	1780
James Montgomery	Lieut	2 June	1780
Abraham Chaplin	Lieut	3 June	1780
Richard Clark	Lieut	4 June	1780

Figure 4.1 Muster roll. From Draper Papers, "George Rogers Clark Papers," vol. 46, series J, p. 39.

enlisted [in] the service of the United States as a volunteer and under Cpt. Berry and Col. Thomas, Col. Richardson having the chief command and served a six weeks campaign in 1775." Collins also served in 1778 and 1780.[5]

CIVIL WAR

The American Civil War was the bloodiest conflict on North American shores. Neighbor fought against neighbor, and brother fought against brother. The United States had a regular army, but most soldiers who fought in the Civil War, Union and Confederate, were from state-raised volunteer units. As the Northern state volunteer troops joined forces with the army, they were "mustered in," meaning they enlisted in or joined the regular army. Southern state-raised units joined forces with the Confederate army and were mustered in as well. Indexes to the consolidated service records exist for both Union and Confederate soldiers. Each soldier's consolidated record comprises a "packet" of index cards. The jacket or cover is a folded envelope that contains all the cards. You will often find a card in the packet that says the soldier was found on a muster roll. Figure 4.2 shows the envelope in which index cards were placed for Abraham (Abram) Ebersole of the 13th Missouri Cavalry (Union), Company C.[6] There are twelve cards in his consolidated record. One of the cards (a portion of which is shown in figure 4.3) indicates he was a private. He appeared on a company muster roll during March and

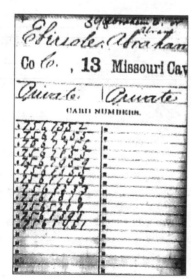

Figure 4.2 Jacket for a consolidated service record. From Compiled Service Records of Volunteer Union Soldiers Who Served in Organizations from the State of Missouri, National Archives, microfilm publication no. M405, roll 268.

Figure 4.3 Service record card showing rank of service member. From Compiled Service Records of Volunteer Union Soldiers Who Served in Organizations from the State of Missouri, National Archives, microfilm publication no. M405, roll 268.

April of 1866. Another card, shown in figure 4.4, indicates he was absent in September and October of 1865. He was "detached and nursed at Regtl Hospt Camp Wardnell C. T. [Colorado Territory] since Oct. 12, 1865." Private Ebersole enrolled for duty on February 28, 1864, and mustered in the US Army on February 29, 1864, in Springfield, Missouri (see figure 4.5).

Many, but not all, of the service records have been microfilmed by the National Archives. Those that have not been filmed must be ordered from the National Archives using Form 86 or by ordering online at www.archives.gov/veterans/military-service-records/pre-ww-1-records.html. Be sure to click on Order Online under Military Service Records. The microfilmed copies are available at libraries and through the Family History Library. You can find

Figure 4.4 [left] Service record card showing absence from duty. From Compiled Service Records of Volunteer Union Soldiers Who Served in Organizations from the State of Missouri, National Archives, microfilm publication no. M405, roll 268.
Figure 4.5 [right] Service record card showing dates joined and mustered in. From Compiled Service Records of Volunteer Union Soldiers Who Served in Organizations from the State of Missouri, National Archives, microfilm publication no. M405, roll 268.

some of the military records on Ancestry.com, Ancestry Library Edition, and Fold3. The Civil War Soldiers and Sailors System, a database of the National Park Service (www.nps.gov/civilwar/soldiers-and-sailors-database.htm), has an index to all Union and Confederate soldiers and sailors who gave service during the war. The free site also gives information about regiments, battles, prisoners, cemeteries, and Medal of Honor recipients. Many books have been compiled to give the same type of information.

To find information for soldiers in the regular army, look in the microfilmed *Registers of Enlistments in the U.S. Army, 1798–1914* (National Archives series M233). Records are in chronological order, then in loose alphabetical order (only alphabetical by the first letter of the last name), and then by date of enlistment. These records can also be found on Ancestry.com and Ancestry Library Edition.

Pension records are available for Union veterans or their widows and are textual records held at the National Archives. They have not been

Civil War Sources: A Brief Bibliography

Dyer, Frederick H. *A Compendium of the War of Rebellion.* New York: T. Yoseloff, 1959. This three-volume set, later reprinted in two volumes, lists the names of Union units, gives brief regimental histories, and lists battles. Names of soldiers are not given.

Hewett, Janet, ed. *The Roster of Confederate Soldiers, 1861–1865.* Wilmington, NC: Broadfoot Publishing, 1995–. This ten-volume set lists the names of Confederate soldiers and the state, rank, and unit to which they belonged.

Hewett, Janet, ed. *The Roster of Union Soldiers, 1861–1865.* Wilmington, NC: Broadfoot Publishing, 1997–. This multivolume set contains information for each state that had Union soldiers. The name of each soldier plus rank, state, and unit are given.

Morebeck, Nancy Justus. *Locating Union and Confederate Records: A Guide to the Most Commonly Used Civil War Records of the National Archives and Family History Library.* North Salt Lake, UT: HeritageQuest, 2001.

United States. War Department. *The War of the Rebellion: A Compilation of the Official Records of the Union and Confederate Armies.* Harrisburg, PA: National Historical Society, 1971. This multivolume set is often referred to as the "ORs." There is no personal information about soldiers. Rather, the volumes contain accounts of battles and correspondence between units.

filmed, but they are slowly being digitized by Fold3. Federal pension records are available for the veteran, if he qualified, or his widow. If a veteran fought for the South, applications for pensions were accepted by states in the former Confederate States of America but were not always granted. Don't look for Confederate pension applications at the National Archives because the federal government did not offer pensions to veterans who had not been Union soldiers. A Confederate veteran was eligible to apply for a pension to the state in which he lived at the time of the application, and that state is where the pension application will be found. If he was living in a state that did not offer a Confederate pension (meaning a Northern state), there will be no pension application. More information about Confederate pension records can be found on the National Archives website, www.archives .gov/research/military/civil-war/civil-war-genealogy-resources/ confederate/pension.html.

Another place to look for information about a Union Civil War veteran is the special 1890 census schedule of Union Civil War veterans or their widows. This separate enumeration was taken at the same time as the 1890 census. However, these records were subject to the same fire that affected the 1890 census. Fortunately, the special schedules for the states of Kentucky through Wyoming survived the fire. When a Union veteran was found to be in the household at the time of the 1890 enumeration, the additional schedule was completed. It contains the name of the soldier (or his widow), his unit of service, and his rank. Additional information is found regarding any disability incurred because of the war. Occasionally the names of Confederate veterans can be found on the pages of the special schedule, but they will be marked through. The names are usually readable through the markings.

Should you wish to find the burial place of a Union Civil War soldier, a couple of sources are available. Shortly after the Civil War, families of deceased Union veterans were allowed to request a tombstone for their loved one. As families applied for the headstones, index card files were created. Each card contains the name of the soldier or veteran, his unit and state, and the place of burial. Some of the cemeteries named on the cards are national cemeteries and some are not. The applications were amassed from about 1879 to about 1903. The image in figure 4.6, from microfilm, shows an application for a headstone for John W. Colyer who served as a private in Company B, 9th Regiment, Pennsylvania

Cavalry. He died on May 3, 1883, and is buried at Oak Hill Cemetery in Millersburg, Dauphin County, Pennsylvania.[7] The National Archives filmed the card files, and Ancestry.com has digitized the film and placed the images on its website.

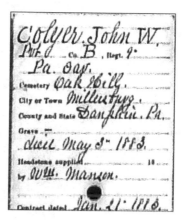

Figure 4.6 Application for a headstone. From Card Records of Headstones Provided for Deceased Union Civil War Veterans, ca. 1879–ca. 1903, *National Archives, microfilm publication no. M1845, roll 1.*

To help you find soldiers buried at national cemeteries—soldiers who fought in the Civil War and those who were in other conflicts— the US Department of Veterans Affairs maintains a web page called "Nationwide Gravesite Locator" at http://gravelocator.cem.va.gov/ j2ee/servlet/NGL_v1. You can search for names in specific cemeteries or in all cemeteries. The only required field in which to enter information is the last name. The website will search for veterans in national and state veterans' cemeteries and also in private cemeteries when the grave has a government grave marker. The results will show the name of the soldier, rank and unit, the war in which the individual served, date of death, the name and address of the cemetery, and, possibly, the location of the grave within the cemetery. If a cemetery map is available, a link will bring up that image.

Civil War records can also be found on the state level. Muster-out records containing the names of soldiers for a particular state were given to the adjutant general of that state. The adjutant general would publish the names either yearly or compiled into a multiyear volume (see figure 4.7). These books of names can be found in libraries and

FIRST REGIMENT KANSAS VOLUNTEERS — INFANTRY — *Continued.*

COMPANY G — *Continued.*

Names and rank.	Residence.	Date of enlistment.	Date of muster.	Remarks.
PRIVATES. Cole, Joseph............	Leavenworth.	May 29, '61	May 29, '61	Shot for murder of Michael Stein, July 14, 1861, by order of Gen. Lyon.
Conley, George F.....	"	"	"	Des. Chillicothe, Mo., Oct. 6, '61.
Caswell, Wm. H......	"	"	"	Des. Trenton, Aug. 10, '62.
DeGraff, Wm. H......	"	"	"	Dis. by order Gen. Fremont, Nov. 10, '62, Tipton, Mo.
Evans, Jeremiah......	"	"	"	Mus. out with reg. June 17, '64.
Funk, Abraham......	"	"	"	Pro. Serg. May 29, '61.
Ford, Wm. W.,......	"	"	"	Mus. out with reg. June 17, '64.
Friend, Asa,.........	"	"	"	Des. Spr'gfield, Mo., Aug. 2, '62
Frederick, Armil.....	"	"	"	Dishonorably dis. by sentence of court martial, Oct. 28, '62, Corinth, Miss.
Fisher, Charles M....	"	"	"	Transf'd to Co. K, Oct. 1, '61.
Fitzgerald, Michael...	"	"	"	Pro. Corp. Mar. 1, '62.
Folsom, George H....	"	"	"	Dis. for disability, June 7, '62, Leavenworth, Kan.
Green, George B.....	"	"	"	Pro. Serg. May 29, '61; des. Trenton, Tenn., Aug. 1, '62.
Gladden, Wm. R.....	"	"	"	Transf'd to Co. B, July 1, '61; mus. out with Co. B, June 16, '64.
Gross, Christian W...	"	"	"	Died, Lake Providence, La., July 27, '63.
Hendelong, John,....	"	"	"	Pro. Serg. May 29, '61.
Hepworth, Jeremiah,	"	"	"	Pro. Corp. May 29, '61; trans. Co. K, Nov. 1, '61.
Harrison, Chas. T....	"	"	"	Pro. Corp. May 29, '61.
Hinckley, Reuben,...	"	"	"	Pro. Corp. Oct. 25, '61.
Hemerith, Gotleib...	"	"	"	Died of congestive fever, Lake Providence, La., June 29, '63; wounded in action.
Henry, John A.......	"	"	"	Pro. Serg. Maj. May 1, 62.
Hart, Henry P.......	"	"	"	Des., Rolla, Mo., Aug. 23, '61.
Hicklin, John........	"	"	"	Died of typhoid fever, St. Louis, Mo., Jan. 30, '62.
Holbush, Wm. S.....	"	"	"	Des., Rolla, Mo., Aug. 19, '61.
Johnson, Edwin S....	"	"	"	Mus. out with reg. June 17, '64.
Kline, Christian.....	"	"	"	App. Musician May 29, '61.
Kirwin, Michael.....	"	"	"	Trans. to Co. K, Nov. 1, '61.
Lareaux, Henry.....	"	"	"	Des. Leavenworth, May 30, '61.
Lowry, James M.....	"	"	"	Des. Memphis, Tenn., June 20, '63; wounded in action.
Lantz, John........	"	"	"	Mus. out with reg. June 17, '64.
Milburn, Phil'nder E.	"	"	"	Pro. Corp. May 29, '61; mus. out with reg. June 17, '64.
Morton, Wm. A......	"	"	"	Dis. for disability Nov. 10, '61, by order Gen. Fremont.
Meyer, Christian.....	"	"	"	Died, St. Louis, Feb. 26, '62.
May, Pierce	"	"	"	Died, Lake Providence, La., July 15, '63.
Morrison, James.....	"	"	"	Re-enlisted vet.; was wounded in action.
Munroe, James......	"	"	"	Re-enlisted veteran.
Miller, Jacob........	"	"	"	Des. Gr. Riv., Mo., July 12, '63

Figure 4.7 Muster-out records for Kansas volunteers. From Report of the Adjutant General of the State of Kansas, 1861–'65, *vol. 1 (Salem, MA: Higginson, 1998; Topeka: Kansas State Printing, 1896).*

archives under the title *Report of the Adjutant General of the State of [name of state], [year or years encompassed]*.

More information about Confederate soldiers can be found in a periodical entitled *The Confederate Veteran*. It was published between 1893 and 1932 and can be found in some libraries and historical societies. Issues have also been digitized and can be found online at the Family History Books website (http://books.familysearch.org). Veterans of the Union army often joined other veterans in a fraternal organization called the Grand Army of the Republic. Rosters of some of those state organizations can be found in scattered books in libraries and historical societies. Look at WorldCat (www.worldcat.org) to locate copies of the rosters. If copies have been digitized, WorldCat will indicate that. Look on the left side of the screen and limit by e-book. Links to online versions will appear below the book record.

SPANISH-AMERICAN WAR

The muster rolls and general index cards to the compiled service records for the Spanish-American War are available as textual records at the National Archives and can be ordered using NATF Form 86 (www.archives.gov/veterans/military-service-records/pre-ww-1-records.html). The compiled military service records for 1,235 Rough Riders, under the command of Theodore Roosevelt, have been digitized and can be found on the National Archives website. Instructions for searching the records and a link to the search site can be found at www.archives.gov/research/arc/topics/spanish-american-war. Adjutant general muster-out records for various states can now be found on the Internet and are available for soldiers of the Spanish-American War and other wars. Try a Google search with the search terms "Spanish-American War records" and the name of the state.

Figures 4.8–4.11 show images from the pension file of Fred E. Williams who was a Spanish-American War veteran. He obtained an invalid pension.

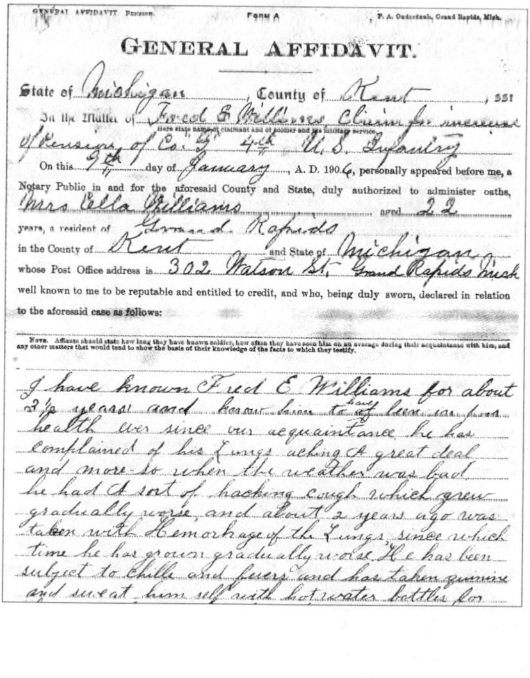

GENERAL AFFIDAVIT. Pension. FORM A P. A. Onderdonk, Grand Rapids, Mich.

GENERAL AFFIDAVIT.

State of Michigan, County of Kent, ss:

In the Matter of Fred E. Williams Claim for increase of Pension, of Co. "G" 4th U.S. Infantry

On this 9th day of January, A. D. 1906, personally appeared before me, a Notary Public in and for the aforesaid County and State, duly authorized to administer oaths, Mrs Ella Williams aged 22 years, a resident of Grand Rapids in the County of Kent and State of Michigan, whose Post Office address is 302 Watson St. Grand Rapids Mich well known to me to be reputable and entitled to credit, and who, being duly sworn, declared in relation to the aforesaid case as follows:

NOTE. Affiants should state how long they have known soldier, how often they have seen him on an average during their acquaintance with him, and any other matters that would tend to show the basis of their knowledge of the facts to which they testify.

I have known Fred E. Williams for about 3½ years and know him to have been in poor health ever since our acquaintance he has complained of his Lungs aching A great deal and more so when the weather was bad he had A sort of hacking cough which grew gradually worse, and about 2 years ago was taken with Hemorhage of the Lungs, since which time he has grown gradually worse. He has been subject to chills and fevers and has taken quinine and sweat him self with hot water bottles for

Figure 4.8 Testimony supporting Fred Williams's application for an invalid pension. From record for Fred E. Williams (Pvt., Co. G, 4th U.S. Inf., Spanish-American War), pension no. Inv. 1051909, Civil War and Later Pension Files, Department of Veterans Affairs, Record Group 15, National Archives.

Santa Cruz } S. S.
Cavite Luzon P.I. }
Philippine Islands

Personally appeared before me, the undersigned authority. Private Lewis Turley. Co. G. 4th Infantry. who being duly sworn deposes and says, than on or about December 22nd 1898, he was on Fatigue duty with Fred Williams, then a private in Company G. 4th Infantry. that the duty consisted in the carrying of coal into the basement of the company quarters at Fort Sheridan, Illinois. That upon reaching the stairs leading into the basement Pvt Williams slipped and fell, with a sack of coal he was carrying, to the bottom of the stairs, that he complained then and afterwards of great pain, as resulting from the fall.
Further deponent sayeth not.

Lewis Turley
Private, Co. G. 4th Infantry

Sworn to and subscribed before me this 3rd day of July in the year of our Lord, one thousand nine hundred and one.

Dwight E. Holley

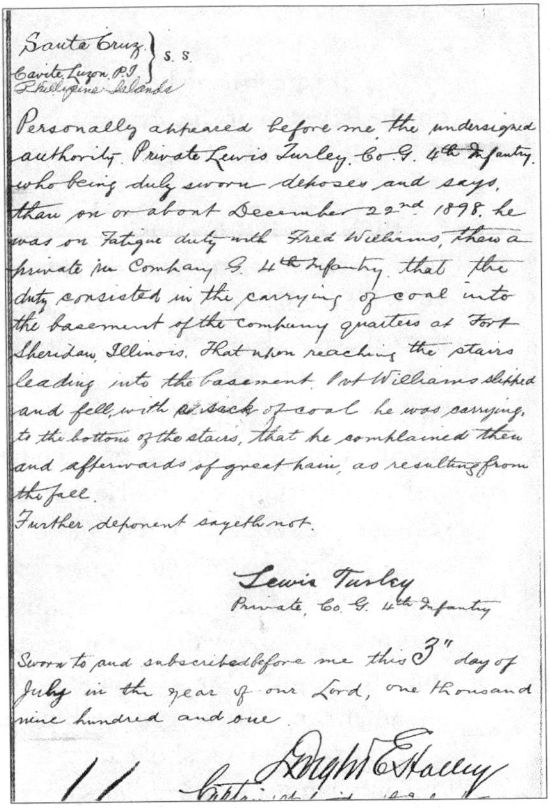

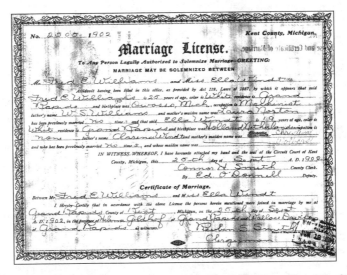

Figure 4.9 *Pension testimony of an injury occurring in the Philippines during Fred Williams's tour of duty. From record for Fred E. Williams (Pvt., Co. G, 4th U.S. Inf., Spanish-American War), pension no. Inv. 1051909, Civil War and Later Pension Files, Department of Veterans Affairs, Record Group 15, National Archives.*

No. 2500 1902 Kent County, Michigan.

Marriage License.

To Any Person Legally Authorized to Solemnize Marriage—GREETING:

MARRIAGE MAY BE SOLEMNIZED BETWEEN

Mr. Fred E. Williams and Miss Ella Windt

Affidavit having been filed in this office, as provided by Act 128, Laws of 1887, by which it appears that said Fred E. Williams is 25 years of age, color is White, residence is Grand Rapids and birthplace was Owosso, Mich., occupation is Machinist father's name W. S. Williams and mother's maiden name was Laura Norton has been previously married no times, and that said Ella Windt is 19 years of age, color is White residence is Grand Rapids and birthplace was Holland Netherlands occupation is none father's name Clarence Windt and mother's maiden name was Christina Wolters and who has been previously married no times, and whose maiden name was

IN WITNESS WHEREOF, I have hereunto attached my hand and the seal of the Circuit Court of Kent County, Michigan, this 20th day of Sept A. D. 1902

Connor H. Smith County Clerk.
By Ed. O'Donnell Deputy.

Certificate of Marriage.

Between Mr. Fred E. Williams and Miss Ella Windt

I Hereby Certify that in accordance with the above License the persons herein mentioned were joined in marriage by me at Grand Rapids County of Kent, Michigan, on the 25th day of Sept A. D. 1902, in the presence of Helena Geldhof of Grand Rapids and Wallace Davis of Grand Rapids as witnesses.

Reuben S. Smith
Clergyman

Figure 4.10 *This marriage certificate was included in the pension file of Fred Williams. From record for Fred E. Williams (Pvt., Co. G, 4th U.S. Inf., Spanish-American War), pension no. Inv. 1051909, Civil War and Later Pension Files, Department of Veterans Affairs, Record Group 15, National Archives.*

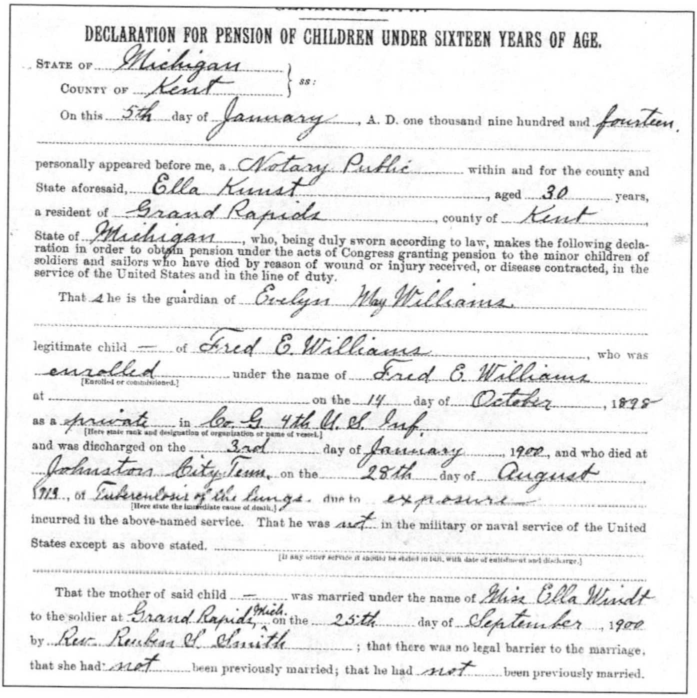

DECLARATION FOR PENSION OF CHILDREN UNDER SIXTEEN YEARS OF AGE.

STATE OF Michigan
COUNTY OF Kent } ss:

On this 5th day of January, A. D. one thousand nine hundred and fourteen.

personally appeared before me, a Notary Public within and for the county and State aforesaid, Ella Kunst, aged 30 years, a resident of Grand Rapids, county of Kent, State of Michigan, who, being duly sworn according to law, makes the following declaration in order to obtain pension under the acts of Congress granting pension to the minor children of soldiers and sailors who have died by reason of wound or injury received, or disease contracted, in the service of the United States and in the line of duty.

That she is the guardian of Evelyn May Williams

legitimate child — of Fred E. Williams, who was enrolled [Enrolled or commissioned.] under the name of Fred E. Williams at .... on the 14 day of October, 1898 as a private in Co. G. 4th U. S. Inf. [Here state rank and designation of organization or name of vessel.] and was discharged on the 3rd day of January, 1900, and who died at Johnston City Tenn. on the 28th day of August 1913, of Tuberculosis of the lungs. [Here state the immediate cause of death.] due to exposure incurred in the above-named service. That he was not in the military or naval service of the United States except as above stated. [If any other service it should be stated in full, with date of enlistment and discharge.]

That the mother of said child — was married under the name of Miss Ella Windt to the soldier at Grand Rapids, Mich. on the 25th day of September, 1900 by Rev. Reuben S. Smith; that there was no legal barrier to the marriage, that she had not been previously married; that he had not been previously married.

Figure 4.11 Application for benefits for Fred Williams's minor child. From record for Fred E. Williams (Pvt., Co. G, 4th U.S. Inf., Spanish-American War), pension no. Inv. 1051909, Civil War and Later Pension Files, Department of Veterans Affairs, Record Group 15, National Archives.

WORLD WAR I

World War I records are available at the National Personnel Records Center in St. Louis, Missouri, and can be viewed by appointment. The World War I draft registrations have been filmed by the National Archives. They have been digitized by Ancestry.com, and the images can be viewed on that site. The Selective Service Act required men to sign up at their local draft board to provide the needed number of men in the armed forces. There were three registrations. The first registration was on June 5, 1917, and was required of those men who were ages 21 to 31. The second registration was on June 5, 1918, for those who had become 21 years old since the previous registration. The third registration, on September 12, 1918, expanded the ages required to 18 through 45. The draft registrations contain the following information: name, birth date, birth place, mailing address, occupation, employer, name

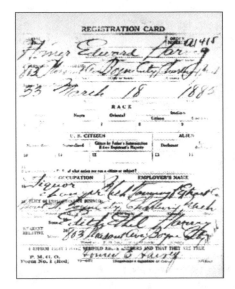
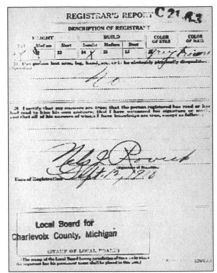

Figure 4.12 Front (left) and back (right) of World War I draft registration card for Homer Edward Harvey, Charlevoix County, Michigan. From Ancestry.com, World War I Draft Registration Cards, 1917–1918 [online database] (Provo, UT: Ancestry.com Operations, 2005).

and address of next of kin (a great place to find the name of the wife or parents), and general description. (See figure 4.12.)

WORLD WAR II AND LATER

As mentioned earlier in this chapter, World War II and later records have not been declassified and are not public record. The soldier or his (or her) next of kin (if the solder is deceased) may obtain copies of the records. Those records, including the records of World War I, are at the National Personnel Records Center in St. Louis, Missouri. A fire at the records center in July 1973 destroyed many personnel files. Records for army personnel who separated from service between November 1, 1912, and January 1, 1960, were 80 percent destroyed. Records for air force personnel who separated from service between September 25, 1947, and January 1, 1964 (with names alphabetically after Hubbard, James E.) were 75 percent destroyed.[8] "Access to Archival Databases," a National Archives web page, has some brief military personnel records for World War II, the Korean War, and the Vietnam War (http://aad

.archives.gov/aad). For those service personnel whose names are in the World War II records, you will find serial number, name, residence (state and county), place of enlistment, date of enlistment, rank upon enlistment, term of enlistment, place and year of birth, race and citizenship, education, civilian occupation, and marital status. The record in figure 4.13 shows the army enlistment record for my father. It is from Ancestry's database, but the information is from NARA's "Access to Archival Databases" web page.

Ancestry.com has a list of World War II draft registrations for the fourth registration, which is the only registration open to the public due to privacy laws. The registration took place in 1942 for men born between the years 1877 and 1897. The information found on these records is similar to that found on the World War I draft registration cards.

To find locations of the final resting places of those who were killed in action on foreign soil, see the American Battle Monuments Com-

Name:	Alan I Lindgren
Birth Year:	1917
Race:	White, Citizen (White)
Nativity State or Country:	Michigan
State of Residence:	Michigan
County or City:	Houghton
Enlistment Date:	11 Jul 1942
Enlistment State:	Michigan
Enlistment City:	Traverse City
Branch:	Branch Immaterial - Warrant Officers, USA
Branch Code:	Branch Immaterial - Warrant Officers, USA
Grade:	Private
Grade Code:	Private
Term of Enlistment:	Enlistment for the duration of the War or other emergency, plus six months, subject to the discretion of the President or otherwise according to law
Component:	Selectees (Enlisted Men)
Source:	Civil Life
Education:	1 year of college
Civil Occupation:	Bookkeepers and cashiers, except bank cashiers
Marital Status:	Single, without dependents
Height:	72
Weight:	143

Figure 4.13 Army enlistment record for Alan Lindgren. From National Archives and Records Administration, US World War II Army Enlistment Records, 1938–1946 [online database] (Provo, UT: Ancestry.com Operations, 2005).

mission (ABMC) website, www.abmc.gov/home.php. You can search for World War I, World War II, and Korean War deaths. Only those buried in US burying grounds on foreign soil are listed. My uncle, Melvin Lindgren, is buried in the Philippines. The ABMC website indicates he was a second lieutenant in the US Army; his service number is given, along with his unit and regiment. The website also indicates he entered the service from Michigan, he died 12 May 1945, and he is buried at the Manila American Cemetery in the Philippines. The plot, row, and grave number are given. The site also shows a photograph of the cemetery.

· · ·

Finding our ancestors in military records helps us "flesh out" their life stories. Our country was founded on patriotism, and from the Revolution to today our ancestors have put themselves in harm's way to protect our freedom. How exciting to find out that people from our own family were involved in those efforts. Finding military records can help place our ancestors in history, help us define their character, and give us a richer view of history.

THE INTERNET

Many military records are available on the Internet. Here are some of the sources discussed in this chapter.

- American Battle Monuments Commission (ABMC): www.abmc .gov/home.php
- Compiled military service records for 1,235 Rough Riders, under the command of Theodore Roosevelt: www.archives.gov/ research/arc/topics/spanish-american-war
- Confederate pension records: www.archives.gov/research/ military/civil-war/civil-war-genealogy-resources/confederate/ pension.html
- Internet Archive digitized copy of *Alphabetical List of Battles: 1754–1900*: www.archive.org/details/alphabeticallist00stra
- NARA's "Access to Archival Databases" (AAD): http://aad .archives.gov/aad

GENEALOGY: TWENTY MINUTES A DAY

Look at the timeline of your ancestor's life. Compare the years he was of military age with the wars and conflicts taking place at that time. If you have family tradition or oral history indicating that your ancestor was in the military, you can eliminate the creation of a timeline. What military records are available for that time? Use Fold3 or Ancestry.com to find the military records, if available, or order them from the National Archives.

- NARA's eVetRecs System: www.archives.gov/veterans/ military-service-records (to order military records)
- NARA's microfilm catalog: www.archives.gov/research/start/ online-tools.html (select Go to the Microfilm Catalog)
- NARA's "Online Public Access" page: www.archives.gov/research/ search
- NARA's pre–World War I records: www.archives.gov/veterans/ military-service-records/pre-ww-1-records.html
- National Personnel Records Center in St. Louis, Missouri: www.archives.gov/st-louis/military-personnel/visitors-and -researchers.html
- Nationwide Gravesite Locator: http://gravelocator.cem.va.gov/ j2ee/servlet/NGL_v1
- Soldiers and Sailors System, National Park Service: www.itd.nps .gov/cwss
- War of 1812 pension files: www.fold3.com/title_761/war_of _1812_pension_files

CHURCH RECORDS

Many of our ancestors came to America for religious freedom. Life in countries where membership in a "state" church was required often caused those with a differing view to find a home elsewhere. Religious freedom was such an important issue that the First Amendment of the US Constitution states, "Congress shall make no law respecting an establishment of religion, or prohibiting the free exercise thereof; . . ."[9] As churches grew and developed, important events were recorded. Church records are one of the best genealogical resources available for finding information about our families. In the United States, church records often preceded civil registrations and were usually more complete. Therefore, church records can be a substitute for missing vital records. The types of items found in church records will vary by religion, but the most common types of records are baptisms and christenings, marriages, deaths and burials, memberships, church minutes, and ministers' records.

Types of Church Records

Substitutes for birth records are church records of baptisms, christenings, and confirmations. A baptism is a sacred rite or ceremony proclaiming one to be a Christian and involves water, either through sprinkling or immersion (submersing a person in water). A christening is a form of baptism but is usually performed on infants. The early term for *christening* meant "to give a name" (*Webster's*). Both baptismal and christening records, at the very least, give the name of the individual and the date of the event. A baptismal record will sometimes give the age of the individual while a christening often records the date of birth. Also on a christening record will usually be found the residence, names of the parents, and names of the sponsors or godparents. Confirmations can be a supplemental event following the baptism or a "rite of passage" for children of age who have prepared to receive their first communion. Knowing the age at which the first communion is normally taken can help determine the approximate year of birth of the child. Another rite of passage can be found in the Jewish faith. A Bar Mitzvah (for males) or Bat Mitzvah (for females) occurs about the age of 12 or 13 and involves the young person's reading of the Torah or Haftarah portion, or both, of the Shabbat service. Again, knowing when this event occurred can help determine the year of birth.

Marriage activities found in church records can be banns, bonds, announcements, ceremonies, and blessings. Marriage banns are notices of an upcoming wedding and are either read or posted in the church. Enough time is given to ensure that there is no known reason for the marriage not to occur. Not all religions require marriage banns. Marriage bonds were contracted by friends, relatives, or the groom to compensate the church if there were any reason the marriage could not occur, perhaps because of infidelity. Announcements can be found in church bulletins and publications, often inviting the congregation to the wedding. The ceremony itself provided a written record that the wedding occurred. The minister recorded the event in the church record book. Marriage blessings are often given following civil ceremonies.

Information about deaths may be found in church records. Some denominations keep records of deceased members either as a record or in a historian's report. If the denomination has or has had a news-letter or periodical publication, you will often find obituaries there. My great-grandfather made front page news when he died. He was hit by a train but, although the newspaper account was very interesting, there was no obituary printed. I found the obituary, which listed the names of his wife and children, in a church periodical. Now I have a detailed account of his death and an obituary for my genealogy records. Min-isters' records often contain information about the funerals that were preached. Some churches have adjacent cemeteries, and lists of those buried there can be found in the church records along with the names of the owners of the cemetery plots.

Records of members are often kept at both the local and denomi-national levels. Admissions into membership, removals, dismissals, admonishments, trials, and letters of transfer are among the types of membership records kept. Some churches, usually on the local level, publish yearly membership directories. Many times the directory will contain photographs of the parishioners, and often those are pictures of family units.

As with any organization, church meetings are often held to deter-mine the yearly budget, elect officers, and vote on a potential minister. The minutes of those meetings can be found locally or on the denom-inational level, or both. In colonial America, the Protestant Episcopal Church, a part of the Church of England, kept vestry books. *Vestry* means "a body of persons entrusted with the administration of the temporal affairs of a parish in the Church of England or in the Protes-tant Episcopal Church" (*Webster's*). Vestry books recorded information

GENEALOGY: TWENTY MINUTES A DAY

If you do not know the declared faith of your ancestors, talk to family members about their knowledge of the subject. Once you have determined the religion, research further to discover what records may be available. Look for repositories on the Internet to find out where the records may be held.

of a civil nature, such as the names of the poor who were helped and taxes collected.

Locating Church Records

Many church records have been filmed and can be found in the Family History Library in Salt Lake City. You might be able to find some church records online, though they are likely to be older church records from the nineteenth century or before. Others can only be found at the church itself or in a denominational repository. College and university libraries (especially if they are sponsored by a particular religious denomination) and historical societies may also have church records. I particularly like *A Survey of American Church Records*.[10] Denominations are listed with their repositories. Though the book is dated, I use the information as a guide. Once I know about the repository, I can do an online search for the current information. You might also want to look at PERSI, the Periodical Source Index, found on HeritageQuest, which is available at public libraries. Many church records have been transcribed in genealogy periodicals, and by searching PERSI you can find in which periodical the material was recorded. For more information about PERSI, see chapter 5.

When trying to locate church records for your ancestor, the most difficult task can be in determining the denomination. Family tradition may indicate the church to which your ancestors belonged. Look at biographical sketches in county histories for clues. Also in county histories look at the names of those who were charter members of the pioneer churches. Look at the name of the person who performed your ancestor's marriage. If the marriage record merely indicates the minister was a "minister of the gospel," look for information about the minister in a county history or city directory. Family histories and genealogies will also give clues as to the denomination of the family. If the ancestor stayed true to his or her religion, the country of origin can give clues. In Scandinavian countries the Lutheran church was the state church. France was a Catholic country, but your French ancestor could have been a Protestant. The French Protestants were called Huguenots. Ancestors from England could be found worshipping in the Church of England, also called the Anglican Church, or the Protestant Episcopal Church. In Germany an individual could have been Lutheran or Catholic depending on the parish in which he or she lived. Individuals in one parish would be Catholic, and individuals in another would be Lutheran. A series of books to help you determine the type of parish, if you know the locality, is *Map Guide to German Parish Registers*.[11] There are currently forty volumes in the series. A map for each parish is listed with an indication of denomination. Do be aware that your ancestors did not always stay true to the faith in which they started life. Sometimes they changed religions through conversion or convenience.

Selected Books for Information about Church Records

Betit, Kyle, and Beverly Whitaker. *Researching American Religious Records*. Toronto: Heritage Productions, 2002.
Carter-Walker, Fran. *Searching American Church Records*. Bradenton, FL: printed by author, 1995.
Heisey, John W. *Church and Tombstone Research*. York, PA: printed by author, 1987.

Quaker Records

Quaker Church records are well documented. Swarthmore College is one of the repositories of Quaker records (www.swarthmore.edu/academics/friends-historical-library/quaker-meeting-records.xml). The Quaker monthly meeting records are excellent, and you can find information about entire family units in them. William Wade Hinshaw abstracted many Quaker records in the *Encyclopedia of American Quaker*

Genealogy.[12] Records of monthly meetings from the states of New Jersey, New York, North Carolina, Ohio, and Pennsylvania are included in the five-volume set. (See figure 4.14.)

```
Page 103.
John T. Pearson, s. Lazarus & Sarah, b.   3-21-
                                              1837.
Dicene S. Pearson, dt. Joseph & Ruth Newlin,
              Alamance Co., b.  3-19-1836.
Ch: Joseph L.        b.   6- 2-1859.
    John N.           "  11- 8-1861.
    William E.        "   8-20-1863.
    Emily R.          "   9-29-1865.
    James R.          "   6- 8-1868.
    Minnie Whitaker   "   5- 5-1871. (d.  7- 3-
                                    1872, p. 119-D)
    Mary Achsah       "   4-10-1874.
    Thomas O.         "   3-16-1877.
Page 119-D.
John T. Pearson, s. Lazarus & Sarah, d. 10-29-
              1877, aged 40 yrs. 7 mos. 8 das.

Page 108.
Jonathan Pearson, s. Ichabod & Elizabeth, b.
                                   3-17-1823.
Sallie Pearson, dt. Warren & Sallie Woodard, b.
                                   1-22-1831.
```

Figure 4.14 Sample section from Encyclopedia of American Quaker Genealogy, vol. 1: North Carolina *by William Wade Hinshaw (Baltimore: Genealogical Publishing, 1991–).*

THE INTERNET

Look at links to church records on Cyndi's List (www.cyndislist.com/religion).

CEMETERY RECORDS

Cemeteries are resting places of the dead and provide a unique genealogy research experience. Families are often buried side by side, and you can re-create the family unit just by walking through the cemetery. The information contained on tombstones varies. Many provide only the birth year and death year. If you are lucky, the full birth and death dates will be shown. Some tombstones have the names of both the husband and wife on the same stone. If the husband and wife have separate stones, there may be an indication of relationship such as "loving wife of" followed by the husband's name. Similarly, a child's headstone may indicate "child of." Cemetery art can determine facts about a person's life. Look for crosses, stars of David, and Masonic symbols. Not every grave is marked, and some, even if the grave is marked, have unreadable stones. If the cemetery has an office, you will still be able to pinpoint the location of burial in the cemetery. Cemetery records also give the interment date and identify who paid for the lot.

There are different types of cemeteries. Sometimes the cemetery can be found next to a church. Other cemeteries may be owned by a municipality or a private company. Still others are found on private land, part of a family burial plot. Also look for potter's fields, sanatorium cemeteries, and national cemeteries. Records for a church cemetery can be found at the church or in a church's archives. Records for municipal cemeteries may be found in a town or city clerk's office. Look for cemetery deeds, which will show the purchaser's name, cost of the plot, location of the plot, and date of sale. Private cemeteries, owned by companies or corporations, usually have an office, assuming they are still active (meaning they are still actively selling plots and burying people). Again, look for cemetery deeds and records in the office. For older cemeteries, those no longer active, you might be able to find sextons' records in an archive or on microfilm at the Family History Library. The sexton was in charge of the upkeep of the cemetery and kept records of those buried in the cemetery, owners of cemetery plots, and details of those interred in each plot. He was also responsible for groundskeeping and for the opening and closing of all graves. Churches also used sextons to oversee their cemeteries. Unfortunately, many family burial plots no longer exist. As land changes hands from one family to another, burying grounds are susceptible to destruction either by plowing under or vandalism. Most states have laws regarding accessibility to burying grounds on private land favoring ancestors of the dead over current landowners. Most large cities at one time or another have had a potter's field. *Potter's field* is an old term meaning the burial place for the indigent or the unknown. Records of those buried there are extremely hard to locate. If an ancestor spent time in a sanatorium and died while there, he or she may be buried in the cemetery next to the medical facility. Those records will be found with the facility, if it still exists. If your ancestor died during active duty with the armed forces, he or she would have qualified to be buried in a national cemetery. Those with honorable discharges might also have qualified for burial. To find someone buried in a national cemetery, use the Nationwide Gravesite Locator on the Internet (http://gravelocator.cem.va.gov/j2ee/servlet/NGL_v1).

Cemetery records have long been a source of articles in genealogy periodicals and books published by genealogical societies and lineage societies. Lineage societies, such as the Daughters of the American Revolution (DAR), constantly seek out burying grounds and publish the names found on the tombstones. The publications are usually given to the society's state organization and to the society's national repository, if there is one. If duplicate copies are made they are frequently given to libraries. In fact, most lineage societies give each chapter "credit" for donating books to libraries. An excellent Internet site for finding burial information is Find a Grave (www.findagrave.com). This is a free social networking site on which people can put information about any burial. The information might cover an entire cemetery that someone has "read" or merely list the names of a person's direct ancestors. To submit information you must create an account. The pages vary in content. Some only state the information found on the tombstone. Others contain photographs of headstones or genealogy information or both. If there is no photograph of a headstone for an individual, you can request one. Volunteers receive the requests and photograph tombstones in cemeteries near them. These pages can tell a lot about a family. (See figure 4.15.)

Some municipalities require, or have required, burial permits. Look for these in the town or city hall. Look at death certificates to find places of burial. Death certificates usually show the name of the cemetery and funeral home. Look in obituaries for burial information. Be aware when looking at tombstones that the marker may have been placed many years after the burial. If that is true, the information on the stone may be incorrect. One of my husband's ancestral lines is buried in Vermont. There is a large stone on the family plot. The front of the stone shows the name of the mother and father and gives their birth and death years. On the back of the stone are the names of all the children with their birth and death years. The monument was obviously not placed in the plot when the mother and father died because the names of all the

Figure 4.15 Record for Ella Sarah Brown Flora with photographs. From Find a Grave, www.findagrave.com.

children are on the tombstone. It was placed there many years later. If you find a stone like that, make sure you verify the information with another source.

A good place to look for cemetery records is PERSI. (Again, you will find out more about PERSI in chapter 5.) Because many genealogy publications contain cemetery records, using PERSI will help you locate the publication in which those records can be found. Finding the location of a cemetery, assuming you know its name, is as easy as using Google maps (http://maps.google.com). You can type in the name of the cemetery as well as the city and state. A map will be displayed pinpointing the location of the cemetery. For more information about finding and researching cemetery records, use *Researching American Cemetery Records*.[13] It contains a good summary.

GENEALOGY: TWENTY MINUTES A DAY

Look at your pedigree or family unit charts. Record the names of all cemeteries in your data. Does anyone in your family have photographs of any of the tombstones? Does anyone in the family live close enough to the cemetery to take a photograph? Look on Internet sites and in periodicals to find burial information. If you are lacking burial locations, look in obituaries, in periodicals, in books, and on the Internet for clues.

Proper care of tombstones is needed for preservation. When a marker is made from a soft stone, weather, moss, and lichens can deteriorate the stone making it unreadable. Deterioration can be further enhanced by human hands. Many genealogists like to photograph the tombstones of their ancestors. When a tombstone is hard to read, many have tried to improve the image by cleaning the headstone with shaving cream. This practice is not recommended. Others have tried putting flour on the stone to enhance the writing on it. This method is controversial. I have talked to several genealogists who have experimented, quite successfully, with mirrors. If the mirrors are placed just right to bounce the sun's light onto the tombstone, you can get a good picture that illuminates the writing on the stone. The Association for Gravestone Studies (www.gravestonestudies.org/welcome.htm) has several ideas for tombstone preservation. The organization also publishes *Markers*, a periodical that comes free with membership. One of the best books for learning about tombstone preservation is *A Graveyard Preservation Primer*.[14]

THE INTERNET

Several Internet sites are available for finding burial information. Here are some websites that have been discussed in this chapter, as well as others.

CEMETERIES AND BURIALS
- www.findagrave.com
- www.interment.net

- www.usgwtombstones.org/index.html (USGenWeb Tombstone Transcription Project)
- Tombstone preservation: www.gravestonestudies.org/welcome .htm
- Nationwide Gravesite Locator: http://gravelocator.cem.va.gov/ j2ee/servlet/NGL_v1 (for finding burials in national cemeteries)

CEMETERY AND BURIAL LOCATIONS
- http://maps.google.com
- www.bing.com/maps
- http://nationalmap.gov/ustopo/index.html (click on Download Maps)

• • •

In this chapter we have discussed military, church, and cemetery records. These are all important records to find for your ancestors. They can provide information on births, marriages, and deaths and give added details about your ancestor's life. Finding information about all aspects of your ancestor's life will help you discover who he or she really was.

NOTES

1. Newton A. Strait, *Alphabetical List of Battles: 1754–1900* (Washington, DC: printed by author, 1905).

2. James C. Neagles, *U.S. Military Records: A Guide to Federal and State Sources, Colonial America to the Present* (Salt Lake City, UT: Ancestry, 1994).

3. Virgil D. White, *Index to War of 1812 Pension Files* (Waynesboro, TN: National Historical Publishing, 1992).

4. Josephine L. Harper, *Guide to the Draper Manuscripts* (Madison: State Historical Society of Wisconsin, 1983).

5. Draper Manuscripts, series DD, vol. 3, p. 197 (Madison: Wisconsin Historical Society).

6. *Compiled Service Records of Volunteer Union Soldiers Who Served in Organizations from the State of Missouri*, microfilm publication no.

M405, roll 268 (Washington, DC: National Archives and Records Administration).

7. *Card Records of Headstones Provided for Deceased Union Civil War Veterans ca. 1879–ca. 1903*, microfilm publication no. M1845, roll 4 (Washington, DC: National Archives and Records Administration).

8. www.archives.gov/st-louis/military-personnel/fire-1973.html

9. "The Bill of Rights," Amendment 1, www.archives.gov/exhibits/charters/bill_of_rights_transcript.html.

10. E. Kay Kirkham, *A Survey of American Church Records*, 4th ed. (Logan, UT: Everton, 1978).

11. Kevan M. Hansen, *Map Guide to German Parish Registers* (North Salt Lake City, UT: Heritage Creations, 2004–2005; Bountiful, UT: Family Roots Publishing, 2007–).

12. William Wade Hinshaw, *Encyclopedia of American Quaker Genealogy*, vol. 1: *North Carolina* (Baltimore: Genealogical Publishing, 1991–).

13. Scott Andrew Bartley, *Researching American Cemetery Records* (Toronto: Heritage Productions, 2005).

14. Lynette Strangstad, *A Graveyard Preservation Primer* (Walnut Creek, CA: AltaMira Press, 1995).

chapter five

Printed and Internet Sources

PRINTED AND INTERNET SOURCES OF GENEALOGICAL MATERIAL ARE often easier to access than original records. The courthouse, church, or cemetery that has the record you are seeking may be hundreds or thousands of miles away. Unless you are willing to travel, you may have to rely on a professional researcher or contact the record keeper in that area to help you obtain copies of the documents. But since Americans first started showing an interest in the European origins of their families, researchers have been copying information from records repositories and publishing that data. The information may have been published in a book or periodical. Today a lot of genealogical research is being published on the Internet as well.

Printed and Internet sources have allowed greater access to information. You may find exact copies of original documents that have been photocopied, microfilmed, or digitized, and you may find transcribed, extracted, abstracted, or translated material from original documents. Indexes are another possibility. Nothing is better than an original document. It is the most reliable information, and you know exactly what the author of the document intended to say. But because it is not always easy to view the original, what we find in print and online serves as a helpful research substitute.

DERIVATIVE RECORDS

Material from original documents can be presented in several ways. Transcribed material is a word-for-word copy of an original document. It can be typed or handwritten. For a transcription to be correct, the transcriber has to both read the original document correctly and make no errors in the process of copying it, such as hitting the wrong computer key or transposing letters. Extracted material is a significant portion of the original document that has been copied and left in the same format. The same caveats apply as with transcribed material. Abstracted material is a significant portion of the original document that has been copied but not in the same format as the original. Abstracted material gives the gist of the original and usually gives names, places, and dates. The abstractor has to understand what the original document says to correctly give an account of it. Original documents can also be translated. A translation is a word-for-word transcription from one language to another. When a document is indexed, names, subjects, or places are copied from that document and put into alphabetical order. As with a transcription, the indexer must be able to read correctly the words being indexed.

Be especially cautious when looking at copies of documents that were originally handwritten. Names, dates, places, or other important words can be misread and written down incorrectly. For example, I have found numerous spellings for the first name of my great-grandfather, Irus Homes Harvey. The name is not always consistent in original documents but, aside from that, the name is not a common one, and transcribers "see" that which is familiar to them. I have found his name spelled, in original and transcribed documents, as Irus, Iris, and Iras. The last spelling is one that I found only recently. After many years of searching I found out, from some information a relative had, his place of death and approximate year of death. I was told he died in Boyne City, Michigan, which is in Charlevoix County, in 1918. I looked at

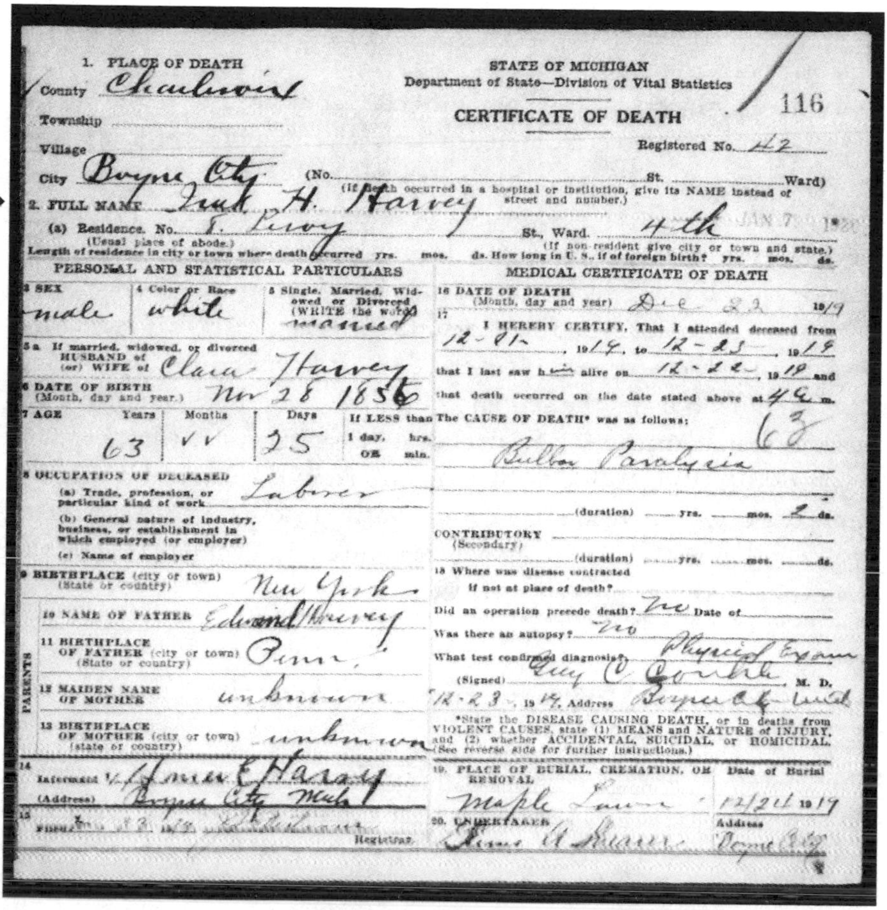
1. PLACE OF DEATH
County Charlevoix
Township
Village
City Boyne City (No. St. Ward)
(If death occurred in a hospital or institution, give its NAME instead of street and number.)

STATE OF MICHIGAN
Department of State—Division of Vital Statistics
CERTIFICATE OF DEATH
116
Registered No. 42

2. FULL NAME Irus H. Harvey
(a) Residence. No. E. Leroy St., Ward. 4th
(Usual place of abode.) (If non-resident give city or town and state.)
Length of residence in city or town where death occurred yrs. mos. ds. How long in U. S., if of foreign birth? yrs. mos. ds.

PERSONAL AND STATISTICAL PARTICULARS
3 SEX male
4 Color or Race white
5 Single, Married, Widowed or Divorced (WRITE the word) married
5a If married, widowed, or divorced HUSBAND of (or) WIFE of Clara Harvey
6 DATE OF BIRTH (Month, day and year.) Nov 28 1856
7 AGE Years 63 Months " Days 25 If LESS than 1 day, hrs. OR min.
8 OCCUPATION OF DECEASED
(a) Trade, profession, or particular kind of work Laborer
(b) General nature of industry, business, or establishment in which employed (or employer)
(c) Name of employer
9 BIRTHPLACE (city or town) (State or country) New York
PARENTS
10 NAME OF FATHER Edward Harvey
11 BIRTHPLACE OF FATHER (city or town) (State or country) Penn.
12 MAIDEN NAME OF MOTHER unknown
13 BIRTHPLACE OF MOTHER (city or town) (state or country) unknown
14 Informant Amon E Harvey
(Address) Boyne City Mich
15 Filed ... Registrar.

MEDICAL CERTIFICATE OF DEATH
16 DATE OF DEATH (Month, day and year) Dec 23 1919
17 I HEREBY CERTIFY, That I attended deceased from 12-21 1919, to 12-23 1919
that I last saw him alive on 12-22 1919 and
that death occurred on the date stated above at 4 a.m.
The CAUSE OF DEATH* was as follows:
Bulbar Paralysis
(duration) yrs. mos. 2 ds.
CONTRIBUTORY (Secondary)
(duration) yrs. mos. ds.
18 Where was disease contracted
If not at place of death?
Did an operation precede death? No Date of
Was there an autopsy? No
What test confirmed diagnosis? Physical Exam
(Signed) Guy C. Conkle M. D.
12-23, 1919. Address Boyne City Mich
*State the DISEASE CAUSING DEATH, or in deaths from VIOLENT CAUSES, state (1) MEANS and NATURE of INJURY, and (2) whether ACCIDENTAL, SUICIDAL, or HOMICIDAL. (See reverse side for further instructions.)
19. PLACE OF BURIAL, CREMATION, OR REMOVAL Maple Lawn
Date of Burial 12/26 1919
20. UNDERTAKER
Address Boyne City

Figure 5.1 Death certificate of Irus H. Harvey. From Seeking Michigan, "Death Records, 1897–1920," http://cdm16317.contentdm.oclc.org/cdm/search/collection/p129401coll7.

Michigan death certificates from 1897 through 1920, which are digitized online at Seeking Michigan (http://cdm16317.contentdm.oclc.org/cdm/search/collection/p129401coll7; see figure 5.1). I did not find his death certificate when looking for the exact spelling of Irus Harvey. I then searched for the surname Harvey with the keyword Charlevoix. His death was indexed under *Iras* H. Harvey. On the digitized copy, his first name clearly reads *Irus*. As I often tell beginning genealogists, if you don't find what you are looking for in an index, it just means that the name is not in the index. It does not mean that the name is not in the original document.

When looking at printed and Internet sources it is important to remember that there is a difference between original records and anything other than original records (transcribed, extracted, abstracted, translated, and indexed records). If it is not an original record, it is a derivative form of the record. As a child you probably played a game called Telephone. In that game several people are in a line. One person whispers a sentence in another person's ear. That person whispers what was heard in the next person's ear, and so on down the line. By the time the last person hears the sentence and restates it out loud, it usually has no resemblance to the original sentence. This is also what happens in derivative records. The farther you are from the original record the more deviations there may be. But derivative records are a necessity for the genealogist, for reasons previously stated. Knowing that you can't believe everything you read is also a necessity.

FAMILY HISTORIES AND BIOGRAPHIES

The goal of a genealogist should be to share the information found. Sometimes that comes in the form of a published family history or genealogy. In chapter 1, I noted the difference between a genealogy and a family history. A published genealogy would, in its truest sense, be a pedigree listing the names and dates of a person's ancestors. A family history would also include social history, historical events, and family stories. It would truly be a history of one's family.

For example, *The Reams, Reames Family and Allied Families*,[1] privately published in 1956, tells the story of, with various spellings, the Reames family. The Reams/Reames family was among the early settlers in Virginia. One of the Reames family lines moved to North Carolina and were Quakers. At that point they began a connection with the Samuel Colyar family (one of my family lines). According to other sources the Reames and Colyar families, along with several other families, removed to Logan County, Ohio, and later to Cass County, Michigan. Moses Reames (1797–1878) married into the Colyar family. He was actually married four times due to the deaths of his first three wives. His second wife was Mary Colyar (1812–1884). His third wife was Mary Colyar's sister, Huldah (1815–1900).[2] I have yet to find a book written specifically on my Colyar family, but *The Reams, Reames Family* helps answer some questions about their migration pattern and gives some information on a couple of members of the Colyar family. Therefore the book aids Colyar researchers in their quest for information.

The quality of information found in family histories is varied. Anyone can publish his or her family's genealogy, but not everyone does high-quality research. Look for documentation when viewing such a publication. If there is no documentation for the data found within the pages, then look at it suspiciously. The presentation of the data also varies. Some researchers do nothing more than put together a printout of their family group records (literally a genealogy). Others "flesh out" the subjects with family stories, social history, and photographs. Then there is the quality of printing. I have seen family histories published years ago that were produced on mimeograph machines or reproduced with carbon paper. Other writers have their work printed by a professional printing company. Today, it is easy to duplicate pages with one's own computer and laser printer. Books can be found hardbound or softbound, stapled or spiraled, or in three-ring binders. In producing a family history, anything goes as long as it gets published.

Many genealogists have published the results of their research in one form or another, but the publication is not always easy to find. Genealogies are always privately published. Immediate family members are often given notice of the publication, but only at the time of publication and only those families of which the author is aware. Trying to find a copy of the publication years later can be daunting. If you are lucky, the author will have donated a copy to his or her local library or to the Family History Library in Salt Lake City, Utah. Fortunately, many avenues are available today to help you find genealogy and family history publications.

One place to start looking is the Family History Library in Salt Lake City, Utah. This library has the world's largest collection of family histories. You can search the catalog at https://familysearch.org. If the book is free of copyright protection, you may find a link to a digital image of the original. If the author gave permission to have the book filmed, you can borrow the film through your local FamilySearch center. The list of centers can be found at https://familysearch.org/locations. If those options are not available, you will have to visit the library in Salt Lake City to view the book.

The Library of Congress has a number of family histories in its collection. When an author desires to copyright his or her publication, a copy of that book is given to the Library of Congress. You can search the catalog at http://catalog.loc.gov. However, the library's genealogy material cannot be borrowed and must be viewed at the library in Washington, D.C. *Genealogies in the Library of Congress: A Bibliography*[3] was published in 1972 to let researchers know the titles of books in the Library of Congress, which also makes genealogy researchers aware of the titles of family publications. This, of course, was before online library catalogs came into being, but the book is still a useful resource. Two additional works followed this publication: *A Complement to the Genealogies in the Library of Congress: A Bibliography*[4] and *Genealogies Cataloged by the Library of Congress Since 1986.*[5] This last publication is helpful because it lists family histories that have been microfilmed. Even though book copies of genealogies cannot be borrowed from the facility, microfilms can.

Family History Books on the FamilySearch website (http://books.familysearch.org) is a joint venture between the Family History Library and several other public and university libraries to digitize family history books that are out of copyright. The collection is growing and provides a good opportunity to find a book about your family. Libraries partnering with the Family History Library are the Allen County (Indiana) Public Library, Brigham Young University–Hawaii, Brigham Young University–Idaho, the LDS Church History Library, the Harold B. Lee Library at Brigham Young University, the Houston (Texas) Public Library—Clayton Library Center for Genealogical Research, and the Mid-Continent Public Library (Missouri)—Midwest Genealogy Center.

Google Books (http://books.google.com) is a venture of Google and partner libraries to digitize books, whether in copyright or not. Those that are free of copyright are shown full-text on the site. Books that are still under copyright protection can be viewed in snippets, but you will be unable to view them in their entirety online. There are also books for which no preview is available. When there is no full-text version of the book, look for the option to buy a copy with a Get This Book link for a physical copy or the e-book link. Partner libraries are many and include libraries worldwide.

Some paid database projects are available for digital images of family history books. Two major players are NewsBank and ProQuest. NewsBank's product is called Genealogy Bank. It has numerous digital books in its database holdings, as well as other elements. The database is available through library subscriptions and by personal subscription. ProQuest's product is called HeritageQuest. It, too, has a growing number of digital books available for viewing, as well as other elements in its collection. HeritageQuest is available only through a library that subscribes to it.

Another option for finding family genealogies or histories is World-Cat. WorldCat is the public face of OCLC (Online Computer Library Center). It is available to users as a library database or as a free Internet site, www.worldcat.org. As you search for books and find one or more that are of interest, follow the link to the libraries that have the item in their collection. OCLC member libraries have hyperlinks to their online catalogs. Don't neglect to follow through on this step. Looking at the library's catalog can help you determine if the book is in open stacks or in closed collections. Usually a book in open stacks is available through interlibrary loan. WorldCat also has links to online digital copies of books. In WorldCat, limit your search to e-books if you are looking for online books.

The genealogy holdings at most public libraries are reference books and cannot be borrowed. There are, however, a couple of options open to you.

Mid-Continent Public Library's Midwest Genealogy Center, in Independence, Missouri, has a collection of circulating genealogy books, many of which are family histories (www.mymcpl.org/catalog). The growing collection has resulted from the donation of the collections of several genealogical organizations—the American Family Records Association (no longer in existence), the Missouri State Genealogical Association, the Heart of America Genealogical Society (no longer in existence), and the Gann Family Historical Society—as well as donations from individuals. When searching the catalog, look for titles that are a part of the Genealogy from the Heartland collection, which is indicated in the catalog record, or in the list of holdings that are indicated as Circulating GE Book (Special Collection). Procedures for borrowing books from the collection can be found on the library's website (www.mymcpl.org/genealogy/how-request-books).

The National Genealogical Society houses its book loan collection at the Saint Louis County (Missouri) Library. The collection of over twenty thousand circulating books can be searched from the library's online catalog (http://webpac.slcl.org). Look for items that do not include an "R" at the beginning of the call number. The procedures for borrowing can be found on the library's website (www.slcl.org/genealogy-and -local-history/services).

Biographies are another genre that can aid in a person's quest for genealogical information. Even though you will find out more about an individual's life than his or her genealogy, biographies can provide genealogical clues. You will usually find out when and where the individual was born, names of parents and siblings, and names of the spouse and children—all of which have genealogical value. Some biographies will also refer to the grandparents. Most libraries have biography collections, and most can be borrowed through interlibrary loan. If your ancestor was a famous person, you will likely find a biography written about him or her. Most libraries have copies of the *Biography and Genealogy Master Index*,[6] which has been published continuously since 1980 and is also available as a database. Each volume is an index to sources of biographical information on the subjects, who are listed alphabetically. Another source of brief biographical information is *Who's Who*.[7] Select individuals are invited to provide their own biographical information for this annual publication. You will also find varying publications with similar titles: *Who's Who among African Americans*, *Who's Who among American High School Students*, and *Who's Who in American History*, to name a few. Each is published by different publishing companies. *Marquis Who's Who* is a commercial database containing all the biographies published in *Marquis Who's Who* since 1985 and from its historical *Who Was Who* volumes 1607–1985. Figure 5.2 is a sample from a biography about mountain man James Bridger.

Looking for published family histories and genealogies can be a daunting task. The book you are looking for might be easily accessible in your local library, or it may be in the hands of a select few family members. It might be a high-quality product or a sloppy production. It might have lots of information on your direct ancestor or possibly only information on an indirect line. But when you find a book on your ancestor, it may answer the questions you have been asking. People have been

2   JAMES BRIDGER—A HISTORICAL NARRATIVE

seek out the evidences of his entire trail afresh, before
that first crossing of the Mormon and Bridger paths was
seen in proper perspective, and the picturesque moun-
taineer stood revealed.

The few known facts of James Bridger's boyhood have
been rescued from oblivion by General Dodge (1) (see
bibliography) and Captain Chittenden (2). According to
these authorities he was born at Richmond, Va., March
17, 1804, in a family with two other children, a boy and
a girl. His parents, James and Chloe Bridger, were fairly
well established as proprietors of a tavern and a farm,
the father also doing some surveying.

But the family was caught up on the tide of emigration in 1812 and deposited on a farm near St. Louis.
Here the father found much employment at his special
occupation in that new and unsurveyed region, while the
mother, bearing the burdens of the growing children,
also assumed charge of the farm. However, after four
strenuous years of pioneering in those primitive conditions, the mother passed away, and her sister-in-law, the
senior Bridger's sister, came to assume the mother's
responsibilities.

The second son soon followed his mother; and in the
following autumn, of 1817, the father also passed away,
leaving some important problems for solution by the
maiden aunt and foster mother.[1]

James Bridger, Jr., then a lad just under fourteen,
had gained some valuable experience and acquaintance
among the rivermen, and was allowed to take temporary

---

1. Colonel Triplett's aspersions on the Bridger family (3) are evi-
dently not worthy of credence. He says: "The name of Bridger is
familiar to all who have ever crossed the plains, especially to those who
made that trip before the advent of the railroads, Fort Bridger being a
noted resting place for all of the traders, pilgrims and trappers. Bridger
came of an Illinois family, which, if reports of that day are to be believed,
was far from respectable, though they could lay full claim to the first
characteristic with which the genealogical epitaphist, as well as the novel-
ist, endows his heroes—they were very poor.

"Used to rough knocks and plenty of them, at home, the life of the
mountain trapper, when he was old enough to embrace it, presented no
peculiar hardships to this man, upon whose birth and circumstances
fortune had so far only frowned, and he was early in the field of adventure, upon the waters of the great continental divide, the backbone of a
hemisphere.

Figure 5.2 Excerpt from James Bridger, Trapper, Frontiersman, Scout and Guide: A
Historical Narrative *(Illustrated) by J. Cecil Alter (Salt Lake City, UT: Shepard, 1925).*

researching genealogy for years. If someone has been researching your
line, let's hope it has been published.

PERIODICALS

Periodicals are printed materials published at intervals. Publication can
occur annually, quarterly, monthly, or at any other regular (or irreg-
ular) interval. Periodicals have always been an important resource in
genealogical research. Much of the information published in them cannot be found elsewhere. In the genealogy world they are published by

county, state, and national genealogical and historical societies, lineage organizations, surname organizations, special interest groups, ethnic organizations, and some for-profit genealogy vendors. In them you find the most current research, transcriptions, extractions, and indexing projects taking place in these organizations. The types of records you will find are county or state census records, cemetery readings, deeds, probate records, and vital records.

Numerous genealogy periodicals have been published over the years. One of the largest public genealogy libraries, the Allen County Public Library (ACPL) in Fort Wayne, Indiana, maintains a collection of over five thousand active periodical titles as well as some copies of publications that are no longer produced. That is a massive amount of information to wade through to find an article that may be useful. Since 1988 the ACPL has been indexing periodicals and publishing the indexes in the PERiodical Source Index (PERSI). For many years PERSI was an in-print publication reaching sixteen volumes. It is now an online source available through HeritageQuest. PERSI makes the hunt for genealogy periodical articles easier.

Two other publications index genealogy periodical publications:

- Jacobus, Donald Lines. *Donald Lines Jacobus' Index to Genealogical Periodicals*. Newhall, CA: C. Boyer, 1988. Reprint, New Haven, CT: 1932, 1948, 1953. This work is a partial index to eighty-five major genealogy periodicals. Articles are indexed by broad subject.
- Rogers, Ellen Stanley. *Genealogical Periodical Annual Index*. Bowie, MD: Heritage Books, 1962–2001. This forty-volume set indexes periodical articles by broad subject, title of article, principal surname, author, and place name.

Most long-running periodicals publish their own annual indexes, and some have published cumulative indexes. You can find links to genealogical, historical, and lineage societies and more at Cyndi's List (www.cyndislist.com/societies). If the organization publishes a periodical, you will find that information on the society's website, as well as information on how to subscribe. Many times you can purchase a copy of a single back issue to find an article that you are seeking.

BIBLIOGRAPHIES

Bibliographies are published lists of books that are written in specific subject areas. There are bibliographies of genealogies, geographic areas, wars, genders, occupations, and so on. They will aid you in your search for printed material on any given subject. If you are looking for a family genealogy, a bibliography such as the aforementioned *Genealogies in the Library of Congress* can help identify those books. If you want to find books that might help you in your Civil War research, you might try *The Civil War, Slavery, and Reconstruction in Missouri: A Bibliography of Secondary Sources and Selected Primary Sources*.[8] If you want to research Colonial Germans in America, you might try *Bibliography on the Colonial Germans of North America*[9] as shown in figure 5.3. Knowing which

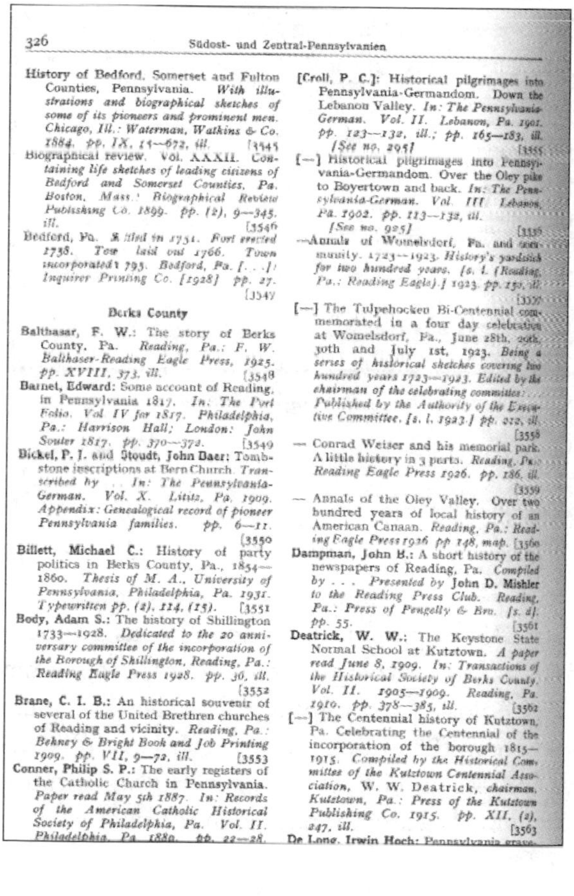

326 Südost- und Zentral-Pennsylvanien

History of Bedford, Somerset and Fulton Counties, Pennsylvania. *With illustrations and biographical sketches of some of its pioneers and prominent men. Chicago, Ill.: Waterman, Watkins & Co. 1884. pp. IX, 15—672, ill.* [3545

Biographical review. Vol. XXXII. Containing *life sketches of leading citizens of Bedford and Somerset Counties, Pa. Boston, Mass.: Biographical Review Publishing Co. 1899. pp. (2), 9—345, ill.* [3546

Bedford, Pa. *Settled in 1751. Fort erected 1758. Town laid out 1766. Town incorporated 1795. Bedford, Pa. [. . .]: Inquirer Printing Co. [1928] pp. 27.* [3547

Berks County

Balthasar, F. W.: The story of Berks County, Pa. *Reading, Pa.: F. W. Balthaser-Reading Eagle Press, 1925. pp. XVIII, 373, ill.* [3548

Barnet, Edward: Some account of Reading, in Pennsylvania 1817. *In: The Port Folio. Vol IV for 1817. Philadelphia, Pa.: Harrison Hall; London: John Souter 1817. pp. 370—372.* [3549

Bickel, P. J. and Stoudt, John Baer: Tombstone inscriptions at Bern Church. *Transcribed by . . In: The Pennsylvania-German. Vol. X. Lititz, Pa. 1909. Appendix: Genealogical record of pioneer Pennsylvania families. pp. 6—11.* [3550

Billett, Michael C.: History of party politics in Berks County, Pa., 1854—1860. *Thesis of M. A., University of Pennsylvania, Philadelphia, Pa. 1931. Typewritten pp. (2), 114, (15).* [3551

Body, Adam S.: The history of Shillington 1733—1928. *Dedicated to the 20 anniversary committee of the incorporation of the Borough of Shillington, Reading, Pa.: Reading Eagle Press 1928. pp. 36, ill.* [3552

Brane, C. I. B.: An historical souvenir of several of the United Brethren churches of Reading and vicinity. *Reading, Pa.: Behney & Bright Book and Job Printing 1909. pp. VII, 9—72, ill.* [3553

Conner, Philip S. P.: The early registers of the Catholic Church in Pennsylvania. *Paper read May 5th 1887. In: Records of the American Catholic Historical Society of Philadelphia, Pa. Vol. II. Philadelphia, Pa. 1880. pp. 22—28.*

[Croll, P. C.]: Historical pilgrimages into Pennsylvania-Germandom. Down the Lebanon Valley. *In: The Pennsylvania-German. Vol. II. Lebanon, Pa. 1901. pp. 123—132, ill.; pp. 165—183, ill. [See no. 295]* [3555

[—] Historical pilgrimages into Pennsylvania-Germandom. Over the Oley pike to Boyertown and back. *In: The Pennsylvania-German. Vol. III. Lebanon, Pa. 1902. pp. 113—132, ill. [See no. 925]* [3556

— Annals of Womelsdorf, Pa. and community. 1723—1923. *History's yardstick for two hundred years. [s. l. (Reading, Pa.: Reading Eagle).] 1923. pp. 150, ill.* [3557

[—] The Tulpehocken Bi-Centennial commemorated in a four day celebration at Womelsdorf, Pa., June 28th, 29th, 30th and July 1st, 1923. *Being a series of historical sketches covering two hundred years 1723—1923. Edited by the chairman of the celebrating committee. Published by the Authority of the Executive Committee. [s. l. 1923.] pp. 212, ill.* [3558

— Conrad Weiser and his memorial park. A little history in 3 parts. *Reading, Pa.: Reading Eagle Press 1926. pp. 186, ill.* [3559

— Annals of the Oley Valley. Over two hundred years of local history of an American Canaan. *Reading, Pa.: Reading Eagle Press 1926. pp. 148, map.* [3560

Dampman, John B.: A short history of the newspapers of Reading, Pa. *Compiled by . . . Presented by* **John D. Mishler** *to the Reading Press Club. Reading, Pa.: Press of Pengelly & Bro. [s. d.] pp. 55.* [3561

Deatrick, W. W.: The Keystone State Normal School at Kutztown. *A paper read June 8, 1909. In: Transactions of the Historical Society of Berks County. Vol. II. 1905—1909. Reading, Pa. 1910. pp. 378—385, ill.* [3562

[—] The Centennial history of Kutztown, Pa. Celebrating the Centennial of the incorporation of the borough 1815—1915. *Compiled by the Historical Committee of the Kutztown Centennial Association, W. W. Deatrick, chairman. Kutztown, Pa.: Press of the Kutztown Publishing Co. 1915. pp. XII, (2), 247, ill.* [3563

De Long, Irwin Hoch: Pennsylvania grave-

Figure 5.3 Sample page from Bibliography on the Colonial Germans of North America: Especially the Pennsylvania Germans and Their Descendants, *edited by Emil Meynen (Baltimore: Genealogical Publishing, 1982; originally published as* Bibliography on German Settlements in Colonial North America *[Liepzig, Germany, 1937]).*

books have been written can help immensely in discovering resources for any research project.

You can also use WorldCat as a bibliographic tool. By creating a free account at www.worldcat.org, you can easily create your own bibliographies, which can be kept private or shared with the public. Figure 5.4 is a screenshot of a simple bibliography I created of Logan County, Ohio, genealogy books.

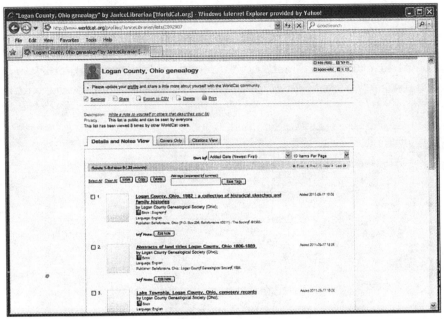

Figure 5.4   Bibliography of Logan County, Ohio, genealogy books.

PHONE BOOKS AND CITY DIRECTORIES

Would you like to be able to trace an ancestor year by year? Phone books and city directories can offer that opportunity. Phone books are published yearly and provide a listing of the phone numbers and, sometimes, addresses of all households in a community. Residents, usually those whose names are shown on the phone bill, are listed in alphabetical order followed by the address and phone number. However, those who do not want their number listed are not named in the phone book.

Businesses, schools, and government offices are also listed. These listings are called the "white pages." Businesses who wish to advertise are listed in the "yellow pages." Phone books were first published in large cities in the early 1900s. Rural community phone books were published much later. Keeping track of a person's movements can be difficult if he or she frequently moved. Phone books can help you trace an ancestor year by year. Knowing where that person was in a particular year can help you find additional records for him or her. Figure 5.5 shows individuals from the surname Mathonet to Matney who were living in the greater Kansas City, Missouri, area in 1941.

```
Mathonet H H Mrs r
                  3724  Valentine. VA lentine-2975
Mathy Jos Mrs  r  931  Paseo. . . . . . . . .GR and-1683
Matjoy Lillian  r  1407  Vine. . . . . . . . . VI ctor-0376
Matkin Dewey  r  3112  Wabash. . . . .LI nwood-2271
Matlaw Julius mens frngs 1601  E  18  GR and-9674
Matlaw Julius r 103  E  Meyer. . . . . . . . HI land-6379
Matlock Herbert E  r  2922  Cherry. VA lentine-3430
Matlock Joe  r  1511  Woodlnd. . . . .HA rrison-4146
Matlock Marie  r  4014  Prospct. . . . . WA bath-5946
Matlock N P Mrs  r  2200  Bunker. . . .FA irfax-5320
Matlock Norris B  r  247  N  33. . . . . .FA irfax-7487
Matlock W W  r  4125  St  John. . . .CH estnut-0924
Matney D E  r  4462  Francis. . . . . . . . .LO gan-3958
Matney E W  r  3424  Chestnt. . . . . . .LI nwood-8448
Matney F S  r  4122  Gibbs  rd. . . . . . . .FA irfax-9158
Matney Geo D  612  Delaware. . . . . . .HA rrison-6893
Matney Goldie  r  3900  Shawnee rd. . . . FA irfax-8819
Matney Harold  r  3712  Ruby. . . . . . . OR earl-4695
Matney J C  electl  contr
                  102  &  Wornall . ①Springdale-5900
Matney Lewis  r  247  E  32  terr  . . .VA lentine-2920
```

Figure 5.5   Section from the Greater Kansas City Telephone Directory, December 1941.

City directories are often called "crisscross" directories. They allow you to search by name, phone number, or address. Many of them were published yearly by the R. L. Polk Company. You can search for residents and businesses. The "white pages," or resident listings, contain a list of adult residents, including students over 18 years of age, living in the city and out-of-town residents employed in the city. You will find

- the full name of the resident with his unemployed spouse's name in parentheses (employed married women will have a separate entry; widows will be listed with their deceased husband's name in parentheses);
- occupation; and
- complete street address, including the apartment number (a letter r before the address signifies that the person is a "roomer").

Businesses included in the white pages will be listed by the name of the business, the name of the owner of the business, or, in the case of a corporation, the names of the corporate officers. Church listings will indicate the name of the pastor.

The "green pages" are the street guide section. Street names are listed in alphabetical order. Numbered streets may be listed before or after the named streets. Under each street name you will find the house numbers in numerical order with an indication of cross streets as they occur. After each house number is the name of the resident. If the individual is a homeowner, the status is indicated with an *o* inside a circle. The telephone number follows. If a house is unoccupied it is listed as "vacant." If the building contains separate apartments, each resident is listed separately after the house number. Figure 5.6 shows individuals living on Park Avenue in Kansas City, Missouri, in 1947.

Figure 5.6 Section from Polk's Kansas City (Jackson County, Missouri) Directory (Kansas City, MO: Gate City Directory, 1947).

The "blue pages" are the telephone listings, in numerical order. The exchange is listed first (for example, CH2 or 242-). Under the exchange are the next four digits of the phone number. After the four digits is the name of the person or business assigned to that phone number.

The city directory also has a "yellow pages" section listing classified businesses, or a buyers' guide. In these pages you can find a list of professions, clubs, societies, hospitals, cemeteries, labor organizations, libraries, parks, and schools. Businesses were listed at no charge with their complete address and owner's name. Paid classified advertisements are also found in the city directory, such as the advertisement for the

Figure 5.7 Department store advertisement. From Polk's Kansas City (Jackson County, Missouri) Directory (Kansas City, MO: Gate City Directory, 1947).

Emery, Bird, Thayer Department Store in Kansas City, Missouri, in 1947 (see figure 5.7).

City directories offer the genealogist an opportunity to not only search for a person year-by-year but also find out where the person was living, where he or she was employed, who the neighbors were, and the names of the businesses, churches, hospitals, clubs, and other organizations in the community. These directories provide a wealth of information for the researcher. You can find some city directories online on Fold3.

OTHER DIRECTORIES

Directories of organizations, associations, professions, libraries, and so on can help you find the who, what, when, where, and why of the organizations listed. In a large library you can find various types of directories going back many years. Here are some examples of the types of directories you may find in your local library.

- *Directory of Alumni, Clemson University*
- *Avondale United Methodist Church (Kansas City, Missouri)*
- *Directory of Churches in New Jersey*
- *1984 Directory of Dentists, Dental Specialists and Dental Hygienists (Missouri Dental Board)*
- *Directory of Family Associations*
- *Johnson County, Kansas, Farmers, 1921*
- *Directory of Higher Education Institutions in Missouri, 1980–81*

DICTIONARIES

Dictionaries tell us the definitions of words. Many of us have a dictionary in our own homes. If you look carefully, you will see that it is probably an abridged dictionary. Abridged dictionaries have the definitions of commonly used words in our language. Libraries often have unabridged dictionaries. These contain all the words in the English language, even archaic words. In genealogy we often come across words unfamiliar to us. For example, you might see on the tombstone for Mary Jones that she was the *consort* of John Jones. *Consort* means "spouse." This tells you that Mary's husband, John, was alive when Mary died. What if the tombstone for Mary Jones said that she was a *relict* of John Jones? *Relict* means "widow," meaning that John Jones preceded Mary in death and that she was a widow at the time of her passing. A death record or obituary may indicate that a person died of *consumption*. *Consumption* is commonly defined as tuberculosis. Don't bypass an unabridged dictionary when doing genealogical research.

HOW-TO BOOKS

How to do genealogy is a popular subject. Many authors, like myself, have published books about how to get started doing genealogy, where to go for resources, how to do "long distance" genealogy, online genealogy, and more. These books will give you guiding principles for wise genealogy research. You can also find out how to do genealogy from numerous online sites. Ancestry.com has an excellent Learning Center to guide you on all elements of research. The Learning Center is a free segment of this fee-based database and is one of the tabs on Ancestry's home page.

Selected How-To Books

- Allen, Desmond Walls. *First Steps in Genealogy: A Beginner's Guide to Researching Your Family History.* Cincinnati, OH: Betterway Books, 1998.
- Crandall, Ralph J. *Shaking Your Family Tree: A Basic Guide to Tracing Your Family's Genealogy.* 2nd ed. Boston: New England Historic Genealogical Society, 2001.
- Croom, Emily Anne. *Unpuzzling Your Past: The Best-Selling Basic Guide to Genealogy.* 4th ed. Cincinnati, OH: Betterway Books, 2001.
- Dowell, David R. *Crash Course in Genealogy.* Santa Barbara, CA: Libraries Unlimited, 2011.

GUIDES TO RESEARCH

Guides to research differ from how-to books. These books guide you in research in different subject or geographic areas. Every time you begin searching in a new state or country, it is wise to look at a guide for that area. Searching for records in Missouri is entirely different than searching for records in New York State. A good guide will tell you about the availability of records and give you names and addresses of records repositories. The *Red Book* and the *Handybook for Genealogists*,

TABLE OF CONTENTS

Figure 5.8 Table of contents. From A Guide to Texas Research *by Carolyn R. and Joe E. Ericson (Nocogdoches, TX: Ericson Books, 1993).*

mentioned in chapter 1, give a brief overview of records in US states but are not as thorough as a guide for any one particular state. Searching for records overseas can be difficult, but finding a guide to research in a specific country, such as Germany, will make you aware of the records available and how to search for them. A good online source for research guidance is the FamilySearch Research Wiki (https://family search.org/learn/wiki/en/Main_Page). Type in the name of a locality and then search through the results list for the topic that best matches your query. Figure 5.8 shows the table of contents for a guide to Texas research. You can see from the table of contents the type of information a guide like this can give you.

GAZETTEERS

A gazetteer is a dictionary of place names. The description of each local-ity varies, but you will often find the longitude and latitude coordinates and some historical information. You can find a gazetteer of a state, such as *The North Carolina Gazetteer: A Dictionary of Tar Heel Places and Their History*,[10] a gazetteer of the United States, such as *Historical Gazetteer of the United States*,[11] or a gazetteer of another country, such as *Genealogi-cal Gazetteer for the Kingdom of Hungary*.[12] A gazetteer will often include places that no longer exist. I particularly like the *Omni Gazetteer of the United States of America*[13] and refer to it often. I use it to find obscure place names. For instance, in Jackson County, Missouri, is a place called "Englewood." Those who live nearby know where it is, but it is no longer on any map. In the *Omni Gazetteer* it is listed as a "population place," the longitude and latitude coordinates are given, and the quadrangle name of the USGS topographical map where one can find it is listed (see figure 5.9). Using the *Omni Gazetteer* I have frequently been able to find a place name that is listed on the census but is no longer on any map.

OMNI GAZETTEER OF THE UNITED STATES • 203 • Missouri					
Name (ZIP) or Variant Name	Type or Pop.	County	USGS Map (7.5' series)	Lat/Long Coordinates	Source(s) & Other Data
Englewood	pop. pl.	Jackson	Independence	3905 13N-0942721W	G F
Englewood 64052	uninc. pl.	Jackson			F
Englewood Cem	cemetery	Henry	boones	3821 45N-0934 40 JOW	b
Englewood Park	park	Clay	North Kansas City	29 11 34N-094 34 0RW	R
Englewood Sch	school	Clay	North Kansas City	39 11 43N-094 34 37W	G

Figure 5.9 Listing for Englewood, Missouri, in the Omni Gazetteer.

There are also now several online gazetteer options. One of those is *Columbia Gazetteer of the World Online*, which was also published in print until 1998. If I type in "Kirkenes," I first see a brief summary of the place in question. The type of place is "village," the country is Norway, and the region is Finnmark. Clicking on the place name I see that the longitude and latitude coordinates are 69°43' N, 30°03' E. The description is as follows:

> **Kirkenes** (KIR–kuh–nais), village, Finnmark county, NE Nor-way, near Russian border, on Bøkfjorden (S arm of Varanger-fjorden), at mouth of Pasvikelva River, 160 mi/257 km ESE of Hammerfest, 90 mi/145 km NW of Murmansk; 69°43'N 30°03'E.

NORTH CAROLINA. 127

Left-hand column shows compensation of Postmaster. Right-hand one, net revenue of Office to Department.

Davidson County.

Office	Postmaster	Comp.	Rev.
Abbott's Creek	Elisha Raper	$15.31	$9.48
Brummell's	Daniel F. Morris	15.01	9.35
Clemmonsville	Evander McIver	38.33	20.58
Cotton Grove	John Miller	8.98	8.41
Fair Grove	Green H. Lee	6.58	10.88
Healing Springs	William C. Buie	4.00	2.70
Jackson Hill	Edmund B. Clark	11.25	6.62
Lexington (c. h.)	Alexander C. Hege	184.77	166.92
Midway	William Q. Beard	18.62	7.98
Pennfield	Jeremiah Piggott	10.06	7.00
Rich Fork	E. D. C. Harris	12.26	4.55
Silver Hill	Thomas Symons	24.19	6.86
Spencer	Seth Ward	5.30	2.91
Thomasville	Henry E. Rounsaville	87.11	5.87
Walser's Mill	William A. Owen		

Davie County.

Office	Postmaster	Comp.	Rev.
Clarksville	William O. Smith	6.00	2.50
County Line	Henry C. Eccles	12.63	5.75
Farmington	George W. Johnson	36.29	16.89
Fulton	William R. Sharpe	20.13	8.49
Jerusalem	Joseph W. Hodge	4.58	3.14
Mocksville	Calvin U. Rich	98.23	109.91
Smith Grove	Albert Sheek	14.81	8.92

Duplin County.

Office	Postmaster	Comp.	Rev.
Albertson's	Amos W. Simmons	5.61	8.49
Bear Swamp	Luther R. Loftin	11.98	7.98
Branch Store	James G. Branch	8.20	5.43
Bowen Vista	Stephen M. Grady	4.82	2.58
Chinkapin	Julius Scott	12.71	11.44
Faison's Depot	Isham R. Faison	51.62	16.31
Hallsville	Edward Armstrong	19.55	5.69
Kenansville (c. h.)	Alsa B. Southerland	96.67	121.56
Outlaw's Bridge	John W. Whitfield	5.75	4.54
Reason	Hugh Maxwell	2.50	2.00
Strickland's Depot	Leonard A. Merriman	94.96	41.47
Teachey's	Cornelius McMillan	36.00	12.00
Warsaw	John B. Southerland	92.52	17.94

Edgecombe County.

Office	Postmaster	Comp.	Rev.
Battleboro'	Isaac W. Ricks	49.23	15.65
Joyner's Depot	William D. Farmer	53.62	9.94
Rocky Mount	Charles C. Bonner	134.70	8.92
Saratoga	Nathan Webb	7.98	.44
Sparta	James Carney	58.97	50.10
Stantonsburgh	John Wilkinson	54.96	17.56
Tarboro' (c. h.)	David Pender	386.16	564.84
Wilson	Edwin G. Clark	222.25	238.29

Forsyth County.

Office	Postmaster	Comp.	Rev.
Bethania	Eugene C. Lehman	38.62	14.85
Flint Hill	John H. Kreeger	1.00	.50
Kernersville	John F. Kerner	37.00	14.90
Lebanon	Daniel Reick		
Muddy Creek	Samuel Alspaugh	6.15	2.72
Old Richmond	Washington Payne	1.41	1.10
Rural Hall	Anthony Bitting	2.50	1.93
Salem	Orestes A. Keehln	425.74	539.28
Sedges Garden	Joseph Waggoner	7.15	2.89
Walkertown	Robert L. Walker	3.77	2.70
Waughtown	Henry M. Lash	18.42	3.14
White Road	George Y. Fulp	6.20	4.59
Winston (c. h.)	Peter A. Wilson	65.29	32.69

Franklin County.

Office	Postmaster	Comp.	Rev.
Franklinton	Addison D. Ellis	178.11	197.67
Hall's Roads	Richard T. Harris	6.86	4.01
Harris' Roads	Samuel Harriss	7.89	5.84
Louisburgh (c. h.)	William Arendell	287.66	267.15
Pacific	John Young, Jr.	19.79	7.05
Wrightsville	Ransom H. Duke	10.00	6.00

Gaston County—Continued.

Office	Postmaster	Comp.	Rev.
Dallas (c. h.)	Andrew Hoyl	$67.50	$94.92
Erasmus	Manuel Ford	2.75	2.03
King's Mountain	Benjamin F. Briggs	14.93	6.54
Mountain Island	John Tate	11.00	6.00
Nail Factory	Thomas Darling	11.62	3.72
Old Furnace	John E. White	5.46	3.74
South Point	Samuel W. Craig	9.00	4.49
Stanley's Creek	Valentine Derr		
Stowesville	Edwin B. Stowe	16.50	8.25
White Pine	Benjamin Black	4.91	3.58
Woodlawn	James C. Rudisill	13.93	9.83

Gates County.

Office	Postmaster	Comp.	Rev.
Buckland	Samuel E. Smith	15.70	11.87
Gatesville	Shadrach W. Worrell	67.95	43.64
Mintonsville	John C. Troutman	23.29	15.07
Reynoldson	Dempsey Langston		
Sunbury	Costen Jordan	20.51	16.14

Granville County.

Office	Postmaster	Comp.	Rev.
Asylum	John F. Harris	15.94	10.85
Berea	Richard S. Wood	12.57	6.43
Blue Wing	Detron T. Walker	19.05	14.00
Brookville	Samuel H. Cannaday	8.85	4.96
Brownsville	Mary C. Gridlin	16.96	8.01
Dutchville	Elijah Hester	13.66	8.00
Fairport	Donalds'n F. Paschall	9.00	8.00
Gregory's Mill	Thomas J. Gregory	8.22	6.77
Henderson	William W. Reaves	187.51	186.60
Kittrell	Elisha H. Overton	29.54	12.55
Knap of Reeds	Logan W. Umstead	11.66	7.49
Millbank	Eaton Davis	8.48	2.54
Oak Hill	William H. Puryear	36.44	22.11
Oxford (c. h.)	A. T. T. Jones	315.00	277.16
Sassafras Fork	James A. Satterwhite	15.23	8.73
Tabb's Creek	Thomas D. Harris	4.75	1.20
Tally Ho	Augustus H. Cooke	24.00	15.15
Tar River	Cameron W. Allen	11.09	10.65
Townesville	William H. Hughes	10.88	1.79
Tranquility	Nathan'l E. Cannady	9.41	6.93
Waterloo	William O. Gregory	5.82	5.21
Williamsboro'	Elijah Satterwhite	69.50	22.70
Wilton	Lewis T. Smith	10.88	4.84
Woodworths	James O. K. Paschall		
Young's Roads	Marcus D. Royster	20.68	18.57

Greene County.

Office	Postmaster	Comp.	Rev.
Bull Head	John J. Edmunson		
Hookerstown	Jesse W. Moore	71.80	27.09
Maysville	George W. Moore	14.80	4.52
Snow Hill (c. h.)	John T. Freeman	54.47	86.70
Speight's Bridge	William A. Darden	26.22	16.00

Guilford County.

Office	Postmaster	Comp.	Rev.
Allemance	William R. Smith	26.92	11.96
Brick Church	Thomas H. Wharton	8.81	3.19
Centre	Andrew C. Murrow	31.71	15.32
Deep River	Cyrus J. Wheeler	12.64	5.46
Fentriss	Frederick Fentriss	6.78	3.80
Friendship	John Hunt	22.48	10.37
Gibsonville	Jerden A. Neese		
Gilmer's Store	Joseph W. Gilmer	14.49	7.55
Greensboro'	Branson G. Graham	754.96	932.92
High Point	Austin H. Welch	11.00	3.00
Hillsdale	Anselom Reed	15.40	8.59
Hunt's Store	Nathan Hunt, Jr	101.90	48.96
Jamestown	Pinckney N. Wheeler	14.31	24.54
McLeansville	James McLean		
Monticello	C. W. Thacker	15.21	6.61
New Garden	John Russell	74.15	
Oak Ridge	Thomas Graham	35.00	11.88
Shaw's Mills	Finley Shaw	6.81	4.61
Summerfield	Sydner A. Powell	20.50	9.98
Summer's Mill	James M. Wharton	8.99	2.30
Westminster	David Beard, Jr	15.48	7.44

Figure 5.10   Post offices in North Carolina, 1856. From Colton's United States Post Office Directory, 1856.

Port and commercial center for Norway's main iron-mining region, until the mines closed in 1997. A shipbuilding industry and medical services remain. Seaplane base and airport; terminus for the coastal steamer from Bergen. Village grew since beginning (1910) of mining operations in region. German base in World War II, it was largely destroyed by air raids. Captured by USSR (Oct., 1944) and occupied by the Russians until shortly after the end of hostilities. Has central library and hospital.[14]

This information aided my understanding of the area that my great-grandfather left in the 1860s.

Other books useful for locating places in the United States are post office guides. These guides are published by the United States Postal Service but are often reprinted by others. You can find guides for many different years, such as *Colton's United States Post Office Directory, 1856*.[15] Of what benefit are these postal guides? In each census record, a post office locality is given on each page of the schedule. Many of these post offices have disappeared over time. Knowing more about the post office can help you pinpoint the location where your ancestors were living. Figure 5.10 shows some of the post offices in North Carolina in 1856.

NEWSPAPERS

Newspaper research is very beneficial to a genealogist. This type of printed record is also now an online resource. Most, if not all, newspaper publications also have an online presence. Genealogists use newspapers primarily to find obituaries. The obituary may tell you about your ancestor's migration into the area, parents' names, age at the time of death, the names of surviving family members and where they lived at the time, religious denomination, occupation, name of the funeral home, place of burial, and much more. Or it may tell you very little (see figure 5.11). There is no standard when it comes to obituaries.

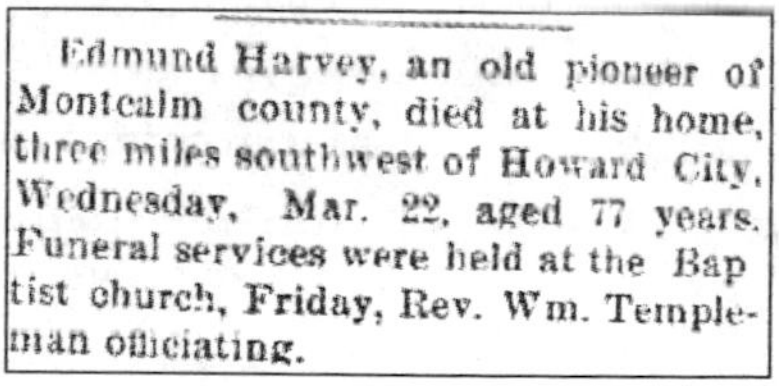

Edmund Harvey, an old pioneer of Montcalm county, died at his home, three miles southwest of Howard City, Wednesday, Mar. 22, aged 77 years. Funeral services were held at the Baptist church, Friday, Rev. Wm. Templeman officiating.

Figure 5.11   Obituary appearing in the Howard City [Michigan] Record, 30 March 1899.

The items you can find in a newspaper are limitless. You can find marriage announcements, birth announcements, the names of residents in the hospital on a particular date, names of visiting relatives and friends, announcements of probate, and events happening in the community (see figure 5.12). Newspapers are a fun printed source to search.

> Chas. Campbell is a grippe victim this week.
>
> Prin. Chas. Meach, of Lakeview, is in town today.
>
> Victor Van Popple, the Waverly agent has sold 13 new wheels this spring.
>
> Chas. O'Donald and wife will soon occupy the Soules house vacated this week by S. V. Bullock.
>
> Rev. Reed is in Grand Rapids this week assisting Rev. C. S. Wheeler at the Epworth M. E. church in special meetings.
>
> Burt Fraker, formerly employed in the Heath drug store at Hastings, has accepted a position in Nagler's Drug store.

Figure 5.12   Announcements appearing in the Howard City [Michigan] Record, 30 March 1899.

Libraries frequently have their local newspaper on microfilm or will at least be able to tell you where the state newspaper repository is located. Some libraries will help you get the microfilmed newspaper through interlibrary loan. Online options are also available but are not universal. Some of those options are

- GenealogyBank (subscription or library access)
- Nineteenth Century US Newspapers (Infotrac; library access only)
- Historical Newspapers (ProQuest; library access only)
- Chronicling America: Historic American Newspapers (Library of Congress; free at http://chroniclingamerica.loc.gov)
- Wikipedia's list of online newspaper archives (http://en.wikipedia .org/wiki/Wikipedia:List_of_online_newspaper_archives)

MAPS

Maps are a wonderful resource for genealogists, and many historic maps are now online. ProQuest has a product entitled *Historic Map Works* available to libraries that has many historic and plat maps of interest to genealogists. One of the best free Internet sites for finding historic maps is www.davidrumsey.com. Finding a map for the time in which your ancestor lived in an area will help you determine where he

Christensen, W. M., Pleasant View Farm, S. 17, T. 62, R. 13, P. O. Brashear. 1907. Mr. Christensen was born in Iowa in 1884, and married Odelia Clarkson. They have two children.

Figure 5.13 Plat book directory page. From Standard Atlas of Adair County, Missouri *(Chicago: Geo. A. Ogle, 1919).*

or she lived. A common map that genealogists use is a plat map. A plat map shows ownership of land at the time the map was published. These maps frequently are published as a county atlas with each civil township map on a different page in the atlas or plat book. In addition, these maps often have "patron" lists. Patrons were residents and businesses that paid to have the plat book printed. There is a lot of detail on these patrons—in addition to an individual's name, you may find out how long he has been a resident of the county, his previous residence, his occupation, the name of his wife, and how many children they have. For instance, directory page 1 in the plat book of Adair County, Missouri (1919), shows that W. M. Christensen of Pleasant View Farm had lived in the county since 1907. His farm was in section 17, township 62, and range 13. His post office was Brashear. He was born in Iowa in 1884 and married to Odella Clarkson. They had two children.[16] (See figure 5.13.) In addition, many plat books have line drawings or photographs of some of the farms. The plat of Mr. Christensen's land is shown in figure 5.14, in section 17.

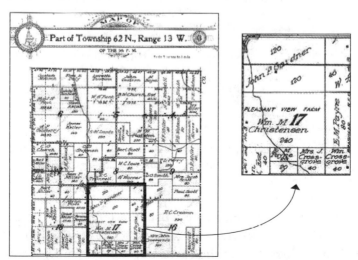

Figure 5.14 Plat map. From Standard Atlas of Adair County, Missouri *(Chicago: Geo. A. Ogle, 1919).*

COUNTY AND TOWN HISTORIES

Histories of counties and towns are an important component of genealogical research. They take us back in time and allow us a glimpse of
life in that area and the people who lived there. Your ancestor's name
may be found in a county history, and the information you find may
help you answer some questions or help you understand your ancestor
better. It is also very likely that your ancestor's name will not appear in
the history, but if you want an overall picture of what your ancestor's
life was like, read the county history. (See figure 5.15.)

> Samuel Colyar was raised in North Carolina, from
> which place he removed to Logan County, Ohio, and
> from there to Penn, in the spring of 1831, and made
> a crop on Young's Prairie. In the fall he went after
> his family, which consisted of his wife and fourteen
> children, ten of whom came with him, and settled on
> Section 11. When en route the streams were so
> swollen that it was necessary to unload the goods and
> ferry them across and reload them again; on one oc-
> casion the wagon-box floated off and was making rapid
> descent down the river when it was caught by them
> after a lively pursuit in a pirogue that was near at
> hand. In November, that year, long before farmers
> were ready for it, there came an immense fall of snow,
> burying everything beneath sight, and the cattle, as
> they wallowed through it, were encased up to their
> sides; it was finally dissipated by the sun. Mr. Col-
> yar helped very considerably in the development of
> the country, and was always ready to assist in every
> good cause. As a christian, he was a zealous ad-
> vocate of christianity, and assisted very materially
> in establishing and maintaining the Baptist Church,
> of which he was a member. He was esteemed by all
> his neighbors for his many good qualities of mind and
> heart, and passed away deeply lamented. Of his
> large family of children, but three remain in the
> county—Phœbe, Mrs. R. Reams, in Cassopolis;
> Mary, Mrs. Reams, in Jefferson, and Jonathan, also
> in Jefferson, he being twenty-one years of age when
> coming into the county.

Figure 5.15 Account from History of Cass County, Michigan: With Illustrations
and Biographical Sketches of Some of Its Prominent Men and Pioneers *(Chicago:
Waterman, Watkins, 1882), p. 369.*

County histories began to be published after the centennial of the
United States. It is purported that President Grant asked counties and
towns to publish a history of their area. Several companies responded to
the challenge. One of those publishing companies was Goodspeed. The

company would send a representative into the county and announce that a history was going to be published. If a family wished to prepay to receive a copy, they could write a biographical sketch about a family member who had lived in the county to be printed in the volume. Because these biographical sketches were composed by the family, they were written in glowing terms. Don't believe everything you read about your ancestor. You should verify the information found. Other content in the history was contributed by members of the community. These early county and town histories were published as early as 1880 but seldom before. The interest in county histories began to fade around 1920.

A resurgence of interest began in earnest with the bicentennial celebration of the United States and continues today. In this case a book committee is usually formed by interested citizens—often members of the historical society. Several companies offer their publishing services, but the content is always written by the citizens in that community.

What is in a county history? The first thing you will want to look at is the date of publication. Was your family in the county at the time of publication to aid in the creation of the content? Next, look at the table of contents. In the early county histories, you will usually find a history of the state. The publishing companies included the same content about the state in the county history of each county in that state.

If we look at the table of contents of the *History of Boone County, Missouri*, published in 1882 by the Western Historical Company, we will see that the first 124 pages are about the history of Missouri: the Louisiana Purchase, description and geography, geology, early settlers, territorial organization, admission into the Union, Missouri as a state, the Civil War in Missouri, an early military record of the state, agriculture and mineral wealth, education and the public school system, religious denominations, and Governor Crittenden's administration. Following the history of Missouri are a history of St. Louis, the laws of Missouri, and statistics. It isn't until page 125 that the history of the county begins. The history is broken down into segments: early history before 1820, 1820 to 1830, 1830 to 1840, 1840 to 1850, 1850 to 1860, the Civil War years, 1860 to 1870, and 1870 to 1882. The book also includes a history of Missouri State University, geology of the county, township histories, livestock interests, a list of county officials, and a list of illustrations.

The main thing every genealogist hopes to find in a county history is a biographical sketch of his or her ancestor. Sometimes the biographical sketches were of well-to-do citizens. In the *Portrait and Biographical Record of Waukesha, Wisconsin,* published in 1894 is a biographical sketch of W. D. Bacon. The three-page biography says that W. D. Bacon came to Waukesha in 1841 from Stillwater, Saratoga County, New York. His grandfather, Samuel Bacon, was a native of England. His full name was Winchell D. Bacon, and he was born August 21, 1816. The names of his children and siblings are listed. He married Delia Blackwell on July 4, 1838. He came from Utica by canal to Buffalo, took a steamer to Milwaukee, and used a team and wagon to get to Prairieville, which is now Waukesha. He was a wagon maker and blacksmith and later operated a sawmill. During the Civil War he was a paymaster for the Union Army. Post–Civil War he organized the Farmer's National Bank. He was a Whig, a Mason, and a Baptist. His first wife died in 1880, and he married Mrs. Clara Campbell in 1883. Mr. Bacon died March 20, 1894.

What if your ancestor did not have a biographical sketch in a town or county history? What else can you find? Here are some examples:

- In the *Biographical and Historical Memoirs of Northeast Arkansas* (published in 1889) we can find out about the organization of Fulton County. It was established in 1843 from land that had formerly been a part of Izard County. Its first town was Salem. The first log courthouse in Salem was destroyed during the Civil War. The next log courthouse was built in 1870.
- You may find a list of the cemeteries, the early settlements, names of the churches, when those churches were established and who the charter members were, the names of the first settlers and the section of land they owned, names of the clubs and who the charter members were, names of the newspapers and who established them, and the names of the ladies in the library association.
- The names of the men in military service are usually shown. In eastern states you will often find the names of those who served in the Revolutionary War and the War of 1812. In states farther west you will usually find the names of those who were enrolled in units of the Civil War.

- Natural disasters are often listed. If your family relocated to another state or county, was it due to a drought that destroyed all the crops? Are some of the children in a family missing from one census to another, and you don't know what happened to them? Perhaps there was typhoid fever in the county, and the children died. What happened in the county happened to your family as well.
- The 1882 *History of Boone County, Missouri*, lists the names of the men who went to the gold fields in 1850.[17] Some of them never returned. (See figure 5.16.)

> CALIFORNIA GOLD FEVER.
>
> The discovery of gold in California in 1849 greatly excited the people all over the West, and of course the people of Boone county caught the infection. Early in the spring of that year, but larger numbers of them during 1850, abandoned their homes and business — some of them, alas! never to return — for the gold fields of the new Eldorado. During the month of April the emigrants from this county took up the line of march in wagons and on horseback for their toilsome journey to the Pacific. So far as we have been able to learn, the following are their names : —
>
> Francis T. Russell, R. E. Lusk, Dan'l Grosse, Jerre Orear, Dr. W. B. Lenoir, M. Boyle, Thos. A. Russell, David Guitar, Wm. T. Russell, John Chadwick, Wm. B. Royall, T. A. Garth, Samuel Kennon, A. N. Willhite, Madison D. Stone, Eli Pulliam, Lawrence Rochford, Rev. Francis Hart, John W. Carter, M. P. Wills, Jr., G. W. Nichols, James M. Wilcox, W. J. Hitt, Nathaniel Torbitt, W. G. Tuttle, ———Elliott, A. E. West, Arch. Goin, W. H. Stone, Samuel R. Tuttle, Thos. A. Sims, Hugh T. Plant, Jas. B. Furnish, James M. Wright, David R. Doyle, Dr. John B. Isbell, G. L. Russell, John M. Willis, Moss P. Foffe, Thomas Orear, John Scott, Chas. R. Thomas, ——— Harris, Samuel D. Lamme, Andrew Trumbaugh, Benj. T. Orear, Lemuel Noble, Thos. J. O'Neal, Wm. Bentley, John H.

Figure 5.16 *Excerpt from History of Boone County, Missouri.*

Where to Find County and Town Histories

Public libraries will usually have the county or town histories that have been published for their area. University libraries and historical societies are other places to look, as well as libraries with large genealogy collections. If the history was published before 1923, it is free of copyright and is probably online. Some places to look for county histories online are

- Google Books: http://books.google.com
- Family History Books: http://books.familysearch.org

GENEALOGY: TWENTY MINUTES A DAY

Visit your local library and explore the sources discussed in this chapter. The library may not have a book about your family, but it may have a printed source that tells about the time in which your ancestor lived. Explore online for historic maps, county histories, and other out-of-print sources that may have been digitized.

- HeritageQuest Online: www.heritagequestonline.com (select Search Books)

County histories can provide vast information on your family. It is like having a conversation with someone who lived long ago and who can provide you with answers to questions you may have about your ancestors. Knowing the geography and climate may give you an idea of why your ancestors settled where they did. Knowing more about the experiences people had in a county or town will help you know what your ancestors endured. Don't neglect this important part of your ancestors' history.

THE INTERNET

Genealogy information can be found in courthouses, in libraries, in cemeteries, in archives, and on the Internet. On the Internet you may find information compiled by a researcher (documented and undocumented), digitized records, transcriptions of records (see figure 5.17), and indexes. It is impossible to know about all the genealogy websites on the Internet. In *The Wizard of Oz*, Judy Garland, as Dorothy Gale, says of Oz, "My! People come and go so quickly here!"[18] I feel that way about the Internet. Websites come and go quickly. Others are tried and true and have lasted, in online terms, a long time.

I like to use search engines to find new websites. Some of the standards are Google, Yahoo!, Gigablast, and Dogpile. Cyndi's List (www.cyndislist.com) is an important genealogy website. Genealogy websites are categorized by subject, which makes finding new websites easy—just look for the subject. A similar website is Linkpendium: The

Be it remembered this Thirtieth day of the seventh month one
Thousand Eight Hundred and Seven, that I SAMUEL COLYAR
being of sound and disposing mind and memory do make and
publish this my Last will and testament in manner and form as
follows.

ITEM I give and bequeath to my son JOSEPH COLYAR the
Plantation whereon I now live with the Lands belonging thereto;
I also give him one bed and furniture.
ITEM I give and bequeath to my Daughter MIRIAM HALL the
old plantation I bought of John Grace with all the lands that lies
on the upper side of the Hide Branch.
ITEM I give and bequeath unto my son SAMUEL COLYAR all
my Lands that I have below the said Hide Branch.
ITEM I give and bequeath unto SARAH COLYAR my grand
Daughter one bed and Furniture, also I give to my grand Daughter
ELIZABETH HALL one bed and furniture, and the choice of beds
and furniture.
And the remaining part of my Estate I desire to be Equally divide
between all my children, ZACHARIAH, JAMES, MIRIAM, JOHN,
SAMUEL & JOSEPH, my wearing apparel, I desire my son
ZACHARIAH to have one half and the other half to be Equally
Divided between all the rest of my sons.
Lastly I nominate & appoint NATHAN PIKE and my son SAMUEL
COLYAR Executors to this my Last will and Testament Revoking
and disannulling all wills heretofore made by me, Ratifying and
Confirming this and no other to be my last will and Testament, in
witness whereof I the testator have hereunto set my hand and seal

Signed and acknowledged SAMUEL COLYAR Seal
In presence of us
Samuel Colyar
John Grace

Wills 1776-1927
CR 103.801.__
Folder 1807
NC State Archives, Raleigh, NC

Copyright. All rights reserved.
http://www.usgwarchives.org/copyright.htm

This file was contributed for use in the USGenWeb Archives by
Judy Ginn - PossumnMaHen@aol.com[20]

Figure 5.17 Transcription of the will of Samuel Colyar. From USGenWeb Archives.

Definitive Directory (www.linkpendium.com). *Eastman's Online Genealogy Newsletter* (http://blog.eogn.com) is a newsletter/blog that keeps genealogists up-to-date on the latest genealogy websites and technology. Google alerts are another way to keep tabs on the latest websites. You will have to create a free Google account and after you are logged on go to www.google.com/alerts?hl–en. Type in the search terms for which you want to be alerted, and those alerts will go to your mailbox. You will then be able to keep up with the latest, most relevant Google results. Be aware that if you type in *genealogy* as your alert term, you will get many and frequent alerts in your mailbox. I would suggest that you be very specific.

Some of my favorite websites are the following:

- Seeking Michigan: http://seekingmichigan.org. You may have realized by now that I have Michigan connections. This website has digital Michigan death records from 1897 through 1920.
- Illinois State Archives: www.cyberdriveillinois.com/departments/ archives/databases/home.html. The Illinois secretary of state's website has been around a long time and keeps getting better. You can find indexes to deaths, marriages, military records, and more.
- Online Searchable Death Indexes and Records: www.death indexes.com. This site has online searchable death indexes with links to all states.
- Missouri Death Certificates: www.sos.mo.gov/archives/ resources/deathcertificates/. Missouri digital death certificates from 1910 to 1962 are now online. Missouri law allows death certificates older than 50 years to be public record. Each January another year is digitized, indexed, and posted.

I frequently check the following sites to see if there is anything new. I'm usually not looking for anything specific—I'm just surfing.

- CastleGarden.org: www.castlegarden.org (Castle Garden passenger arrivals)
- FamilySearch: https://familysearch.org
- One-Step Webpages by Stephen P. Morse: www.stevemorse.org. This website is a mishmash of interesting data. Morse is famous for his "one-step" pages, making existing websites easier to search.
- RootsWeb: www.rootsweb.ancestry.com (free)
- The Statue of Liberty–Ellis Island Foundation: http://ellisisland .org (Ellis Island passenger arrivals)
- USGenWeb Project: http://usgenweb.org (includes state pages and several projects, including the Tombstone Transcription Project)
- USGenWeb Free Census Project: www.usgwcensus.org (free census images)

Other websites mentioned in this chapter are

- David Rumsey Map Collection: www.davidrumsey.com (search historic maps free online)
- Family History Books: http://books.familysearch.org (online books at FamilySearch)
- Google Books: http://books.google.com (online books at Google)
- Library of Congress Online Catalog: http://catalog.loc.gov
- Mid-Continent Public Library: www.mymcpl.org/catalog (genealogy books are available for interlibrary loan from the Midwest Genealogy Center; to learn how to request the books on interlibrary loan, go to www.mymcpl.org/genealogy/how-request -books)
- Research Wiki: https://familysearch.org/learn/wiki/en/Main _Page (learn how to do genealogy research)
- St. Louis County Library: www.slcl.org/genealogy-and-local -history/services#ill (genealogy books are available for interlibrary loan from the National Genealogical Society Book Loan Collection)
- Wikipedia's list of online newspaper archives: http://en.wikipedia .org/wiki/Wikipedia:List_of_online_newspaper_archives
- WorldCat: www.worldcat.org (create your own bibliography or just search for books in libraries)

· · ·

In this chapter we have looked at printed and Internet sources of genealogy material. Original records are not always easily accessible. One way to discover information from the documents is through print materials and online websites. As you have also seen, not all the print materials that genealogists use are considered "genealogy materials." There are many materials you can find in the reference section of your local library. Finding information about your ancestors can take many varied paths. I hope you venture onto some new ones.

NOTES

1. Harry Clyde Smith, *The Reams, Reames Family and Allied Families* (Glendale, CA: printed by author, 1956).

2. Ibid., 105.

3. Library of Congress, *Genealogies in the Library of Congress: A Bibliography* (Baltimore: Magna Carta, 1972).

4. Marion J. Kaminkow, *A Complement to the Genealogies in the Library of Congress: A Bibliography* (Baltimore: Magna Carta, 1981).

5. Library of Congress, *Genealogies Cataloged by the Library of Congress Since 1986: With a List of Established Forms of Family Names and a List of Genealogies Converted to Microform Since 1983* (Washington, DC: Cataloging Distribution Service, Library of Congress, 1991).

6. *Biography and Genealogy Master Index* (Detroit, MI: Gale Research, 1980–).

7. *Who's Who . . . an Annual Biographical Dictionary* (New York: St. Martin's Press, 1849–).

8. Gary W. Shearer, *The Civil War, Slavery, and Reconstruction in Missouri: A Bibliography of Secondary Sources and Selected Primary Sources* (Angwin, CA: printed by author, 2000).

9. Emil Meynen, ed., *Bibliography on the Colonial Germans of North America: Especially the Pennsylvania Germans and Their Descendants* (Baltimore: Genealogical Publishing, 1982). Originally published as *Bibliography on German Settlements in Colonial North America* (Liepzig, Germany, 1937).

10. William Stevens Powell, *The North Carolina Gazetteer: A Dictionary of Tar Heel Places and Their History* (Chapel Hill: University of North Carolina Press, 2010).

11. Paul T. Hellmann, *Historical Gazetteer of the United States* (New York: Routledge, 2005).

12. Jordan Auslander, *Genealogical Gazetteer for the Kingdom of Hungary* (Bergenfield, NJ: Avotaynu, 2005).

13. Frank R. Abate, ed., *Omni Gazetteer of the United States of America* (Detroit, MI: Omnigraphics, 1991).

14. "Kirkenes," *The Columbia Gazetteer of the World Online*, Columbia University Press, accessed October 7, 2011, www.columbiagazetteer .org/main/ViewPlace/70830.

15. Theron Wierenga, *Colton's United States Post Office Directory, 1856* (Muskegon, MI: printed by author, 1985). Originally published as *Post Office Directory or Business Man's Guide to the Post Offices in the United States*, compiled by D. D. T. Leech (New York: J. H. Colton, 1856).

16. *Standard Atlas of Adair County, Missouri: Including a Plat Book of the Villages, Cities and Townships of the County, Map of the United States and the World, Patrons' Directory, Reference Business Directory and Departments Devoted to General Information, Analysis of the System of U.S. Land Surveys, Digest of the System of Civil Government, Etc., Etc.* (Chicago: Geo. A. Ogle, 1919).

17. *History of Boone County, Missouri: Written and Compiled from the Most Official and Private Sources;* . . . (St. Louis, MO: Western Historical Co., 1882; repr., Cape Girardeau, MO: Ramfre Press, 1970).

18. *The Wizard of Oz* (Metro-Goldwyn-Mayer, 1939).

chapter six

Immigration Records and Foreign, Native American, and African American Research

THE UNITED STATES IS A NATION OF IMMIGRANTS. FINDING THE SOURCE of our ethnicity comes from researching back in time until we find an immigrant ancestor. The number of immigrant ancestors you will find depends on the number of generations you need to go back before you find a foreign-born ancestor. On my father's side, I need only to go back to his father to find an immigrant. My paternal grandfather emigrated from Sweden in 1901. If your ancestry goes back to colonial America, you will have a large number of immigrant ancestors.

PASSENGER LISTS

A passenger list, although it may not tell you everything you need to know, gives you a definite link from the old country to the new. There are things you will need to know before you begin searching passenger lists: the first and last name of the immigrant, his or her age or approximate age upon arrival, and the approximate date of arrival. The closer you can come to a date, the easier your search will be. It may seem obvious that you need to know the name of your immigrant, but this is very important. We can't look for all arrivals having the last name of Schmidt. It would be a futile effort because you would not be able to identify your ancestor among all those arriving. In addition to the first and last name, it helps to have an approximate age and year of immigration. If your Johann Schmidt was born in approximately 1862 and his arrival was approximately 1890, you would be looking for a Johann Schmidt arriving about 1890 who was about 28 years old. How do you determine the year of immigration? First of all, look for your ancestor on the 1900, 1910, 1920, or 1930 census. If he or she was on a census in one of those years, the census will tell you the year of immigration, based on the answer given the enumerator by that individual. If you can't pinpoint the immigration year exactly, try to find a window in time in which he or she arrived. Let's say your ancestor was born on foreign soil in 1832 and died in the United States in 1885. We know that he immigrated after 1832 and before 1885. If he had a child who was born in the United States in 1855, then the immigration year was between 1832 and 1855. If that same ancestor was married in the United States in 1854, then the window in time narrows a little more. The answers to the following questions, though not necessary, are good to know: Did your ancestor travel alone or with others? Did he bring his family? Did he come as a child? Was someone waiting for him in the United States, or was he the first of his family or friends to arrive?

There is one important thing to remember in your search for passenger lists and that is the pivotal year of 1820. Overcrowding on immigrants ships was leading to many deaths en route to the United States. In March 1819 Congress enacted a law requiring only two passengers for every five tons of a ship's register.[1] The result was an enumeration of all ships' passengers that was to be sent to the US secretary of state. These lists are called Customs Passenger Lists. The law took effect in 1820. If your ancestor arrived before 1820, the passenger list will not be an arrival list into the United States. It will be a printed re-creation of a list: it may be a license to pass overseas, a will record, or a land record—any document that gives a date when an immigrant came to this country. Look for an index to published lists.

Locating Passenger Lists Before 1820

In searching for lists of passengers arriving prior to the official keeping of customs lists, you will be looking at books. In 1962 the New York Public Library published a bibliography of books that contain re-created passenger lists called *A Bibliography of Ship Passenger Lists, 1538–1825*.[2] The bibliography is divided by colony (later state), and within each colony titles are sorted by year. Figure 6.1 shows Massachusetts for the years 1620–1623. The source for the year 1620 shows "Passengers of the Mayflower" from *History of Plymouth Plantation* by William Bradford. The contents contain the names of those who sailed on the *Mayflower* in 1620. The next work covers the years 1620–1623: *The English Ancestry and Homes of the Pilgrim Fathers Who Came to Plymouth on the "Mayflower" in 1620* . . . This book shows passengers on the *Mayflower*,

MASSACHUSETTS

1620

"Passengers of the Mayflower; the Names of Those Which Came Over First, in the Year 1620 and Were by the Blessing of God the First Beginers and (in a sort) the Foundation of All the Plantations and Colonies in New England; and Their Families" (*In* William Bradford *History of Plymouth Plantation*, 1620–1647, Boston, Massachusetts Historical Society 1912 II 397–412)   33

   There are several editions of Bradford's *History*, all of which have this list as an appendix. Of these, the ed of 1898 is the most easily obtainable on the out-of-print market.

   Mayflower passenger lists are also printed in 33A Nathaniel Bradstreet Shurtleff, "The Passengers of the May Flower in 1620," *The New England Historical and Genealogical Register* I (1847) 47–53; 33B Algernon Aikin Aspinwall, "The Mayflower Passengers," *National Genealogical Society Quarterly* VI (1917) 56–57; 33C Azel Ames, *The May-Flower and Her Log, July 15, 1620 – May 6, 1621, Chiefly from Original Sources* (Boston, Houghton, Mifflin & Co 1907) 166–195; 33D "List of Passengers to America. From Authentic Sources," *The Genealogist's Note Book* I (1899) 66–67; 33E "The Mayflower Series of Papers: 2," *The Historical Bulletin* IV (1904) 101–103; 33F *List of Passengers Who Came to Plymouth in The "Mayflower" on Her First Trip in 1620* (New York, Society of Mayflower Descendants 1896); 33G *Mayflower Descendants and Their Marriages* (Baltimore, Southern Book Co 1956).

1620–1623

Charles Edward Banks, *The English Ancestry and Homes of the Pilgrim Fathers Who Came to Plymouth on the "Mayflower" in 1620, the "Fortune" in 1621, and the "Anne" and the "Little James" in 1623* (New York, The Grafton Press 1929) 187 p   34

   Names of the various passengers, together with valuable information on their origin and later history, grouped alphabetically under the ship in which they arrived. Contains an appended list of the female passengers on the Anne and Little James.

   Passenger lists of the Anne and Fortune may also be found in 34A "The Mayflower Series of Papers: 5," *The Historical Bulletin* V (1904) 34–36. The lists of all four vessels also appear in: 34B John A. Goodwin, *The Pilgrim Republic* (Boston, Tickner and Co 1888; 2d ed, Boston and New York, Houghton Mifflin Co 1920) 183–186, 190–191, 242–244, 297–300; in 34C Leon Clark Hills, *History and Genealogy of the Mayflower Planters and First Comers to Ye Olde Colonie* (Washington, Hills Publishing Co 1936) 20–22, 79–80, 84–86; and in 34D an unidentified, 2-page pamphlet (n p, n d) which commences "List of Passengers in the Mayflower" and which has been pasted into a red-rope cover and bound into a pamphlet volume (IQH p v 34, no 14) in The New York Public Library.

   Reissued in facsimile by the Genealogical Publishing Co, Baltimore, 1962.

Figure 6.1 Excerpt from A Bibliography of Ship Passenger Lists, 1538–1825, *compiled by Harold Lancour (New York: New York Public Library, 1963).*

Fortune, *Anne*, and *Little James*. Lancour's *Bibliography* was a boon to genealogists who suddenly had the names of books that contain immigration information. However, it was a tedious task to go through each book in hopes of finding the name of an ancestor.

The bibliography was expanded several years later by P. William Filby in *Passenger and Immigration Lists Bibliography, 1538–1900*,[3] and the number of books included was greatly increased. Filby then indexed the names found in the books in his bibliography. This endeavor resulted in a multivolume work entitled *Passenger and Immigration Lists Index: A Guide to Published Records of About 500,000 Passengers Who Came to the United States and Canada in the Seventeenth, Eighteenth, and Nineteenth Centuries*.[4] This index made the search much easier. Each year a different set of books from the bibliography is indexed. Although the project began over thirty years ago, a researcher must still look through many books to possibly find an ancestor. To make the search a little easier, volumes are combined to make a cumulated supplement about every three years. The volumes contain a bibliography of books that were used to index the names in the volumes and an index that shows the name of the individual, age, year of immigration, port, page number, and book number from the bibliography. Then the researcher has to find the book that was indexed and find the original citation. The task still isn't easy, but the index truly does help narrow down the possibilities.

Figure 6.2 is an excerpt from volume 2 of the three-volume first edition of Filby and Meyers's index. You can see three entries for Gideon Merlit, who immigrated to either New Netherlands or New York (State) in 1662 with a wife and four children. The books in the bibliography are numbers 5635, 6291, and 6520. According to the bibliography, 5635 refers to *Early Immigrants to New Netherlands, 1657–1664* by Carol M. Meyers;[5] 6291 is "Early Immigrants to New Netherlands, 1657–1664" as found in *The Documentary History of the State of New York*;[6] and 6520 is "Passenger Lists 1657 to 1664," from *The Documentary History of New York* as found in a periodical entitled *Year Book of the Holland Society of New York*.[7] These three works seem to come from the same source. So, from the third volume of *The Documentary History of the State of New York*, we see the list shown in figure 6.3. You can see "Gideon Merlit, and Wife and four children" arriving in October on the ship *Purmerland Church*. Unfortunately, for the genealogist who wishes to see more information, there isn't any. This content is similar to what constitutes a reconstructed passenger list prior to 1820. Ancestry.com has placed the Filby indexes on its website but only with the information found in the index. The source of the information is not shown.

Merlit, Gideon n.a.; New Netherlands, 1662 *5635 p19*
with wife & 4 children
Merlit, Gideon n.a.; New Netherlands, 1662 *6291 p60*
with wife & 4 children
Merlit, Gideon n.a.; New York (State), 1662 *6520 p154*
with wife & 4 children

Figure 6.2 Entries for Gideon Merlit. From Passenger and Immigration Lists Index, *vol. 2, edited by P. William Filby and Mary K. Meyers (Detroit: Gale Research, 1981–), p. 1434.*

OCTOBER; *In the Purmerland Church.*
Claus Paulus, from Detmarsum, and Wife.,
Nicolas du Pui, from Artois, and Wife and three children.
Arnout du Tois, from Ryssel, (Lisle,) and Wife and one child.
Gideon Merlit, and Wife and four children.
Louis Louhman, and Wife and three children.
Jacques Cossaris, and Wife and two children.
Jan de Conchilier, (now, Consilyea) and Wife and five childre
Jacob Colff, from Leyden, and Wife and two children.
Judith Jans, from Leyden, maiden.
Carsten Jansen.
Ferdinandus de Mulder.
Isaac Vernlel, and Wife and four children.
Abelis Setshoorn.
Claes Janson van Heynengen.

Figure 6.3 Passenger arrival list. From The Documentary History of the State of New York.

Many books have been published to record re-created passenger lists. Using a bibliography or the Filby indexes, or both sources, is a great time saver. Another project deserves mention here. It is a continuing effort to identify all immigrants arriving to our shores between 1620 and 1640 entitled the Great Migration Study Project, developed by the New England Historic Genealogical Society. The results of the research are published monthly in the *Great Migration Newsletter*. You can find out how to subscribe to the newsletter or learn more about the project at www.greatmigration.org. Two books have resulted from the studies of the organization: *The Great Migration Begins: Immigrants to New England, 1620–1633*[8] and *The Great Migration: Immigrants to New*

CUSTOMS LIST OF PASSENGERS.

District of the City of New York, Port of New York.

I, Edw. P. Buck, Master of the American S.S. Saratoga, do solemnly, sincerely and truly swear that the following List or Manifest subscribed by me, and now delivered by me to the Collector of Customs of the District of the City of New York, is a full and perfect list of all the passengers taken on board said vessel at Tampico & Havana, from which port or ports the said vessel has now arrived; and that on said list is truly designated the age, sex, calling or occupation, the port of embarkation, the number of pieces of baggage, of all the passengers, the date and cause of death of any such passengers who may have died on the voyage, and also a statement, so far as it can be ascertained, with reference to the intention of each immigrant passenger as to a protracted sojourn in this country, and also, in regard to Cabin passengers, the country of which they are citizens, and of passengers other than cabin passengers, their native country, their intended destination or location in the United States, and whether they are citizens of the United States, or not, and the location of the compartment or space occupied by each, as required by the Passenger Act of 1882 and the Regulations of the Secretary of the Treasury. So help me God.

Sworn before me this 24 day of August 1896.

No.	Name in full	Age Years	Age Mths	Sex	Calling or Occupation	Country of which they are Citizens	Native Country	Intended Destination or Location, State or Territory	State of passengers other than Cabin, whether Citizens of the United States	Transient, in Transit or intending protracted sojourn	Location of Compartment or Space occupied forward or aft	Number of pieces of Baggage	Port of Embarkation	Date and Cause of Death
1	Joseph E. Jacobs	45		M	Detective	U.S.	U.S.	U.S.		U.S.	aft	1	Tampico	
2	C. L. McCarthy	32		"	Bookkeeper	"	"	"		"			"	
3	Mrs. C. L. McCarthy	38		F		"	"	"		"		5	"	
4	Lillian McCarthy	8		"		"	"	"		"			"	
5	Mrs. E. A. White	27		"		"	"	"		"		4	"	
6	Geo. Lee	38		M	Professor	England	England	Pittsburg		"		2	"	
7	Louis Troesch	48		"	Builder	Germany	Germany	Germany		Transit		2	"	
8	Robert Loindner	47		"	"	"	"	"		"		1	"	
9	H. R. Gleason	23		"	None	U.S.	U.S.	U.S.	U.S.	U.S.	Fwd	2	"	
10	Conte Maria Marefoschi	49		"	Consul	Italy	Italy	"		Sojourn	aft	3	Havana	1 — 0

Figure 6.4 This passenger list shows arrivals at the port of New York on August 24, 1896, on the ship Saratoga. From Passenger Lists of Vessels Arriving at New York, NY, 1820–1896, National Archives, microfilm publication no. M237, roll 664.

Ticket No.	Name in full	Age Yrs	Age Mos	Sex	Married or Single	Calling or Occupation	Country of which they are Citizens	Native Country	Intended Destination or Location, State or Territory	State of Passengers other than Cabin, whether Citizens of the United States	Transient, in Transit or intending protracted sojourn	Location of Compartment or Space occupied forward or amidships or aft	Number of pieces of Baggage	Port of Embarkation
								Steerage				Steerage		Bremen
494	Ramona Figueroa			f	s.	servant		Cuba	N.Y.	—	U.S.	Steerage N⁰	1	
496	Fred Schmidt	45		m	m	labor.		Germany		yes		I	1	
497	Fried. Hick	16		f	s.			"				II	1	
498	Susana Hick	41		f	m.	none		Hungary		—		II	1	
"	Stefan		2	m	s.			"				II		
499	Annie Lyreman	32		f				Germany		—		II	1	
101	Hugh't Oedar	45		m	m.	privat		"	Chicago	yes		I	1	
102	Anna Orobel-Cornell	18		f	s.	none		Hungary	Buffalo	—		III		
105	Lina Friedmann	20		f	m.			Russia Poland		—		II	2	
"	Stefan		3	m	s.			"		—				
"	Ilse		1	f	s.			"		—				
106	Ilie Syionk	48		m	m.	dealer		"	N.Y.	—			2	
"	Gitte		40	f	m.	none		"		—				

Figure 6.5 This image shows passengers on the SS Lehn from Bremen to New York on August 26, 1896. The word Steerage is written at the top. Most of our ancestors arrived in this country traveling steerage. It was basically the cargo hold and was the cheapest of accommodations on board the ship. From Passenger Lists of Vessels Arriving at New York, NY, 1820–1896, National Archives, microfilm publication no. M237, roll 664.

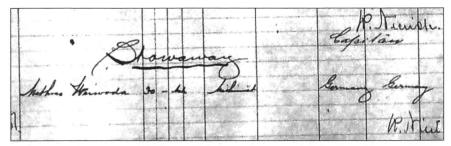

Figure 6.6 The word stowaway appears on this image. This individual was on the SS Emb from Naples to New York on August 26, 1896. Many people have heard family stories about their ancestor being a stowaway and believe that their ancestor would not have been recorded on a passenger list. Very seldom were stowaways undiscovered. From Passenger Lists of Vessels Arriving at New York, NY, 1820–1896, National Archives, microfilm publication no. M237, roll 664.

England, 1634–1635.[9] The latter work is a seven-volume set that took over ten years to complete.

Locating Passenger Lists After 1820

If your ancestor arrived after 1820 there will probably be a passenger list for him or her, provided the arrival was at a US port. The National Archives has filmed the passenger lists that were compiled between 1820 and 1954. Most arrival lists have survived, but not all. Ancestry.com has digitized all the passenger lists filmed by the Archives. If you have access to Ancestry.com or Ancestry Library Edition, the search will be relatively easy, provided you know the name of the immigrant, the approximate year of immigration, the approximate age, and the probable port of arrival. The major ports of entry were Boston, Baltimore, New Orleans, New York, and Philadelphia. There were also numerous minor ports of arrival. The amount of data collected by the customs agents varied depending on the year of arrival. Like the census records, the more recent the record, the more data was collected. (See figures 6.4, 6.5, and 6.6.)

NEW YORK ARRIVALS

The number one port of arrival was New York. Before I started doing my own genealogy I thought all immigrants came through Ellis Island. Not so. Ellis Island was created as an arrival station in 1892. The earlier processing station in New York, beginning in 1855, was Castle Garden. Eighty percent of all arrivals occurred at the port of New York, no matter what processing station was involved. Passenger lists are extant from 1820. From 1846 to 1897 there was no microfilmed index, but with the search capabilities of Ancestry.com it is easy to search the records. Do remember that with any passenger list the name may be recorded differently than that for which you are looking. The difference may be as simple as looking for Johann instead of John. Or the last name may be entirely different. Contrary to popular belief, names were not changed at Ellis Island or at any other port. Names were changed by the individuals themselves for various reasons and at many different times. A couple of free websites to note are CastleGarden.org and EllisIsland.org. The Castle Garden website allows users to search for New York arrivals from 1820 (predating Castle Garden) to 1892. The digitized images of the arrival records are not available, but full detail is. The Ellis Island website allows the user to see digitized images of the passenger lists, but you must pay a fee to obtain a copy of the list.

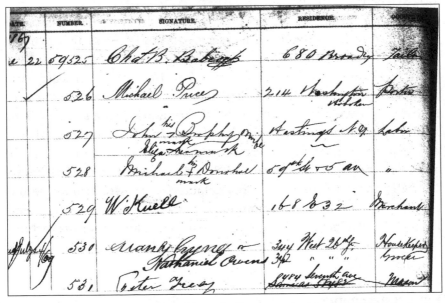

Figure 6.7 *This portion of a record from the Emigrant Savings Bank Records shows the name, address, and occupation of the passbook holders. On the fourth line, account holder 59528, we see Michael Donohue (his mark), who was a laborer. From Emigrant Savings Bank Records, Emigrant Savings Bank, roll 10, June 22, 1867.*

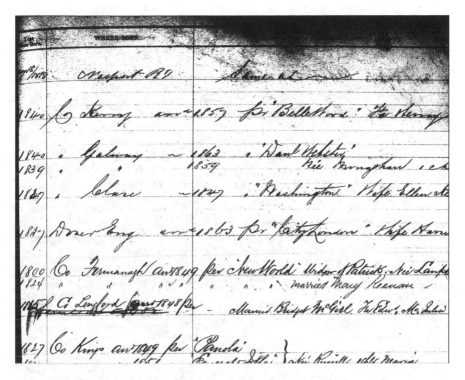

Figure 6.8 This portion of the Emigrant Savings Bank Records shows where account holders were born, when they arrived, and on what ship. Again on the fourth line is more information about Michael Donohuc. He was born in 1827 in County Clare. He arrived in 1847 on the Washington. His wife is Ellen Kelly.

Passenger lists are not the sole source for finding immigrant ancestors in New York. The *Emigrant Savings Bank Records, 1841–1945* are passbook savings account records from the Emigrant Savings Bank in New York. Most of the account holders were Irish, but other nationalities are in these records, as well. Most of the entries tell the name of the boat on which the account holders arrived in this country and the date. Some even tell the names of the account holder's parents, even if the parents did not emigrate. This is a wonderful source for ancestors who arrived and then stayed in New York. It has been filmed by the National Archives and is also on Ancestry.com and Ancestry Library Edition. (See figures 6.7 and 6.8.)

Selected Books to Help You Search New York Arrivals

- Glazier, Ira A., ed. *The Famine Immigrants: Lists of Irish Immigrants Arriving at the Port of New York, 1846–1851.* Baltimore: Genealogical Publishing, 1983–.
- Glazier, Ira A., ed. *Germans to America: Lists of Passengers Arriving at U.S. Ports.* Wilmington, DE: Scholarly Resources, 1988–. This sixty-seven-volume set contains lists of Germans arriving at US ports from 1850 to June 1897, most of whom arrived in New York. To be included in this work, passengers had to be on German ships. If your ancestor sailed across the English Channel to Great Britain and sailed from there, he or she will not be found in these books.
- Glazier, Ira A., ed. *Germans to America—Series II: Lists of Passengers Arriving at U.S. Ports in the 1840s.* Wilmington, DE: Scholarly Resources, [2002–2003]; Lanham, MD: Scarecrow Press, 2004. This seven-volume set was published after the original *Germans to America* volumes to cover the years 1840–1849.
- Glazier, Ira A., ed. *Italians to America: Lists of Passengers Arriving at U.S. Ports.* Baltimore: Genealogical Publishing, 1992–. This series contains twenty-six volumes of Italian arrivals from January 1880 to April 1905.
- Olsson, Nils William. *Swedish Passenger Arrivals in New York, 1820–1850.* Chicago: Swedish Pioneer Historical Society, 1967.
- Wolfert, Marion. *German Immigrants: Lists of Passengers Bound from Bremen to New York, 1868–1871, with Places of Origin.* Baltimore: Genealogical Publishing, 1993.
- Zimmerman, Gary J. *German Immigrants: Lists of Passengers Bound from Bremen to New York, [1847–1867], with Places of Origin.* Baltimore: Genealogical Publishing, 1985–. The two works by Zimmerman and Wolfert were created from microfilmed records of New York passenger arrivals, recording only those passengers on ships that left from Bremen. This was done because of the absence of records of departure from Bremen.

BOSTON ARRIVALS

Boston is the second major port of arrival. All original customs passenger lists prior to 1883 were destroyed by a fire, leaving only transcripts and copies available. Be aware that there are gaps in those records.

However, Massachusetts required a port tax for those who arrived there, resulting in lists of passengers. These lists date from 1848 to 1891. You can search the state lists at www.sec.state.ma.us/arc/arcsrch/passenger manifestsearchcontents.html. Boston was a favored port of arrival of Irish immigrants. After leaving Ireland many became "lost" to friends and family. A newspaper, the *Boston Pilot*, ran frequent advertisements for those looking for missing friends. The names and texts of the advertisements for the years 1831 to 1920 can be found in an eight-volume series of books entitled *The Search for Missing Friends: Irish Immigrant Advertisements Placed in the Boston Pilot*.[10] Boston University has created a website of those same advertisements entitled Information Wanted (http://infowanted.bc.edu). (See figure 6.9.)

---

4 March 1854   *INFORMATION WANTED*

REWARD OF FIFTY DOLLARS will be paid for any information that will lead to the whereabouts of THOMAS RATHWELL, who left the city of Albany about two and a-half years ago. He is about five feet ten or eleven inches high; has fair or light hair, with a mole under his right eye; light blue eyes with heavy eye brows; walk straight with stooped shoulders; has a scar of a large cut on left thumb; age is between thirty-one and thirty-four; his appearance is shy or bashful, and speaks childish, is of a solid complexion, has strong black beard, and when last seen wore no whiskers; he now goes under the name of O'Neil; address, JAMES BRICE, Esq, Albany, N Y.

Figure 6.9 *Advertisement for a missing immigrant. From* The Search for Missing Friends, *edited by Ruth-Ann M. Harris and Donald M. Jacobs (Boston: New England Historic Genealogical Society, 1989–).*

BALTIMORE AND PHILADELPHIA ARRIVALS

Baltimore was the next most active port. Many of Baltimore's customs passenger lists were destroyed by a fire, and quarterly abstracts help to fill the gaps as do the city lists that were gathered between 1833 and 1866. The city lists contain the names of passengers who paid the city surcharge upon arriving.

Philadelphia was fourth in the number of arrivals in the nineteenth century. Available lists for this port begin as early as 1727. These early arrivals were non-English immigrants who were required to sign oaths of allegiance to the British Crown. English immigrants during this period were merely going from one British land to another, and their names were not recorded. Beginning in 1800, the port of Philadelphia

Selected Books about the Immigration Process

- Colletta, John Philip. *They Came In Ships: A Guide to Finding Your Immigrant Ancestor's Arrival Record.* Orem, UT: Ancestry, 2002.
- Eakle, Arlene, and Cerny, Johni, eds. *The Source: A Guidebook of American Genealogy.* Salt Lake City, UT: Ancestry Publishing, 1984. Chapter 15, "Tracking Immigrant Origins," includes a list of maritime museums (page 464). In maritime museums you will find ships' logs.
- Szucs, Loretto Dennis, and Sandra Hargreaves Luebking, eds. *The Source: A Guidebook of American Genealogy.* Rev. ed. Salt Lake City, UT: Ancestry Publishing, 1997. See the chapter on immigration.
- Tepper, Michael. *American Passenger Arrival Records: A Guide to the Records of Immigrants Arriving at American Ports by Sail and Steam.* Baltimore: Genealogical Publishing, 1993.

began keeping baggage lists, recording the names of passengers who were bringing baggage on board. The customs passenger lists begin in 1820 and are extant.

NEW ORLEANS ARRIVALS

New Orleans was the fifth most active port with fewer than 800,000 arrivals between the years 1820 and 1920. The long voyage to New Orleans and the threat of disease (because of swampy conditions) made this an unattractive port of arrival for nineteenth-century immigrants. Transcripts of baggage lists from 1813 to 1849 exist for this port. Passenger lists also exist beginning in 1820 and continuing until 1902 as well as quarterly abstracts of passenger lists from 1820 to 1874. The Louisiana secretary of state's office has posted an online index to New Orleans passenger lists for January 1 to July 7, 1851, in a text file (www .sos.la.gov/Portals/0/archives/gen/passenger.txt).

OTHER PORTS OF ARRIVAL

There were other ports at which immigrant ships landed. Galveston, Texas, was a substantial port. Records can be found on microfilm and on Ancestry.com, and the Texas Seaport Museum has created an online index to Galveston passenger lists (www.galvestonhistory.org/galveston _immigration_database.asp). Other ports along the east and west coasts of the United States have been filmed by the National Archives and can be found on Ancestry.com. But miscellaneous ports were numerous. The National Archives filmed *Copies of Lists of Passengers Arriving at Miscellaneous Ports, on the Atlantic and Gulf Coasts and at Ports on the Great Lakes 1820–1873* (film series M575), which is also on Ancestry. Ports in Virginia, Maryland, Maine, North Carolina, Connecticut, Rhode Island, Massachusetts, New Jersey, Florida, Georgia, and Delaware are among those that are a part of the collection.[11]

What if you still can't find your ancestor's arrival? Look north to Canada. Forty percent of all passengers arriving in Canada were actually bound for the United States.[12] It was often easier to enter Canada, which had fewer immigration restrictions than US ports, and then go across the border into the United States where there were no border crossing restrictions. The first lists were kept at the port of Quebec City in 1865. Earlier records do not exist. The Library and Archives Canada has an online index to Canadian arrivals from 1865 to 1922 (www.collectionscanada.gc.ca/databases/passenger/001045-100.01-e .php). Border crossings from Canada to the United States began being recorded in 1895 with the records being kept in St. Albans, Vermont. These records were also filmed by the National Archives and are found on Ancestry.

Figure 6.10 shows immigrants arriving in Eastport, Idaho, December 1909, as found on the *Manifests of Passengers Arriving in the St. Albans,*

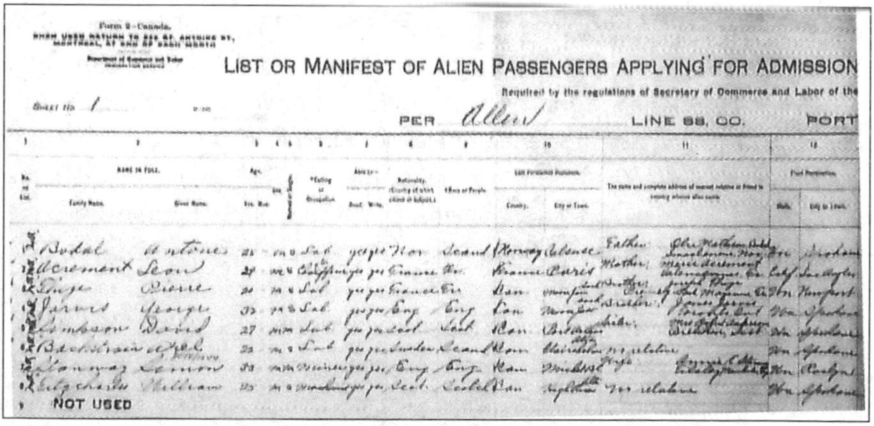
LIST OR MANIFEST OF ALIEN PASSENGERS APPLYING FOR ADMISSION

PER Allan LINE SS. CO. PORT

NOT USED

Figure 6.10 List of immigrants. From Manifests of Passengers Arriving in the St. Albans, VT, District, *National Archives, microfilm publication no. M1464, roll 113.*

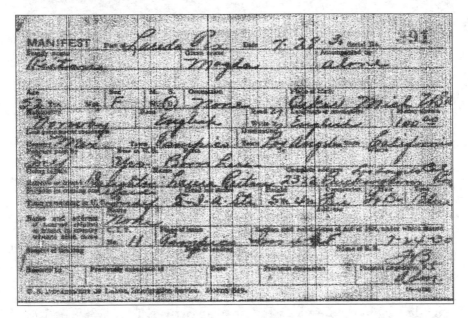

Figure 6.11 *This card shows Magda Reitan entering the United States from Mexico on July 29, 1930, in Laredo, Texas. From Manifests of Statistical and Some Nonstatistical Alien Arrivals at Laredo, Texas, May 1903–April 1955, National Archives, Record Group 85, microfilm publication no. A3437, roll 107; Ancestry.com, Border Crossings: From Mexico to U.S., 1895–1957 [online database] (Provo, UT: Ancestry.com Operations, 2006).*

VT, District.[13] The film title may lead genealogists to think that the arrivals were all in Vermont, but the record included arrivals from Canada anywhere in the United States. The first individual enumerated on the schedule is Antone Bodel, age 25, who was a male laborer. He could read and write. The genealogical gem is that this document shows his nearest relative as his father, Olie Mathison Bodel, of Smaalsnene, Norway. Mr. Bodel's final destination was Spokane, Washington.

Your ancestor may also have come into this country from Mexico. The National Archives has filmed Mexican border crossings from 1895 to 1957, and the images are available on Ancestry.com and Ancestry Library Edition. Every time a person crossed the border during those years, his or her information was documented in official records. The names recorded were Mexicans coming to the United States, other foreign-born individuals entering the United States through Mexico,

GENEALOGY: TWENTY MINUTES A DAY

Look at your pedigree and family unit charts and identify all your immigrant ancestors. Create a spreadsheet with the name of each immigrant, year or time frame of arrival, and port of immigration, if known. Begin looking for the passenger list for each of these individuals. You might try using some of the passenger list websites shown in the next section or in the books that have been mentioned. It can be a tedious process, but it is so rewarding when you find your ancestor on a passenger list.

and Americans working or living or both in Mexico and crossing into the United States for a visit. My grandmother's sister lived with her husband in Mexico for several years. I knew very little about her until I discovered her on the Mexican border crossings database. She and her daughters were recorded several times, and her husband was recorded one time (see figure 6.11).

THE INTERNET

There are lots of resources on the Internet for finding lists of passengers arriving into US ports. These websites come and go so quickly that I find it easiest to refer to Cyndi's List with its links to passenger lists and immigration information: www.cyndislist.com/ships.htm#lists.

The Immigrant Ships Transcribers Guild has a myriad of transcribed ship passenger lists. This volunteer project can be searched at www.immigrantships.net.

Here is a reminder of websites mentioned thus far in this chapter.

- Arrivals into Canada (1865–1922): www.collectionscanada.gc.ca/databases/passenger/001045-100.01-e.php
- Castle Garden (New York passenger arrivals): www.castlegarden.org
- Ellis Island (New York passenger arrivals): http://ellisisland.org
- Galveston passenger lists: www.galvestonhistory.org/galveston_immigration_database.asp
- *Great Migration Newsletter*: www.greatmigration.org

- Information Wanted (Irish immigration): http://infowanted
  .bc.edu
- Massachusetts state lists (passenger arrivals 1841–1891):
  www.sec.state.ma.us/arc/arcsrch/passengermanifest
  searchcontents.html

SEARCHING FOR IMMIGRANT ANCESTORS IN EUROPE—AND ELSEWHERE

Now that we have, it is hoped, found the passenger lists of all our foreign-born ancestors, it is time to look toward their homelands. How do we get there? As with all genealogy, start with yourself and work back in time. Go back one generation at a time until you reach an immigrant ancestor. It is necessary to know the town or parish location in the old country to pursue your ancestor. Look for your ancestors in census records, county histories, cemetery records, birth and death records, marriage records, probate records, and family Bibles for clues to their origins. Look for books and websites that will tell you how to research ancestors in a particular country. Using a guide to research for the country in which you will be searching will help you discover the types of records that are available. I like to use the wiki at FamilySearch to discover more about research in other countries (https://family search.org/learn/wiki/en/Main_Page). Just type in the country about which you wish to know more, and you will find results that will help you in that quest. In European countries you will be looking at church records to determine the names of parents and dates of births, deaths, and marriages. The rest of this chapter will discuss some major ethnic groups and some tips on researching them. It would, unfortunately, be too cumbersome to try to discuss researching ancestors from all countries and backgrounds.

German Genealogy

Germany was a constantly shifting country with changing borders and states. Reading up on German history is a must when looking for your German ancestors. Areas of Germany have been owned by various feudal lords, dukes, and barons and ruled by numerous leaders, dividing

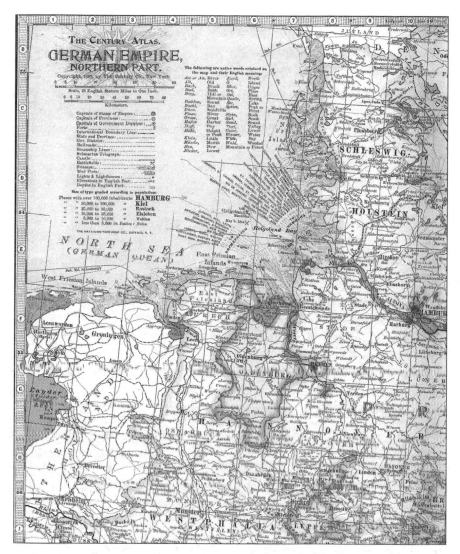

Figure 6.12 Map of Germany, 1911. From The Century Atlas of the World, *edited by Benjamin E. Smith (New York: Century, 1911).*

the country into kingdoms, duchies, estates, and states. To find out what area your ancestors lived in at any given time, it is necessary to look at a map covering that period. The map in figure 6.12 shows a portion of Germany in 1911. German geography changed a great deal a few years later after World War I.

Germany is divided into states and each state into parishes and then towns or cities. Records will be at the parish level, so knowing what parish someone lived in is imperative. Knowing someone was from Bavaria is not good enough. Bavaria is a German state, and that is too large a region in which to search. Use the *Map Guide to German Parish Registers*[14] and *The Atlantic Bridge to Germany*[15] to assist in your research. The *Map Guide* currently has forty volumes, each giving the names of the Lutheran and Catholic parishes for the area discussed in the volume. *The Atlantic Bridge to Germany* has ten volumes for the different German states, with maps and lists of city and parish names. The serious researcher, one who doesn't mind trying to bridge the language barrier and decipher the old German script, can try *Meyers Gazetteer*.[16] Because the full name is very long, the book is generally called *Meyers Gazetteer* or *Meyers Orts*. The book gives detailed information on every German place name, the type of place (whether Evangelical or Catholic), and the types of public services in the place. Information is based on data from the early twentieth century. You can find the book on Ancestry.com if you can't locate a copy in your area, but, again, it is in German and in the old German script. Figure 6.13 shows the village of Eberbach from *Meyers Gazetteer*. Wendy Uncapher has written a book to help the novice researcher understand *Meyers Orts*.[17] Figure 6.14 shows how to decipher an entry such as that shown in figure 6.13.

Meyers Orts- identifies each placename by location, governing bodies, kind of church present, transportation available, what industries and trades are there, population, and what, if any, smaller communities are dependent on this community. The following example shows a typical entry.

Everode, D., Pr., Hann., RB. BKdo. Hildesheim, Kr. AG. Alfeld, E 5,9 km Freden; 605 E., P, StdA., ev. Pfk.; Först.; Zigarrenfbr.

Translation:

The town of Everode, is a dorf (village) in Prussia, Hannover, the government district and district military office are in Hildesheim, the Kreis (district like our counties) and court are in Alfeld, the railroad is 5.9 km away in Freden; the population is 605, there is a post office with a telegraph, it has its own civil registration office and a Evangelical parish. There is a forester's station and a cigar factory.

Figure 6.13 [above] The village of Eberbach. From Meyers Gazetteer. *Figure 6.14 [right] Translation of an entry in* Meyers Gazetteer. *From* How to Read and Understand Meyers Orts *by Wendy K. Uncapher (Janesville, WI: Origins, 2003).*

Selected Resources to Aid Your German Research

- Anderson, Chris. *A Genealogist's Guide to Discovering Your Germanic Ancestors: How to Find and Record Your Unique Heritage.* Cincinnati, OH: Betterway Books, 2000.
- Baxter, Angus. *In Search of Your German Roots: A Complete Guide to Tracing Your Ancestors in the Germanic Areas of Europe.* 4th ed. Baltimore: Genealogical Publishing, 2001.
- Brandt, Edward R. *Genealogical Guide to East and West Prussia (Ost- und Westpreussen): Records, Sources, Publications and Events.* Minneapolis: printed by author, 2002.
- Humphrey, John T. *Finding Your German Ancestors: A Practical Guide for Genealogists.* Washington, DC: Pennsylvania Genealogy Books, 2009.
- Jones, Henry Z. *The Palatine Families of New York: A Study of the German Immigrants Who Arrived in Colonial New York in 1710.* Universal City, CA: printed by author, 1985.
- Minert, Roger P. *German Immigrants in American Church Records.* Rockport, ME: Picton Press, 2005–.
- Riemer, Shirley. *The German Research Companion.* Sacramento, CA: Lorelei Press, 2010.
- A helpful website for German research is www.genealogienetz.de (in German—make sure you click the Translate button).

The records you will use in German research are both civil and church (parish) records. Parish records include births, baptisms, marriages, deaths, and burials. Record keeping began as early as 1650, but the effects of war, weather, and political indifference have left some records damaged and others destroyed.[18] But don't despair—records do exist. The Family History Library has filmed many of the church records and is an excellent place to start your search. Check the library's website for a list of FamilySearch centers (https://familysearch.org/locations). Films can be sent to one of these centers if you do not wish to travel to Salt Lake City to do research. Records kept by the German government are called civil registrations. They are records of births, deaths, and marriages and are an important record type to search. Civil registrations vary by area, but most had begun by 1876 (see https://family search.org/learn/wiki/en/Germany_Civil_Registration). Some civil registrations have been filmed and are available at the Family History Library. When you can't find the film at the Family History Library and you can't visit the record centers in person, the next best thing is to write for information. An excellent guide to writing for records in Germany is called *Writing to Germany* by Kenneth L. Smith.[19]

German immigration to the New World was the result of several factors. First, the Thirty Years' War brought severe poverty. The American colonies were considered a way out of that situation. In addition, land in Germany was held by relatively few people. In order to receive land of their own, many Germans immigrated to the Americas. Finally, a forced military duty impelled many families to leave Germany. German immigration began in the late 1600s to Pennsylvania. Other colonial areas of settlement were New York, Virginia, the Carolinas, and Maryland. During the American Revolutionary War, some Germans came over as Hessian soldiers. Some of those soldiers stayed when the war ended. Clifford Neal Smith has written several books about these Hessian soldiers.[20]

Here is a selected list of books to aid in your German research.

Italian Genealogy

Italy is divided into regions, provinces, and municipalities. Records in Italy are kept at the town level. Because Italy is a Catholic country, the church records are excellent, and many go back into the 1500s. You will find records of births, deaths, marriages, and confirmations. Italy also has civil registrations (government records) that predate 1870— many of which have been filmed by the Family History Library. Each province and town has archives for searching more recent registrations. Your search must begin at this local level.

Selected Resources to Aid Your Italian Research

- Adams, Suzanne Russo. *Finding Your Italian Ancestors: A Beginner's Guide.* Provo, UT: Ancestry, 2008.
- Colleta, John Philip. *Finding Italian Roots: The Complete Guide for Americans.* Baltimore: Genealogical Publishing, 2003.
- Nelson, Lynn. *A Genealogist's Guide to Discovering Your Italian Ancestors: How to Find and Record Your Unique Heritage.* Cincinnati, OH: Betterway Books, 1997.
- The Italian Genealogical Group has a helpful website: www.italiangen.org.

English Genealogy

Sometimes I think, "British research shouldn't be too hard. After all, we speak the same language, don't we?" Well, we may speak the same language, but the laws, the records, and the history are not the same as those in the United States. First, a little bit of history regarding the name. What is it called—England, Great Britain, or the United Kingdom? Paul Milner and Linda Jones describe it perfectly: In 1536, England and Wales united. In 1707, Scotland joined their union, and the three countries became known as Great Britain. In 1801, Ireland united with Great Britain, and the name was changed to the United Kingdom of Great Britain and Ireland. By 1921, Ireland was not too happy with England, and most of the country separated itself from the union. The remaining countries of England, Wales, Scotland, and Northern Ireland are now called the United Kingdom of Great Britain and Northern Ireland, also known as the U.K. The British Isles means England, Wales, Scotland, Northern Ireland, the Republic of Ireland, the Channel Islands, the Isle of Man, and all other surrounding islands.[21]

In researching British roots, again we look to the parish and civil records. Parish record keeping began at the time of King Henry VIII. The king established the Church of England, also called the Anglican Church. A law was established in 1538 requiring the recording of christenings, burials, and marriages within the parish. England is organized by county, parish, and town. Before the nineteenth century the parish church was the center of both religious and civil administration within the geographical parish. During this time the parishes took care of the poor, administered justice, raised militias when needed in fact they did it all, and the records will be in each parish. An older, but still useful, source for determining parishes is *Parish Maps of the Counties of England and Wales*.[22] In addition to giving the dates that parish records have for each parish, the book gives Family History Library film numbers. Be aware, however, that the book was published in 1977 and additional films may have been added to the library's holdings since then. Another helpful guide is *Researching English Parish Records*.[23]

England also has public or county records offices where civil records are kept. In these repositories you will find land, church, tax, and probate records. Sometimes the offices will have indexes to people or places

Selected Books to Aid Your British Research

- Baxter, Angus. *In Search of Your British and Irish Roots: A Complete Guide to Tracing Your English, Welsh, Scottish, and Irish Ancestors.* 4th ed. Baltimore: Genealogical Publishing, 1999.
- Rogers, Colin Darlington. *Family Tree Detective: Tracing Your Ancestors in England and Wales.* 3rd ed. Manchester, NY: Manchester University Press, 1997.

or both. The book *Record Offices: How to Find Them*[24] can help you locate an office in the area where your ancestor lived. You might also want to try *Parishes and Registration Districts in England and Wales*[25] for finding parish locations. England had its first national registration of vital records in 1837, conducted its first census in 1801, and has had a central probate since 1858.[26] Census records of England are on Ancestry.com for the years 1871 to 1901. A helpful free website for finding records of births, marriages, and deaths is www.freebmd.org.uk. More and more British records are showing up on Ancestry.com as well. Another website to try is www.genuki.org.uk (United Kingdom and Ireland).

There are some things to remember about British emigration. Early British settlers in the colonies were either adventurers or convicts. The adventurers, such as those who settled Jamestown, were looking for instant wealth. Many were also looking for the ability to own land because most of the land in England was owned by barons. The colonies also became a solution for easing the overcrowded English jails. The jails held many people who were guilty of what today would be called misdemeanors, such as stealing food, and others who were there because of unpaid debts. The convicts were cheap labor. English investors, those who wanted to capitalize on amassing great holdings of land in the Americas, often brought over indentured servants—those who were given free transportation to the colonies in exchange for labor. Indentured servants would work off the debt for a set period of time and then receive a small portion of land after the debt was paid. Those who came during the colonial period were not naturalized as "Americans." They were moving from one English land to another.

Irish Genealogy

When you are considering Irish research, right away you have a problem—were your ancestors a part of what is now Northern Ireland or the Republic of Ireland? In the previous section on English research, you saw that most of Ireland broke from the United Kingdom in 1921, leaving Northern Ireland a part of the earlier union. This section about Irish research centers on the Republic of Ireland.

Census records were taken in Ireland, but the earliest surviving schedule is 1901. Earlier census records were either destroyed by fire or destroyed by the government after the data was collected. All record keeping in Ireland has been done by civil parishes—the political or administrative division of the land. The country is divided into thirty-two counties. Each county contains several civil parishes. Civil parishes contain twenty-five to thirty townlands each. Townlands are small units of land averaging about 350 acres and may or may not include towns within their borders. Townlands do not have their own unit of government. Look for birth, death, and marriage records at the parish level. Ireland also has religious, or ecclesiastical, divisions—church parishes and dioceses. Dioceses are the larger entities, and there are twenty-eight of them today. Each diocese has several parishes within it. You can find church censuses and tax lists in ecclesiastical parish records.

Ireland is known for its linen trade. The Board of Trustees of the Linen and Hempen Manufactures wanted to encourage the growth of flax and hemp seed. In 1796 spinning wheels were given to those involved in this agricultural venture in proportion to the acreage sown. Lists were kept of those making claims for the spinning wheels. A result is the Spinning Wheel Records of 1796. The index to the entitlements

Selected Books to Aid Your Irish Research

- Collins, E. J. *Irish Family Research Made Simple*. Munroe Falls, OH: Summit Publications, 1980.
- Nevius, Erin. *The Family Tree Guide Book to Europe: Your Passport to Tracing Your Genealogy across Europe*. Cincinnati, OH: Betterway Books, 2003.

		Occupier	Immediate Lessor	Description	Area	Val. Land	Val. Buildings	Total
MONASTEREVIN-BOG. *(Ord. S. 26.)*								
1		William M'Dermott,	Marquis of Drogheda,	Land,	11 1 29	5 0 0	—	
–	a	Michael Duffy,	Same,	House and garden,	0 1 24	0 5 0		0 10 0
2		John Harris,	Same,	Land,	19 1 17	8 0 0	—	
–	a	Thomas Gavin,	Same,	House and garden,	0 0 12	0 1 0		0 5 0
3		Christopher Cusack,	Same,	House and land,	5 0 12	1 10 0		0 5 0
4		James Deering,	Same,	Land,	13 0 25	6 5 0		
–	a	Martin Doolan,	James Deering,	House and garden,	0 3 34	0 15 0		0 5 0
5		James Brennan,	Marquis of Drogheda,	House and land,	7 1 30	2 15 0		0 5 0
6		Robert Gorman,	Same,	Land,	8 1 1	3 0 0	—	
7		Patrick Gorman,	Same,	House and land,	3 2 0	1 5 0		0 5 0
8		Marquis of Drogheda,	In fee,	Land (bog),	55 3 14	4 10 0	—	
9		Charles Deegan,	Marquis of Drogheda,	House and land,	6 0 10	2 5 0		0 5 0
10		Thomas Kelly,	Same,	Land,	10 1 24	4 0 0	—	
11		Michael Murray,	Same,	House and land,	11 0 32	3 15 0		0 5 0
				Total,	153 0 24	43 6 0		2 5 0
MOOREABBEY DEMESNE. *(Ord. S. 26.)*								
1		Marquis of Drogheda,	In fee,	House, offices, steward's and farm houses, office, and land,	1267 0 5	600 0 0	110 0 0	
–	b	Joseph Fleming,	Marquis of Drogheda,	House,	—	—		0 5 0
					1267 0 5	600 0 0	110 5 0	
OGHIL. *(Ord. S. 37.)*								
1 A / – B		Marquis of Drogheda,	In fee,	Land (bog),	56 2 22 / 223 1 25	0 5 0 / 3 10 0	—	
–	a	Thomas Dowd,	Marquis of Drogheda,	House and garden,	0 2 3	0 5 0		0 5 0
2		John Hyland,	James Behan,	House and land,	5 2 5	1 15 0		0 5 0
3 A		James Behan,	Marquis of Drogheda,	House, offices, and land,	247 0 10	107 0 0	5 10 0	

Figure 6.15 A portion of Griffith's Valuation. From www.askaboutireland.ie/search .xml?query=griffiths&radio_filter=images.

has been filmed and is on microfiche. The Family History Library has a copy but it does not circulate outside the Salt Lake City facility. Global-Genealogy.com has a free list of Irish Flax Growers of 1796 (www.failter omhat.com/flax1796.php).

One of the most important nineteenth-century Irish resources is Griffith's Valuation. Between 1847 and 1861 properties were assessed and taxed with the tax used to support the poor. The valuation records list the name of the head of house, the name of the landowner, the amount of acreage, the value of the property, and the amount of the tax assessed (see figure 6.15). Maps are also found in the records. The Ask about Ireland website (www.askaboutireland.ie) has a free search of Griffith's Valuation. Click on Reading Room and under Contents choose History and Heritage and then select Irish Genealogy. Ancestry also has images from Griffith's Valuation.

French Genealogy

Prior to 1790, France was divided into provinces. Some administrative jurisdictions still use the names of the former provinces. France now is divided into departments. You will need to know the department your ancestor's town is in to find the records. Church records of births, marriages, and deaths go back into the 1500s. The Catholic Church was the official church until 1787, so when looking at church records before that date you will need to look at the Catholic records, no matter what religion your ancestor may have been during or after that date.

Not all French citizens were Catholic, even though it was the state religion. Many were Huguenots. They were members of the Protestant Reformed Church of France during the sixteenth and seventeenth centuries. Since the seventeenth century they have been called French Protestants. In 1560, King Charles issued an amnesty to the Huguenots, and Protestant baptism was allowed in 1562. In spite of the change in laws there was still religious persecution, and many Huguenots relocated to other Protestant countries. Some of the countries included England, Denmark, and Switzerland, and the North American colonies.

State registrations of vital records began in 1792. Prior to this, the Catholic Church kept records of all vital events. After 1792 the church was only concerned with the sacraments of baptism, marriage, and burial. Marriages after 1792, to be officially recognized, had to occur at the town hall. Look for marriage records from this point forward in both civil and church records. Civil registers are the best source for finding vital records from 1792 to the present. Notarial records, those records of events recorded by a notary, may be found as early as the 1300s. Notaries were used to record contracts. The types of records you can find are marriage contracts, wills, property divisions among heirs, inventories of property after death, and guardianship agreements for determining the person who would provide for the care of a minor after the death of one or both of the parents. Notarial records may be found in departmental archives. Most of the records are not indexed. A useful book for guiding your research into French records is *Ancestral Research in France: The Simple Guide to Tracing Your Family History through French Records.*[27]

The French were early explorers of the Americas. Some early residents in the areas of what is now Canada and the northern United States were fur trappers and traders. Other early explorers were priests who desired to convert the American Indians to Christianity. If you look at maps drawn by early French cartographers, you will see much detail of the rivers and streams but you will also see the locations of Indian tribes.

Other French settlements in the 1600s were in the area now known as Louisiana and in areas along the Mississippi River.

Scandinavian Genealogy

Many aspects of researching ancestors in Scandinavian countries are similar. Naming patterns is one of them. The names could be patronymic, occupational, characteristic, or military. Patronymic names are those that derive from the first name of the father. (The surname Johnson/ Johannsen meant that the father's name was Johann.) Occupational surnames were given to those in trade, while characteristic surnames could have been used to designate a physical characteristic (perhaps a man had a blue nose). Military names were chosen by a man when he entered military service. You can imagine how difficult it would be to have an army of many Johann Johannsens. Upon leaving service a man could keep his military name or go back to his patronymic name. My maiden name, Lindgren, means "green linden tree" in Swedish and is a military name.

Another element common to Scandinavian countries is the Lutheran Church as the state church. You were considered Lutheran even if you belonged to another religion. The Lutheran Church was in charge of keeping records of christenings, marriages, and burials. As with other European countries, knowing the parish is vital to finding records for your ancestor.

Records in Iceland go back to the ninth century. The country was settled largely by Danes, but there is also a large segment of the population with Scots and Irish ancestry. The country was under Danish rule until 1918. Records prior to 1800 may be in Danish or Latin.

Danish records include census records, church records, civil registrations, and court records. Census records began in 1787 and are available

Selected Websites to Aid Your Icelandic Research

- 1816 Census: www.halfdan.is/vestur/census.htm
- The Emigration from Iceland to North America: www.halfdan.is/vestur/vestur.htm
- Icelandic Archives: www.archives.is (in Icelandic)
- Icelandic Genealogy Society: www.aett.is (in Icelandic)
- Mapping the Icelandic Genome: http://sunsite.berkeley.edu/biotech/iceland/about.html

Selected Resources to Aid Your Danish Research

- Genealogy Research Denmark: http://myweb.cableone.net/really/index.htm
- Tracing Your Danish Ancestors: http://usa.um.dk/en/about-denmark/tracing-your-danish-ancestors/
- Carlberg, Nancy Ellen. *Beginning Danish Research*. Anaheim, CA: Carlberg Press, 1992.
- *The Danish Genealogical Helper*. Logan, UT: Everton Publishers, 1968-1969.
- Smith, Frank. *Genealogical Guidebook and Atlas of Denmark*. Bountiful, UT: Thomsen's Genealogical Center, 1998.

through 1911. The enumerations were sporadic until 1840 when they started being taken every five years. From 1860 to 1880 they were taken every ten years. Civil registrations began in 1874, but the records are generally not available to the public, except that part that was under German rule—those records are available for 1865–1920. Court records include cases regarding land rights, inheritance, and crime.

The official languages of Finland are Finnish and Swedish. The Finnish language is closely related to Estonian and distantly related to Hungarian. Census and church records are available to aid in your research. Finnish passports are available for the years 1820 to 1920 on microfilm at the Family History Library. Also on microfilm are passenger lists for emigrants who left from the port of Hanko from 1892 to 1960.

Selected Resources to Aid Your Finnish Research

- FinlandGenWeb: www.rootsweb.ancestry.com/~finwgw/index.html
- Institute of Migration: www.migrationinstitute.fi/sinst/emigrantregister.php
- Jewish Web Index: http://jewishwebindex.com/Scandinavia.htm. Although geared toward Jewish research, this website has links for Finnish genealogical research as well as for other Scandinavian countries.
- Choquette, Margarita. *The Beginner's Guide to Finnish Genealogical Research*. Bountiful, UT: Thomsen's Genealogical Center, 1985.
- Vincent, Timothy Laitila. *Finnish Genealogical Research*. New Brighton, MN: Finnish Americana, 1994.

Norway has census records available beginning in 1664, and they are available through 1910. Church records began in 1668 and civil registrations in 1876. Emigration lists of passengers, lists of those leaving the country, began in 1867. The major ports for embarkation were Oslo, Bergen, Trondheim, and Stavanger. All but Stavanger have been filmed by the Family History Library. If your ancestors were farmers, you might try locating farm books (Bydgebøker). These books contain a history of the families that owned a particular farm. The farms were named, and while a family lived on that farm they would use that name as a surname.

Selected Resources to Aid Your Norwegian Research

- Ancestors from Norway: http://homepages.rootsweb.ancestry.com/~norway
- Digital Archives from the National Archives of Norway: http://digitalarkivet.uib.no/cgi-win/WebFront.exe?slag=vis&tekst=meldingar&spraak=e
- Norway Genealogy: www.rootsweb.ancestry.com/~wgnorway
- Norwegian American Homepage: www.lawzone.com/half-nor/roots.htm
- Carlberg, Nancy Ellen. *Beginning Norwegian Research*. Anaheim, CA: Carlberg Press, 1991.
- Flom, George T. *A History of Norwegian Immigration to the United States: From the Earliest Beginning Down to the Year 1848.* Baltimore: Reprinted for Clearfield by Genealogical Publishing, 2002.
- Gregerson, Merle Winton. *Norway Family Farm Surname, 1589–1989: Research Lists for Norwegians in USA.* [Onalaska, WI: printed by author, 1989].

Swedish records include parish records beginning in 1750. Included in the parish records are emigration records. These were sent to the government annually, beginning in 1865, by the parish minister and included the names of those arriving from or leaving for another country. In addition, the parish records include clerical survey records, which were yearly examinations by the parish minister to determine if everyone in the household could read and understand the catechism. Census records exist from 1630 to 1860. The parish and census records are available on microfilm from the Family History Library. Swedish parish records are also available on Ancestry.com.

Selected Resources to Aid Your Swedish Research

- Asmundsson.nu: www.asmundsson.nu/English_start.htm
- Clemensson, Per. *Your Swedish Roots: A Step by Step Handbook.* Provo, UT: Ancestry, 2004.
- Johansson, Carl Erik. *Cradled in Sweden.* Logan, UT: Everton Publishers, 1995.
- Olsson, Nils William. *Tracing Your Swedish Ancestry.* New York: Swedish Information Service, 2000.
- Pladsen, Phyllis J., et al. *Swedish Genealogical Dictionary.* White Bear Lake, MN: Pladsen Sveria Press, 2000.
- Thomsen, Finn A. *The Beginner's Guide to Swedish Genealogical Research.* Bountiful, UT: Thomsen's Genealogical Center, 1984.

Canadian Genealogy

Canada had its beginning with the French fur traders. Two major companies were formed with charters from the French government. The Hudson's Bay Company began in 1670 and was given all the land that had rivers that drained into Hudson Bay. The North West Fur Company was formed in 1783. The two companies merged in 1821. Together, they wielded much power and had the authority to make and enforce many of the laws in their domain. In 1870 the Hudson's Bay Company gave up its land to the British Crown, which in turn gave it to the Dominion of Canada.

It is important to know some geographic terms when looking for Canadian ancestors. Canada was originally organized as six separate colonies. Originally the Province of Canada was divided into Upper Canada (Ontario) and Lower Canada (Quebec). Later, Ontario became known as Canada West and Quebec as Canada East. Eventually the Dominion of Canada was divided into provinces. The provinces were formed in the following order: Ontario, Quebec, Nova Scotia, New Brunswick, Manitoba, Northwest Territories, British Columbia, Prince Edward Island, Yukon, Saskatchewan, Alberta, Newfoundland, Labrador, and Nunavut.

Like the United States, Canada was settled by people from many different countries. The first French settlement in Canada was in 1604. In the first 150 years of settlement, almost ten thousand French immigrants came to Canada. During the American Revolution, many people who were loyal to the Crown, called Loyalists, fled to Canada, where they were called the United Empire Loyalists. The first group of Loyalists left Boston for Canada in March 1776.

Native tribes in Canada are called the First Nations. People who are of mixed blood are called the Métis. The Métis are ancestors of French, Scottish, or English fur traders and Cree, Ojibway, or Saulteaux women. As these offspring married among themselves they developed a new culture, neither European nor Indian, but a fusion of the two with an identity as Métis. The Métis of the Northwest formed a Provisional Government under the leadership of Louis Riel in 1869 and laid the foundation for the creation of the Province of Manitoba. Records of Métis land claims from 1870 to 1924 are on microfilm at Library and Archives Canada. In 1982 the Métis were given aboriginal status.

Ontario land records are called Crown land records, or original land grants. Crown land records pertain to property owned by the British Crown. As in US land sales, land grants are considered land registry records once they are sold. The Land Purchase Act of 1853 allowed tenants to purchase their land from the government. A series of payments resulted in a deed, which was recorded in township ledgers. Those who were Loyalists were given land grants for being loyal to the British Crown. In Quebec land estates held by feudal tenure were called *seigneurie*. The land holder was called a *seigneur*.

When looking for Canadian probate, or any court, records, you must remember that there are aspects of both the English and French legal systems. Because Canada was a British colony, acts passed by the British Parliament affected the procedure for wills in Canada. In Quebec before 1760 the will of a deceased person was distributed by a *notaire* (notary).

Lists of immigrants arriving into Canada generally began in 1865, though there are a few earlier records, some as early as 1745. They are housed in the Library and Archives Canada. Passenger lists for the port of Quebec are on microfilm from 1865 to 1900 but are incomplete. Records for the port of Halifax are on microfilm from 1881 to 1899 and, again, are incomplete. Records for the port of Saint John, New Brunswick, began in 1900. Lists for Victoria and Vancouver, British Columbia, for North Sydney, Nova Scotia, and for Montreal begin with the early 1900s. For those arriving in Canada and going to the United States, there are records on the St. Albans lists as discussed earlier in this chapter.

Microfilm of Canadian census records is available through the Library and Archives Canada and the Family History Library. The first Canadian census took place in Quebec in 1666. When Canada underwent confederation in 1867, another census was taken. Beginning in 1871, a census was taken in Canada every ten years. The most recent census available to researchers is the 1911 census. Digitized copies of the census are available on Ancestry. Images for the 1871, 1881, and 1891 censuses are also available on the Library and Archives Canada website, www.collections canada.gc.ca/discover/index-e.html. Choose the Censuses link.

Canadian vital records are sketchy before 1920. A marriage act in Ontario in 1831 allowed for the registrations of marriages and validated all marriages that were performed before that date. Look for church records to find marriages performed before 1831. Some Canadian vital records can be found on the Library and Archives Canada website. Others can be found on Ancestry. A series of books to help in finding Canadian ancestors in vital records, histories, and census is *The Atlantic Canadians, 1600–1900*[28] (people in Nova Scotia, New Brunswick, Prince Edward Island, and Newfoundland), *The French Canadians, 1600–1900*,[29] *The Central Canadians*[30] (people in Ontario and Manitoba), and *The Western Canadians*[31] (people in Alberta, British Columbia, Saskatchewan, Yukon Territory, Nunavut, and Alaska Territory). The names were found in various sources and then indexed.

The Library and Archives Canada is the major repository for Canadian records. Its holdings include family histories, parish registers, census records, passenger lists, naturalization records, land records and grants, newspapers, Métis land claims, and an increasing number of online databases. For information about researching French Canadian families, use *French and French-Canadian Family Research*.[32]

Native American Genealogy

Native American genealogy research can be difficult if your ancestor was not in the right place at the right time. In order for you to trace your American Indian heritage, your ancestor had to be living with the tribe on Indian land. The basics of Native American research are the same as those for researching any ancestor. Begin with yourself and move backward in time until you find someone you feel is the Native American ancestor. You must know the name of the ancestor before you can explore his or her Indian affiliation. Don't assume anything—you need to find the facts. You will need to keep an open mind and separate fact from fiction or family lore. But do listen to the family stories and use them as your guide.

Next, you will need to do some background searching into the history of the suspected tribe. Use the *Gale Encyclopedia of Native American Tribes*.[33] This work has historical information on each tribe and its location. The location of tribal land has changed from time to time. Look at maps in the areas in which your ancestors lived and compare them with maps that show tribal lands. Was your ancestor living in an area where Indian tribes were known to live? Many of these maps are available on the Internet. An excellent website for finding current tribal land is NationalAtlas.gov at http://nationalatlas.gov/printable/fedlands.html.

Use census records to identify someone as "Indian." All censuses beginning with 1870 show the possible race of "Indian." The 1910 federal census, for states with reservations, had additional Indian schedules. They asked for the Indian name, nativity, blood quantum, marital status, citizenship, and type of dwelling. The 1930 federal census showed the name of the tribe in the space where you would find the place of the father's birth and the blood quantum where you would find the birthplace of the mother. *Indian Census Rolls, 1885–1940* contains special census records taken of tribal members. It is available on microfilm at the National Archives and on Ancestry. These special schedules include: the name (Indian or English or both), gender, age, birth date, the person's relationship to the head of family, marital status, name of the tribe, and the names of the agency and reservation. Please note that there is not a census for every reservation or group of Indians for every year. Only persons who maintained a formal affiliation with a tribe under federal supervision are listed on these census rolls.

You can sometimes find Native American people in church records. The Catholic Church did a lot of missionary work among the native tribes. A book that will help you in this area is *History of the Catholic Missions among the Indian Tribes of the United States, 1529–1854*.[34] This book has been digitized. You can find it on Google Books (http://books.google.com) and read it in its entirety online. The areas encompassed by the archdioceses were larger in the time of the early Catholic missions than they are today. For instance, the Archdiocese of Detroit has records for Indians in the upper Midwest, especially Wisconsin, Michigan, and the lower part of Ontario while the Archdiocese of San Antonio has Indian records for Texas and the upper part of Mexico. Other religious bodies who gave ministry to the tribes were Baptist, Presbyterian, Dutch Reformed, Mormon, and Moravian. The records of the Moravian Church have been filmed and are available through the Family History Library.

For the most part, American Indians did not have a written language. The exception was the Cherokee. With no written language, there is only oral tradition. This is the most difficult roadblock when searching Native American ancestry. When the federal government came in contact with native people, records were created. Searching federal documents is a worthwhile endeavor for the Native American genealogy researcher. When treaties were signed, the principal chief and the braves and warriors were to sign as well. For a list of treaties, see *Documents of American Indian Diplomacy: Treaties, Agreements, and Conventions, 1775–1979*.[35] If you are near a library that has the US Serial Set or the Executive Branch Documents on microfiche, you can find more information on Native American treaties with the US government. When land was being allocated, enrollments were created. Annuity payments as a result of compensation from treaties created lists of recipients. Citizenship rolls and land allotments from the Dawes Act created more records. When the government decided Native American children needed to be educated in "civilized" ways, Indian schools were created and, thus, more records. Many of these documents are housed at the National Archives or its field branches.

Many of the disagreements between the US government (and US citizens) and the Native American tribes occurred over land. Settlers wanted to find new land on which to build a new life. Frequently, the land was Indian land. Land in the east was becoming scarce without the availability of tribal land, and that scarcity led to the removal of the Native American people from land east of the Mississippi River. President Andrew Jackson signed the Indian Removal Act on May 28, 1830. Each tribe was asked to sign a removal treaty. The act included all Indian tribes, but the tribe most associated with the removal—and the Trail of Tears—was the Cherokee tribe. There are more records available for searching Cherokee Indians than for any other tribe.

> ## Selected Resources to Aid Your Native American Research
>
> - Carpenter, Cecelia Syinth. *How to Research American Indian Blood Lines: A Manual on Indian Genealogical Research*. Bountiful, UT: HeritageQuest, 2000.
> - Native American Genealogy: Reconnecting with Your American Indian Heritage: www.native-languages.org/genealogy.htm
> - Native American Nations: www.nativeculturelinks.com/nations .html. This website has links to the home pages of Native American tribes. Look on each Native American website for a link to Genealogy or Enrollment. You might have to search hard and long to find the right link, but you should be able to find one.

In 1882 the Dawes Act was passed. It applied to all Indian tribes, though only those of the Five Civilized Tribes (Choctaw, Chickasaw, Cherokee, Creek, and Seminole) have documentation. The act provided an allotment of lands on Indian reservations and extended protection of US laws over all Indians. Basically, the government gave the tribal lands to the individual tribal members. Heads of families received 160 acres, single individuals over the age of 18 received 80 acres, orphans under the age of 18 received 80 acres, and other individuals under the age of 18 received 40 acres. Citizenship was promised to those registering for land, providing they gave up their allegiance to the tribe.

For more information about researching Native American ancestors, see the following.

African American Genealogy

Researching African American ancestors can be daunting at best. The first thing to remember is that tracing African Americans back to 1870 is like doing any other genealogy research. Start with yourself and work backward in time, using all the usual sources. Pay particular attention when you get to the 1870 federal census. This is the first census that recorded the names of former slaves. Before this date slaves were recorded on the slave schedules, but their names were not shown. Only the slave owner is named on the slave schedules. Knowing the name of the slave owner will help you immensely in your research. If your ancestor was a "free black," meaning the person was not a slave, he or she will continue to be recorded by name on the census as you go backward in time.

Slaves were often documented by name in church records. However, they are most likely to be found in the records of the church that their slave owners attended. The Catholic records of New Orleans contain many names of slaves. Finding slave names in the church records of their owners is one reason why it is good to know the names of your ancestors' masters. If your ancestor was a free black (or a slave who was allowed to attend the church of his or her choice), look in the records of the following religions: African Methodist Episcopal (A.M.E.), African Methodist Episcopal Zion (A.M.E. Zion), Baptist, Catholic, Methodist, Presbyterian, Protestant Episcopal, and Quaker. The oldest black church in America was founded in Philadelphia in 1787 and was called Mother Bethel A.M.E. Church. Many early church records noted whether the individual was a free black or a black slave.[36]

Finding your ancestor in military records is very helpful. African American participation in the military goes back to the Revolutionary War. You can find the names of some of those men in *Forgotten Patriots: African American and American Indian Patriots in the Revolutionary War*[37] and in *Black Courage, 1775–1783: Documentation of Black Participation in the American Revolution.*[38] The Civil War saw much participation by African Americans, especially after the Emancipation Proclamation. On microfilm from the National Archives you can find *Descriptive Recruitment Lists of Volunteers for the United States Colored Troops for the State of Missouri, 1863–1865* (M1894) and *Index to Compiled Service Records of Volunteer Union Soldiers Who Served with U.S. Colored Troops* (M589). The latter can also be found on Ancestry. You will find the name and regiment, company, and rank for each soldier. Copies of the enlistment records can be found on Fold3. The 54th Massachusetts Volunteer Infantry, one of the "colored troops," was made famous in the movie *Glory* (1989).

The Indian wars found much African American participation as well. The soldiers in the US 10th Cavalry Regiment, formed on September 21, 1866, at Fort Leavenworth, Kansas, were nicknamed "Buffalo Soldiers" by the Native American tribes they fought.[39] The term *Buffalo Soldier* later became synonymous with all African American regiments formed in 1866 and was used in other, later military conflicts as well. Similar regiments served in the Spanish-American War, the Philippine Insurrection, World War I, and World War II. You can search for records in the *Register of Enlistments in the U. S. Army, 1798–1914* on National

Selected Resources to Aid Your African American Research
- AfriGeneas: www.afrigeneas.com
- Burroughs, Tony. *Black Roots: A Beginner's Guide to Tracing the African American Family Tree*. New York: Fireside Books, 2001.

Archives microfilm (M233). Records of soldiers will also be found at the National Personnel Records Center in St. Louis, Missouri. Desegregation of the armed forces occurred during President Harry Truman's term of office by Executive Order 9981, signed on July 26, 1948. A timeline, digitized documents, and photographs regarding the desegregation can be found on the Truman Library and Museum website, www.trumanlibrary.org/whistlestop/study_collections/desegregation/large/index.php?action=chronology#1953.

Slave records are not consistently available, but they do exist. You will find information in records of deeds, bills of sale, wills, plantations, manumissions, the Freedmen's Bureau, and the Freedman's Savings and Trust Company, in slave manifests, and in newspaper advertisements. When searching for your slave ancestors, you will have to think of them, unfortunately, as property. When slaves were sold, the deeds of sale were registered in the local courthouse. When a slave was inherited through the death of the owner, he or she was mentioned in a will. A slave could buy his or her own freedom or an owner could set a slave free. Those records of manumission will be filed in a local courthouse. Ancestry.com has a collection of emancipation and manumission records.

Many, but not all, slaves lived on plantations. Plantation owners kept diaries that often mentioned slaves. They also kept deeds of sale and lists of slaves. These records can be found in university repositories, and some have been microfilmed (see figure 6.16). Check your local university library or check WorldCat. If you use the search term "southern plantation records" and limit to "archival materials," you will find a list of some of the microfilmed records and a list of the libraries that have copies of those records.

The Freedmen's Bureau was an agency created by the federal government in 1865 to help former slaves adjust to freedom. The agency helped legalize slave marriages, provided food, clothing, and transpor-

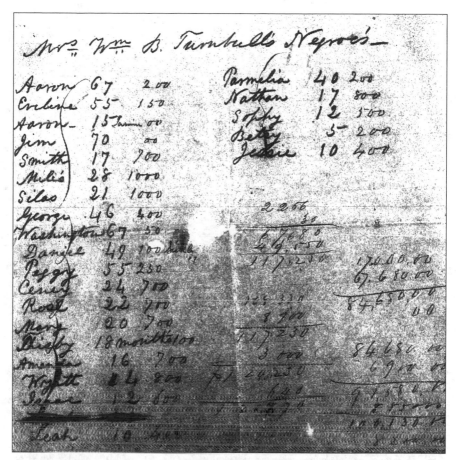

Figure 6.16 *A list of Wm. B. Turnbull's Negroes. From "Turnbull-Bowman-Lyons Family Papers," Records of Ante-Bellum Southern Plantations. From the Revolu tion through the Civil War, series I, part 4, reel 36, frame 444.*

tation, helped in legal matters, helped in relocation, and operated hospitals. This aid was never meant to be permanent, however, and in 1872 the government considered that the agency had met its goal. The records of the field offices have been filmed by the National Archives and can be found on Ancestry. The Freedman's Savings and Trust Company, also known as the Freedman's Bank, was a savings bank for freed slaves that operated in thirty-three cities in the South. It was in operation from 1865 through 1870. The records were microfilmed by the National Archives and can also be found on HeritageQuest.

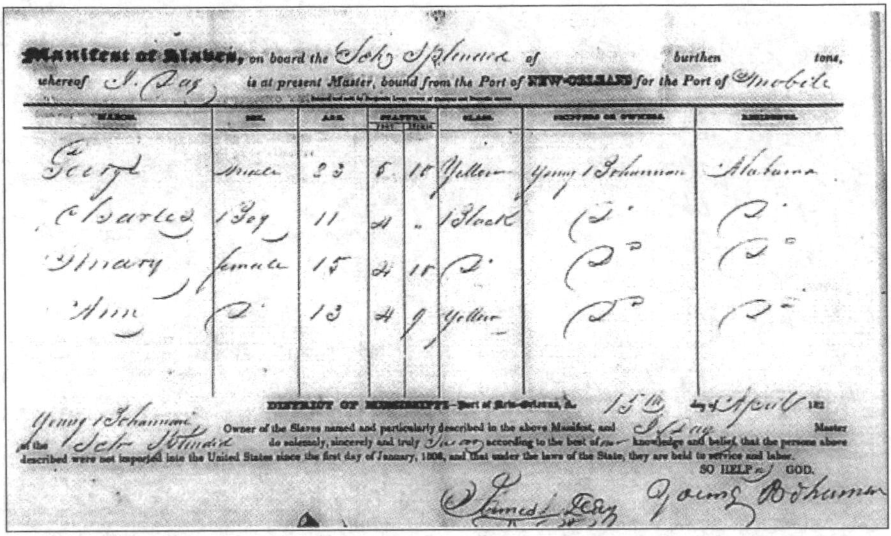

Manifest of Slaves, on board the Sch. Splendid of burthen tons, whereof J. Day is at present Master, bound from the Port of NEW-ORLEANS for the Port of Mobile

NAMES	SEX	AGE	STATURE Feet	STATURE Inches	CLASS	SHIPPERS OR OWNERS	RESIDENCE
George	Male	23	5	10	Yellow	Young Bohannon	Alabama
Charles	Boy	11	4	-	Black	do	do
Mary	female	15	4	10	do	do	do
Ann	do	13	4	9	yellow	do	do

DISTRICT OF MISSISSIPPI—Port of New-Orleans, the 15th day of April 182

Young Bohannon Owner of the Slaves named and particularly described in the above Manifest, and J. Day Master of the Sch. Splendid do solemnly, sincerely and truly swear according to the best of our knowledge and belief, that the persons above described were not imported into the United States since the first day of January, 1808, and that under the laws of the State, they are held to service and labor. SO HELP us GOD.

James Day Young Bohannon

Figure 6.17 Slave manifest, April 1828. From Outward Bound Slave Manifests, 1812–1860, Scholarly Resources, roll 3.

Records of the slaves that were brought to this country from Africa are few. Congress ordered the importation of slaves stopped in 1807, but slaves could still be bought and sold within the country. The port of New Orleans was a major hub for the buying and selling of slaves. Scholarly Resources microfilmed the Outward Bound Slave Manifests (1812–1856), which is a record of the slaves leaving New Orleans (see figure 6.17), and the Inward Slave Manifests (1807–1860), which is a record of the slaves being brought into New Orleans for sale (see figure 6.18). The microfilm for these records can be found in some libraries and also on Ancestry.

...

There are many, many more ethnic ancestral lines that I have not talked about in this chapter. Here are some miscellaneous books and websites.

- Jensen, Cecile Wendt. *Sto Lat: A Modern Guide to Polish Genealogy*. Rochester Hills, MI: Michigan Polonia, 2010.
- Konrad, J. *Mexican and Spanish Family Research*. Indianapolis: Summit, 1993.

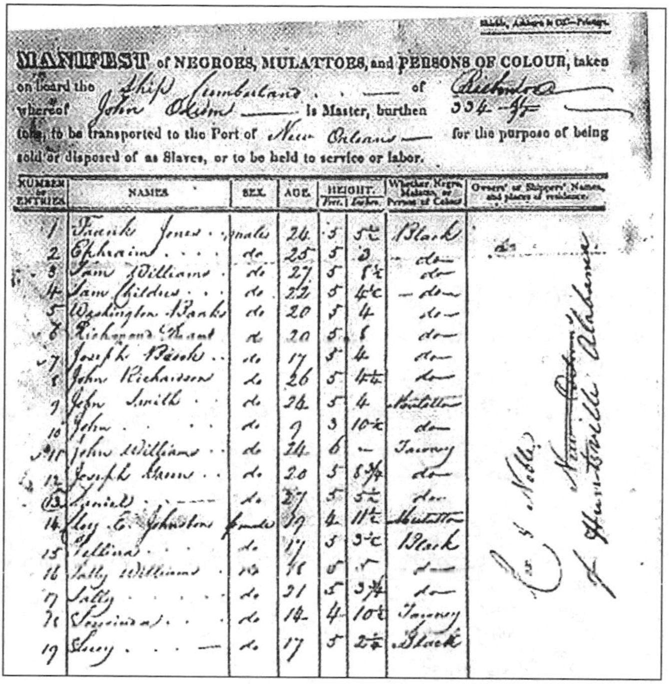
MANIFEST of NEGROES, MULATTOES, and PERSONS OF COLOUR, taken on board the Ship Cumberland . . . — of Richmond whereof John Odiorne — is Master, burthen 334 — tons, to be transported to the Port of New Orleans — for the purpose of being sold or disposed of as Slaves, or to be held to service or labor.

NUMBER of ENTRIES	NAMES	SEX	AGE	HEIGHT Feet	HEIGHT Inches	Whether Negro, Mulatto, or Person of Colour	Owners' or Shippers' Names, and places of residence
1	Frank Jones	male	24	5	5½	Black	do
2	Ephraim	do	25	5	3	do	
3	Sam Williams	do	27	5	8½	do	
4	Sam Childres	do	22	5	4½	do	
5	Washington Banks	do	20	5	4	do	
6	Richmond Grant	do	20	5	6	do	
7	Joseph Brooks	do	17	5	4	do	
8	John Richardson	do	26	5	4¼	do	
9	John Smith	do	26	5	4	Mulatto	
10	John	do	9	3	10½	do	
11	John Williams	do	24	6	—	Tawney	
12	Joseph Mann	do	20	5	8¾	do	
13	Daniel	do	27	5	5½	do	
14	Lucy E. Johnston	female	19	4	11½	Mulatto	
15	Sellina	do	17	5	3½	Black	
16	Sally Williams	do	18	5	5	do	
17	Sally	do	21	5	3¾	do	
18	Susannah	do	14	4	10½	Tawney	
19	Lucy	do	17	5	2½	Black	

E. S. Noble, New Orleans, Huntsville Alabama

Figure 6.18 Slave manifest, December 1821. From Inward Bound Slave Manifests, 1807–1860, Scholarly Resources, roll 2.

- Mokotoff, Gary. *Getting Started in Jewish Genealogy: 2010 Version*. Bergenfield, NJ: Avotaynu, 2010.
- Ryskamp, George R. *Finding Your Mexican Ancestors: A Beginner's Guide*. Provo, UT: Ancestry, 2007.
- Sack, Sallyann Amdur. *Avotaynu Guide to Jewish Genealogy*. Bergenfield, NJ: Avotaynu, 2004.
- The Federation of East European Family History Societies: http://feefhs.org
- The Belgium-Roots Project: http://belgium.rootsweb.ancestry.com (Belgium)
- Hispanic Genealogical Society: www.hispanicgs.com
- IrishAncestors.net: www.IrishAncestors.net or http://freepages.genealogy.rootsweb.ancestry.com/~irishancestors (Ireland)
- JewishGen: www.jewishgen.org (Jewish)

ETHNIC PERIODICALS

Ethnic genealogical societies exist and are good sources of information. The organizations that follow publish a newsletter or journal in a specific area of ethnic research. This is a selected list of periodical publications.

AFRICAN AMERICAN
- *Journal of the Afro-American Historical and Genealogical Society*: www.aahgs.org/journal.htm
- *Black History Bulletin* (Association for the Study of African American Life and History): http://asalh.org/bhb.html

BELGIAN
- *Belgian Laces*: www.rootsweb.ancestry.com/~inbr/belgian_laces .htm
- *Flemish American Heritage*: http://rootsweb.ancestry.com/~gsfa/ gsfainfo.html#publications

CANADIAN
- *American-Canadian Genealogist*: http://acgs.org/genealogist
- *British Columbia Genealogist* (British Columbia Genealogical Society): www.bcgs.ca/?page_id=253
- *Generations* (Manitoba Genealogical Society): www.mbgenealogy .com/index.php?page=generations
- *Generations* (New Brunswick Genealogical Society): www.nbgs .ca/journal.html
- *Nova Scotia Genealogist* (Genealogical Association of Nova Scotia): www.chebucto.ns.ca/Recreation/GANS/nsg.html

CZECH
- *Nase rodina* (Our Family) (Czechoslovak Genealogical Society International): www.cgsi.org/publications

ENGLISH
- *Essex Family Historian* (Essex Society for Family History): www.esfh.org.uk/Historian/Historian.htm

- *Genealogists' Magazine* (Society of Genealogists): www.sog.org .uk/genmag/genmag.shtml
- *Your Family Tree*: www.yourfamilytreemag.co.uk/category/ the-magazine

FRENCH
- *Acadian Descendants* (Acadian Genealogy Exchange): www.acadian-cajun.com/age.htm

GERMAN
- *American/Schleswig-Holstein Heritage Society Newsletter*: www.ashhs.org/Ashhs_membership.html
- *German Genealogical Digest* (Federation of East European Family History Societies): http://feefhs.org/links/Germany/ger-digest/ frg-ggdp.html
- *Journal of the American Historical Society of Germans from Russia*: www.ahsgr.org/Products/journals.htm
- *Palatine Immigrant* and *Palatine Patter* (Palatines to America German Genealogical Society): www.palam.org/publications.php

HISPANIC AMERICAN
- *Hispanic Genealogical Journal* (Hispanic Genealogical Society of Houston): www.hispanicgs.org/journals.html

IRISH
- *Irish Roots Magazine*: www.irishrootsmedia.com
- *The Recorder* (American Irish Historical Society): www.aihs.org/ American_Irish_Historical_Society/Welcome.html
- *The Septs* (Irish Genealogical Society International): http:// irishgenealogical.org/page/septs-1

ITALIAN
- *POINTers* (POINT — Pursuing Our Italian Names Together) www.point-pointers.net/home.html

JEWISH
- *Avotaynu Journal*: www.avotaynu.com/journal.htm

LITHUANIAN
- *Lithuanian Heritage Magazine*: www.lithuanianheritage.com

NATIVE AMERICAN
- *Goingsnake Messenger*: www.goingsnake.org/gsMEMBERSHIP .html

NORWEGIAN
- *Norwegian-American Studies*: www.naha.stolaf.edu/pubs/ nastudies.htm

POLISH
- *Polish Eaglet* (Polish Genealogical Society of Michigan): www.pgsm.org/polisheaglet.htm
- *Rodziny* (Polish Genealogical Society of America) www.pgsa.org/ Publications/publications.php

SCOTTISH
- *The Highlander*: www.highlandermagazine.com/highlander magazine.htm

SWEDISH
- *Swedish American Genealogist* (Augustana College): www.augustana.edu/x13918.xml

THE INTERNET

Ancestry.com or the Ancestry Library Edition and FamilySearch have significant data for researching your ethnic ancestors and are good places to begin. Here is a review of some of the websites mentioned in this chapter.

- FamilySearch centers: https://familysearch.org/locations (find the location of a FamilySearch center near you)
- FamilySearch Germany Civil Registration: https://familysearch .org/learn/wiki/en/Germany_Civil_Registration

GENEALOGY: TWENTY MINUTES A DAY

Look at your pedigree chart for the names of the countries from which your ancestors emigrated. Research the history of the country and of the record keeping. This research will help you prepare yourself for the research to come. Check the Family History Library catalog for available microfilm records and order those films as needed.

- FamilySearch Research Wiki: https://familysearch.org/learn/wiki/en/Main_Page. To find information about how to do research in a foreign country, type in the name of the country in which you wish to do research. You will get many ideas to aid in your search.
- FreeBMD: www.freebmd.org.uk (free website for finding records of British births, marriages, and deaths)
- Tracing Your Danish Ancestors: http://usa.um.dk/en/about-denmark/tracing-your-danish-ancestors/
- Genealogy Research Denmark: http://myweb.cableone.net/really/index.htm
- Institute of Migration (Finland): www.migrationinstitute.fi/sinst/emigrantregister.php
- FinlandGenWeb: www.rootsweb.ancestry.com/~finwgw/index.html
- German Genealogy Server: www.genealogienetz.de (in German — make sure you click the Translate button)
- 1816 Census (Iceland): www.halfdan.is/vestur/census.htm
- The Emigration from Iceland to America: www.halfdan.is/vestur/vestur.htm
- Icelandic Archives: www.archives.is
- Icelandic Genealogy Society: www.aett.is
- Mapping the Icelandic Genome: http://sunsite.berkeley.edu/biotech/iceland/about.html
- Ask about Ireland: www.askaboutireland.ie. Search Griffith's Valuation here. Ancestry.com and Ancestry Library Edition also have Griffith's and many other Irish databases.
- Italian Genealogical Group: www.italiangen.org

- Jewish Web Index: http://jewishwebindex.com/scandinavia.htm. Although geared toward Jewish research, this site has links to Finnish genealogical research, as well as for other Scandinavian countries.
- Norway Genealogy: www.rootsweb.ancestry.com/~wgnorway
- Ancestors from Norway: http://homepages.rootsweb.ancestry .com/~norway/index.html
- Norwegian American Homepage: www.lawzone.com/half-nor/ roots.htm
- Digital Archives from the National Archives of Norway: http://digitalarkivet.uib.no/cgi-win/WebFront.exe?slag=vis& tekst=meldingar&spraak=e
- Asmundsson.Nu: www.asmundsson.nu/English_start.htm. Swedish parish records are also available on Ancestry.

· · ·

The search for your ancestors gets more and more fascinating as you continue your journey. As we begin to discover the rich cultural heritage of our families, we begin to appreciate the struggles they had to overcome to reach this land and often the struggles they had to endure after they arrived. Finding the passenger arrival record is only the beginning. The tough part is to discover where they lived before they left the Old World. But when you find that information, the story will begin to unfold and unravel. As we discover our ancestors, we truly discover the world around us.

NOTES

1. Michael Tepper, *American Passenger Arrival Records: A Guide to the Records of Immigrants Arriving at American Ports by Sail and Steam* (Baltimore: Genealogical Publishing, 1993), 63.

2. Harold Lancour, comp., *A Bibliography of Ship Passenger Lists, 1538–1825: Being a Guide to Published Lists of Early Immigrants to North America* (New York: New York Public Library, 1963).

3. P. William Filby, ed., *Passenger and Immigration Lists Bibliography, 1538–1900: Being a Guide to Published Lists of Arrivals in the United States and Canada*, 2nd ed. (Detroit: Gale Research, 1988).

4. P. William Filby and Mary K. Meyers, eds., *Passenger and Immigration Lists Index: A Guide to Published Records of About 500,000 Passengers Who Came to the United States and Canada in the Seventeenth, Eighteenth, and Nineteenth Centuries* (Detroit: Gale Research, 1981–).

5. Carol M. Meyers, *Early Immigrants to New Netherlands, 1657–1664* (Gardena, CA: RAM Publishers, 1965).

6. Edmund Bailey O'Callaghan, "Early Immigrants to New Netherlands, 1657–1664," in *The Documentary History of the State of New York*, vol. 3 (Albany: Secretary of State, 1850, 33–42; Albany: Weed, Parsons, 1850, 52–63).

7. *Year Book of the Holland Society of New York*, 1896, 141–158.

8. Robert Charles Anderson, *The Great Migration Begins: Immigrants to New England, 1620–1633* (Boston: New England Historic Genealogical Society, 1995).

9. Robert Charles Anderson, *The Great Migration: Immigrants to New England, 1634–1635* (Boston: New England Historic Genealogical Society, 1999–2011).

10. Ruth-Ann M. Harris and Donald M. Jacobs, eds., *The Search for Missing Friends: Irish Immigrant Advertisements Placed in the Boston Pilot* (Boston: New England Historic Genealogical Society, 1989–).

11. National Archives and Records Administration, *Immigrant and Passenger Arrivals*, rev. ed. (Washington, DC: 1991), 4–5.

12. Tepper, *American Passenger Arrival Records*, 121.

13. National Archives and Records Administration, *Manifests of Passengers Arriving in the St. Albans, VT, District through Canadian Pacific and Atlantic Ports*, microfilm publication no. M1464, roll 113.

14. Kevan M. Hansen, *Map Guide to German Parish Registers* (North Salt Lake City, UT: Heritage Creations, 2004–).

15. Charles M. Hall, *The Atlantic Bridge to Germany* (Logan, UT: Everton Publishers, 1974–).

16. Raymond S. Wright, *Meyers Orts und Verkehrs-Lexikon des Deutschen Reichs: With Researcher's Guide and Translations of the Introduction, Instruction for the Use of the Gazetteer and Abbreviations* (Baltimore: Genealogical Publishing, 2000).

17. Wendy K. Uncapher, *How to Read and Understand* Meyers Orts und-Verkehrs-Lexikon des Deutschen Reichs: *Meyers Geographical and Commercial Gazetteer of the German Empire* (Janesville, WI: Origins, 2003).

18. Chris Anderson, *A Genealogist's Guide to Discovering Your Germanic Ancestors: How to Find and Record Your Unique Heritage* (Cincinnati, OH: Betterway Books, 2000), 14.

19. Kenneth L. Smith, *Writing to Germany: A Guide to Genealogical Correspondence with German Sources* (Columbus, OH: printed by author, 1984).

20. Clifford Neal Smith, *Notes on Hessian Soldiers Who Remained in Canada and the United States after the American Revolution, 1775–1784* (McNeal, AZ: Westland, 1992–); *Deserters and Disbanded Soldiers from British, German, and Loyalist Military Units in the South, 1782* (McNeal, AZ: Westland, 1991); *Mercenaries from Hessen-Hanau Who Remained in Canada and the United States after the American Revolution* (McNeal, AZ: Westland, 1976).

21. Paul Milner and Linda Jones, *A Genealogist's Guide to Discovering Your English Ancestors: How to Find and Record Your Unique Heritage* (Cincinnati, OH: Betterway Books, 2000), 13.

22. Institute of Heraldic and Genealogical Studies, *Parish Maps of the Counties of England and Wales* (Logan, UT: Everton, 1977).

23. Penelope Janet Christensen, *Researching English Parish Registers* (Toronto: Heritage Productions, 2001).

24. Jeremy Sumner Wycherly Gibson, *Record Offices: How to Find Them* (Baltimore: Genealogical Publishing, 2002).

25. Penelope Christensen, *Parishes and Registration Districts in England and Wales* (Toronto: Heritage Productions, 2001).

26. Milner and Jones, *A Genealogist's Guide to Discovering Your English Ancestors*, 21.

27. Patrick Pontet, *Ancestral Research in France: The Simple Guide to Tracing Your Family History through French Records* (Andover, Hampshire, Great Britain: printed by author, [1998]).

28. Noel Montgomery Elliott, *The Atlantic Canadians, 1600–1900: An Alphabetized Directory of the People, Places and Vital Dates* (Toronto: Genealogical Research Library, 1994).

29. Noel Montgomery Elliott, *The French Canadians, 1600–1900: An Alphabetized Directory of the People, Places and Vital Dates* (Toronto: Genealogical Research Library, 1992).

30. Noel Montgomery Elliott, *The Central Canadians: An Alphabetized Directory of the People, Places and Vital Dates* (Toronto: Genealogical Research Library, 1994).

31. Noel Montgomery Elliott, *The Western Canadians: An Alphabetized Directory of the People, Places and Vital Dates* (Toronto: Genealogical Research Library, 1994).

32. J. Konrad, *French and French-Canadian Family Research* (Indianapolis: Ye Olde Genealogie Shoppe, 1998).

33. Sharon Malinowski, *The Gale Encyclopedia of Native American Tribes* (Detroit: Gale, 1998).

34. John Dawson Gilmary Shea, *History of the Catholic Missions among the Indian Tribes of the United States, 1529–1854* (New York: J. P. Kennedy, 1854).

35. Vine Deloria and Raymond J. DeMallie, *Documents of American Indian Diplomacy: Treaties, Agreements, and Conventions, 1775–1979* (Norman: University of Oklahoma Press, 1999).

36. Deloris Kitchell Clem, *Tracing African American Roots* (Las Vegas, NV: Gator Publishing, 1999), 79.

37. Eric G. Grudset, *Forgotten Patriots: African American and American Indian Patriots in the Revolutionary War; A Guide to Service, Sources and Studies* (Washington, DC: National Society Daughters of the American Revolution, 2008).

38. Robert Ewell Greene, *Black Courage, 1775–1783: Documentation of Black Participation in the American Revolution* (Washington, DC: National Society Daughters of the American Revolution, 1984).

39. William H. Leckie, *The Buffalo Soldiers: A Narrative of the Black Cavalry in the West* (Norman: University of Oklahoma Press, 2003), 26, 27.

chapter seven

Putting It All Together

LET'S REVIEW WHAT WE HAVE LEARNED SO FAR. FIRST, YOU SHOULD write down everything you already know about your family, going back as far as you can. Enter names, dates, and places onto proper paper forms or into a genealogy computer program. Next, interview family members to find out what they know and look at resources you may have in your home for additional information. Then begin a search of all documents in which you might find information about your ancestors. Use census records; look at federal, state, and county records; search military, church, and cemetery records; use your local library to find printed sources; and scour the Internet for additional records. As you find information you may discover that it just doesn't sound right, or you may find conflicting information. That is where the next step comes in.

BUILDING SOLID EVIDENCE

The Board for Certification of Genealogists (BCG) has created a standard for building a credible pedigree. It is called the Genealogical Proof

Standard (GPS). There is a lot of research that can be found in books and on the Internet. Some of the conclusions, without further research, can look pretty good. You might conclude that because you found the research in a printed source, it is correct. But wait a minute—look at that research carefully. You might find that it is only partially correct. The research is only as good as the researcher. Recently I was helping a patron in the library who did not know how to begin genealogical research. A distant relative had done some research on her family but had only gone back so far. Now this woman wanted to go one step farther back. As I began to verify some of the information in order to have a more solid foundation from which to go backward in time, I found some immediate discrepancies. The woman wanted to find the father of a man who was supposedly born in Kentucky. However, this man was shown on all census records to have been born in Missouri. The man's supposed firstborn child was actually his third child. Mistakes are made every day in genealogical research. Citing your sources and making sound conclusions are the only ways you can be sure you have a solid pedigree.

I have a jigsaw puzzle that is truly a puzzle. At Christmas time we have a family tradition of putting a jigsaw puzzle on a card table and working on it as a family or with friends when they drop by. One year I picked up an inexpensive puzzle at a local pharmacy. We are going to think of this particular puzzle as a genealogical problem. We want to make the puzzle look like the picture on the box. In genealogical research we will call this defining the problem and thinking of a possible solution. As I took pieces out of the box I began my foundation or border. We always need a foundation or a plan before we begin. But I hit my first problem. I could not put all the pieces into the border. I just couldn't tell where they fit. Have you ever had that problem with your genealogy? Maybe you have too much information and are having trouble analyzing where it all fits in. My other problem was that I couldn't tell the top from the bottom and the bottom from the sides. I was very confused.

Then I came upon another problem. I began pulling pieces of blue sky out of the box. The trouble was, there was no blue, not even a hint of it, in the picture on the lid of the box. I was getting pieces that did not belong in this puzzle. This is often our genealogy problem. We find information that just doesn't belong. The GPS is a solution for that. The GPS is used when there is no direct evidence to prove a conclusion or to resolve a case where evidence conflicts. All evidence must point in the same direction—contrary data or evidence must be resolved.

The GPS is a standard of credibility. Can you proudly say that your genealogical research is free of errors? A speaker at a national genealogy conference I attended asked, "Wouldn't it be nice if we could proudly say 'I found my information on the Internet'?" Wow! That does not speak highly of this person's opinion of information found online. More and more information can be found on the Internet, and much of it is correct. But there are also sites where genealogists can post their pedigree for others to view. Very few of those sites show any citations as to where the researcher found the data. Not all genealogists are good researchers, and some will accept anything they find. A good genealogical researcher will look to the GPS as a guide to proper research no matter where it is found.

The steps in the GPS are (a) a reasonable and exhaustive search, (b) complete, clear, and accurate source citations that allow others to replicate the steps taken in research, (c) an analysis of the evidence and correlation of the evidence from each applicable source, (d) a resolution of any conflicting evidence, and (e) a soundly reasoned proof conclusion with an explanation of how the evidence led to the conclusion.[1]

The prerequisites for the GPS are an analysis and definition of the genealogical problem. You should determine what information you hope to find and review what you already know. Your pedigree chart is your road map. Your family group records are supplemental road maps. They chart your course and keep you on the right track in your genealogical research. The blank spaces on your pedigree chart or on your family unit charts are the "problems" for which you hope to find a solution.

One of my problems is finding the name of the mother of my maternal great-grandfather, Irus Homes Harvey. First, I need to review what I already know. I know that Irus was born about 1857 in Michigan, but it might also be New York. His father's name was Edmund. I have a copy of Edmund Harvey's land patent for land in Michigan in 1872. Edmund was supposedly born in New York. The name of his second wife was Elizabeth, but Elizabeth was not Irus's mother (see figure 7.1).

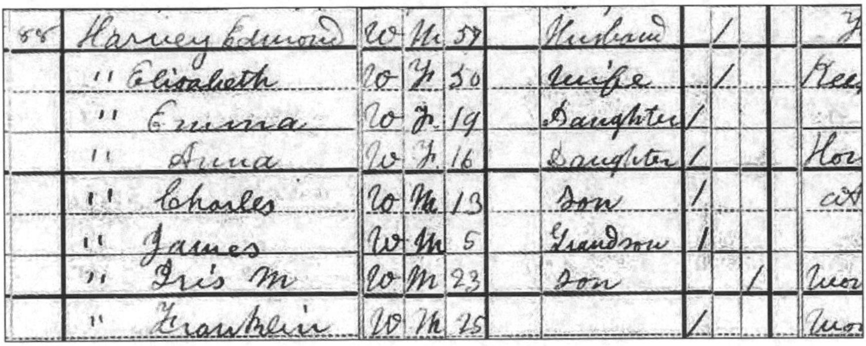

88	Harvey Edmond	W	M	57	Husband	/		
	" Elizabeth	W	F	50	wife	/		Kee
	" Emma	W	F	19	Daughter	/		
	" Anna	W	F	16	Daughter	/		Hou
	" Charles	W	M	13	Son	/		at
	" James	W	M	5	Grandson	/		
	" Iris M	W	M	23	Son		/	wor
	" Franklin	W	M	25		/		wor

Figure 7.1 The 1880 census shown here lists Edmond [sic] *Harvey (age 57), Elizabeth (wife, age 50), Emma (age 19), Anna (age 16), Charles (age 13), James (grandson, age 5), Iris* [sic] *(age 23), and Franklin (age 25). From 1880 US Census, Montcalm County, Michigan, p. 288, National Archives, microfilm publication no. T9, roll 597.*

Figure 7.2, though hard to read, shows the place of birth of each individual, then place of birth of father and place of birth of mother. Elizabeth, wife of Edmond/Edmund (line 2), was born in New York. Iris/Irus and Franklin (lines 7 and 8), sons of Edmund, are sons of a mother born in Pennsylvania. Therefore, this census indicates that Elizabeth is not the mother of Iris/Irus and Franklin. Again, my problem is "Who is the mother of Irus Harvey?"

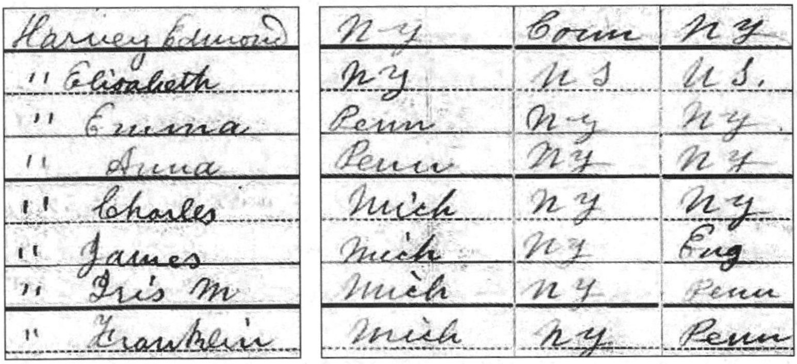

Harvey Edmond	N Y	Conn	N Y
" Elizabeth	N Y	U S	U S.
" Emma	Penn	N Y	N Y
" Anna	Penn	N Y	N Y
" Charles	Mich	N Y	N Y
" James	Mich	N Y	Eng
" Iris M	Mich	N Y	Penn
" Franklin	Mich	N Y	Penn

Figure 7.2 The 1880 census showing places of birth. From 1880 US Census, Montcalm County, Michigan, p. 288, National Archives, microfilm publication no. T9, roll 597.

Now I am ready for the next step. I have thoroughly defined my problem and reviewed what I already know. My next step is to find out what sources are available. A thorough researcher should try to find every record generated in the life of an ancestor. If there are birth records available, then you should find the birth record. If your ancestor lived from 1857 to 1923, you should find him or her on every census record from 1860 through 1920. There will be different sources depending on when your ancestor lived and where he or she lived. The *Handybook for Genealogists* and the *Red Book*, as mentioned in chapter 1, give general information on what is available for each state. However, a regional guide to research will give much more in depth information on the sources available. You should thoroughly research the area in which your ancestor lived and know what resources are available there. Then identify those sources that may be useful and may provide reliable information relevant to the problem or the solution.

After you know what sources are available, you can begin your research. Write down all of the sources you look at by keeping a log. You can create a simple log by using an Excel spreadsheet or creating a Word document. (See figure 7.3 for a Word document I created.) At the top of the sheet write the surname of the person you are researching. Below that, state the problem or research focus. Then list every book, periodical, and Internet site you look at as well as recording visits to cemeteries and courthouses. Next to each source, record the date, the information you found (or did not find), and the place you found that source—the name of the library with the call number of the book or the URL and name of the website. The benefit of keeping a log is that you will not look at the same book or Internet site more than once. There is nothing more frustrating than realizing you have already looked at a particular book previously for the same problem.

Conduct a reasonably exhaustive search. Look at every source imaginable. Think about your ancestor's life or the locale in which he or she lived. Determine the laws that were in place for record keeping. Check history books or websites to determine if a war was taking place during your ancestor's life. Look at research guides to determine what records are available. Look at every record that your ancestor could have generated in his or her lifetime. By using many sources you eliminate the possibility of a too-hasty conclusion.

Learn how to abstract and transcribe if you don't already know how. Abstracting records gleans the important data in a document. In abstracting you are recording the "who, what, when, where, why, and

SURNAME_____

RESEARCH LOG

SEARCH FOCUS/RESEARCH PROBLEM

Date	Repository/Call Number or Internet URL	Title or Website Name	Findings

Figure 7.3 Word document for recording research sources.

how" of the document. You should abstract all names, places, and events you find in the document. When you are transcribing, you record exactly, word for word, what you see written. Transcribing is especially beneficial when a document is too fragile to photocopy or no photocopier is available. Christine Rose, a professional genealogist, author, and lecturer, is one of the best abstracters in the business. In the following references, look at the sections on transcribing and abstracting.

- Rose, Christine. *The Complete Idiot's Guide to Genealogy*. 2nd ed. Indianapolis: Alpha Books, 2005.
- Rose, Christine. *Courthouse Research for Family Historians: Your Guide to Genealogical Treasures*. San Jose, CA: CR Publications, 2004.

While you are researching you must create clear, complete, and accurate source citations. Where did you find this information? How do you know this is true? An excellent book entitled *Evidence Explained: Citing History Sources from Artifacts to Cyberspace*[2] by Elizabeth Shown Mills explains everything you need to know about citing a source. Citing your sources allows others to replicate your steps and evaluate the quality of your research.

You will be making conclusions based on the information or evidence you find. You must analyze the evidence from each source to ensure that the conclusion reflects the evidence. Evaluation leads to additional sources or facts you may want to research. The evidence you find will be either direct or indirect. Let's say we are looking for the parents of James Smith. His birth certificate states that his parents are John and Mary Smith. That is direct evidence. What if there is no birth certificate for James? Let's say you find that James Smith has a brother named Ethan, and you find documentation that Ethan Smith is the son of John and Mary Smith. Indirectly you have linked James to John and Mary. Just make sure your assumption is sound.

The evidence will also be either primary or secondary and original or derivative. A death certificate has both primary and secondary evidence. Primary information is taken at the time of the event (name, death date, location, cause of death) and is provided by the attending physician. The secondary evidence on the record is the age, birth date, birth location, and parents' names. The informant for this information is usually someone who was not present at the time of birth, unless the informant is the mother or father. Each segment must be reviewed and analyzed for accuracy. More information is usually needed to back up secondary evidence. An original piece of evidence is the exact document that has not been copied or altered. A derivative document is a photocopy. A derivative is given less weight than the original but is still considered primary evidence if the original was primary evidence. You should build a case for accuracy with direct evidence or a combination of direct and indirect evidence. If there is no direct evidence, indirect evidence may be used. The important things to remember in building a case for accuracy are that you must do an exhaustive search and that all evidence must point in the same direction. If there is any opposing evidence, it must be researched and either negated or explained.

What should you do if the evidence conflicts? Conflicting evidence, even when it is primary evidence, must be resolved by carefully considering each piece or segment of the document. The search must be exhaustive. When was the document created? Who created the document? Why was it created? A document created close in time to an event usually carries more weight. Assess the information's quality regarding whether or not it can be evidence. For example, microfilm copies and photocopies carry more weight than transcripts or abstracts, and a photo of a tombstone carries more weight than notes taken from inscriptions. Evaluate every piece of information you have.

You should also put your ancestors into the correct historical setting. Using a timeline helps a great deal. We discussed timelines in chapter 1. A timeline helps determine if an event could have happened in the way it is presented. If you feel your ancestor fought in the Revolutionary War, look at the timeline of the war and a timeline of your ancestor's life and compare the two. If you see that your ancestor was 9 years old at the end of the war, there is not a high probability that your information is accurate. The birth date you have for this ancestor may be wrong, or his supposed participation may be wrong. You want an honest portrayal of individuals, their relationships, their records, and all related data.

What do you do if you have conflicting evidence? You must resolve it. There must be soundly reasoned proof that explains how the evidence led to a conclusion. Create another document in Excel or Word and compile your data in a logical sequence with all the source citations and repositories searched. Outline the negative and positive research results and analyze the information. Evaluate the results of the search and determine whether you should continue the plan, modify it, or develop a new plan. It may sound like a lot of work, but genealogical research is a constant process of gathering, compiling, and evaluating evidence. The GPS is considered the minimum in genealogy research.

Here is a selected list of articles by authors who have used the GPS successfully.

- Bockstruck, Lloyd D. "Who Was Mary, the Wife of George Archer?" *Virginia Genealogist* 43 (January–March 1999): 42–47.
- Haines, Jeffrey L. "Under a Spreading Chestnut Tree: Parents for the Village Blacksmith, Nathaniel F. Sullivan of North Carolina." *National Genealogical Society Quarterly* 89 (March 2001): 16–28.
- Jones, Thomas W. "A Conceptual Model of Genealogical Evidence: Linkage between Present-Day Sources and Past Facts." *National Genealogical Society Quarterly* 86 (March 1998): 5–18.
- Jones, Thomas W. "Merging Identities Properly: Jonathan Tucker Demonstrates the Technique." *National Genealogical Society Quarterly* 88 (June 2000): 111–121.

- Leary, Helen F. M. "Resolving Conflicts in Direct Evidence: Identity and Vital Dates of Mary Kittrell." *National Genealogical Society Quarterly* 87 (September 1999): 199–205.

The following is a selected list of resources for learning more about the GPS.

Board for Certification of Genealogists. *The BCG Genealogical Standards Manual.* Orem, UT: Ancestry Publishing, 2000.
- Christensen, Penelope Janet. *How Do I Prove It?* Toronto: Heritage Productions, 2000.
- Jones, Thomas W. "What Is the Standard of Proof in Genealogy?" *2002 NGS Conference in the States: Milwaukee.* Richmond, VA: National Genealogical Society, 2002, 35–38.
- Leary, Helen F. M. "In Conclusion . . ." *2002 NGS Conference in the States: Milwaukee.* Richmond, VA: National Genealogical Society, 2002, 457–460.
- Leary, Helen F. M. "Standards for Success." *2002 NGS Conference in the States: Milwaukee.* Richmond, VA: National Genealogical Society, 2002, 1–4.
- Little, Barbara Vines. "Correlating Evidence." *2002 NGS Conference in the States: Milwaukee.* Richmond, VA: National Genealogical Society, 2002, 361–364.
- Meriman, Brenda Dougall. *About Genealogical Standards of Evidence: A Guide for Genealogists.* Toronto: Ontario Genealogical Society, 1997.
- Rose, Christine. *Genealogical Proof Standard: Building a Solid Case.* San Jose, CA: Rose Family Association, 2001.
- Rose, Christine. "Which Source Is Right?" *2002 NGS Conference in the States: Milwaukee.* Richmond, VA: National Genealogical Society, 2002, 306–309.

IT'S TIME TO SHARE

Now that you have created a high-quality, sound family history, it is time to share it. Decide who your audience will be. Are you writing this for your immediate family, your extended family, or a wider audience? Next, decide what format this sharing might take. You can share your findings in a periodical. Many county genealogical societies gladly share the narrative findings of its members. Perhaps you want to write a book. How much expense do you want to put into it? You can publish it inexpensively or create a high-quality book printed by a professional printing company. The important thing to remember is that you will be publishing it yourself. Some printing companies will help you sell your book, but the immediate outlay in printing costs will come out of your pocket. You can also publish your findings on the Internet. You can find a social networking site or publish your findings on Ancestry .com or RootsWeb.

You will need to decide the scope of your project. Do you want to start your book with the first immigrant into this country and then show all generations descending from the first? That is a massive undertaking, but it can be done. Perhaps you will want to start with your grandparents and only include the first couple of generations of ancestors. It is totally up to you. I completed one book about my family. It had a limited audience—my children, my brothers and their children, and my sister. It is called *Israelson: Norway to America*. It tells the tale of my great-grandfather, Israel Israelson, who came to America from Norway in either 1873 or 1874. I included information on the political conditions in Norway at the time of his emigration that I found in a book about Norway's history to show why he might have emigrated from Norway. The book went from Israel down to his great-grandchildren. I did not include birth dates for those currently living in a desire to keep them safe from identity theft, should the book get into the wrong hands.

Putting a timeline into your book, as well as a pedigree chart, will help readers understand who the people in the book are, when and where they lived, and how they relate to each other. Creating an outline for your book will provide a road map for you to follow in developing an easily understood narrative. You might add to, delete from, or modify your outline as you go along, but the outline will help you keep on track. Interview family members and ask about recent births. Ask for stories you may include in your book, and find out if family members have any documents you could scan and include. Do not wait until you consider your research "finished." There will always be one more document or piece of information to find. If you find information after the book has been published, and believe me you will, you can publish an addendum or a second volume of the book.

Investigate the social history of the era and the places where your ancestors lived. Include any historical events that may have impacted their lives. I included the following in my book:

> One of the contributing factors in the change of life for those in agricultural communities was a law which was passed in 1854 which gave all children equal inheritance in the land. This led to smaller farms which made making a living at farming increasingly difficult.
>
> In 1873, Norway adopted a gold standard. Between the years 1873 and 1896 prices spiraled downward because of the monetary change. During the 1870s the government did some extensive railroad building. Loans from England financed the venture but increased the national debt. On the positive side, it provided credit abroad, stimulated shipping, reduced unemployment, and opened up new trade districts. Perhaps if Israel had stayed in Norway he would have found the economic conditions improving.[3]

Although I did not know why Israel immigrated to the United States, I found some historical facts that may indicate a reason.

Write your family history as though you were telling a story. There is a temptation on the part of genealogists to include pedigree charts and Ahnentafel lists and exclude a lot of narrative. The research process may have been exciting to you, but it will quickly put your reader to sleep. So make sure your book has a beginning, a middle, and an end. As you begin the writing process, there will probably be one or two ancestors who will benefit from the bulk of the narrative. There are always those ancestors for whom you found a lot of data and social history and those ancestors who fascinated you as you were researching. It is alright to give some of your ancestors more space than others. Be considerate about what you write. Do not include birth information on family members still living. Refrain from moralizing or including embarrassing facts. Be prepared for the response you will get from other family members. As soon as your book is published, your family will begin advising you about what you should have included, will give you corrections to names, dates, and spellings, and will come forward with the stories they would not tell you before you published your book. It happens every time. My library receives many donations of family histories. Many of them include errata sheets. You will never get your book completely perfect, but that is okay. If you waited until it was perfect, you would never complete your book.

As I mentioned previously, there are several ways you can publish your genealogy. The easiest way is to print copies from your word processing program or to take the manuscript to a local print shop and have it comb bound. If you are giving away copies, this is the cheapest way to go. If you want a professional-looking book, use a reputable printing company that will print and bind your book. This approach is definitely more expensive, but it creates a nicer product. Many of these companies will also help you prepare your manuscript for publication. I hesitate to list the publishers of which I am aware because they are so numerous and I do not want to endorse anyone. Cyndi's List has a list of publishers for you to explore (www.cyndislist.com/writing/publishers).

The following books will help you in your pursuit of writing your family history.

- Barnes, Donald R. *Write It Right: A Manual for Writing Family Histories and Genealogies*. 2nd ed. Ocala, FL: Lyon Press, 1988.
- Drake, Paul. *You Ought to Write All That Down: A Guide to Organizing and Writing Genealogical Narrative*. Bowie, MD: Heritage Books, 1996.
- Hatcher, Patricia Law. *Producing a Quality Family History*. Salt Lake City, UT: Ancestry, 1996.
- *How to Write and Publish Your Family Book*. Franklin, NC: Genealogy Publishing Service, 1999.
- Morgan, George G. *How to Do Everything with Your Genealogy*. New York: McGraw-Hill/Osborne, 2004.
- Zousmer, Steve. *You Don't Have to Be Famous: How to Write Your Life Story*. Cincinnati, OH: Writer's Digest Books, 2007.

I hope you now have the incentive to put what you have learned into practice. There are many sources available to researchers today. Books have been published on every possible topic of genealogical research.

Records have been digitized, transcribed, indexed, and made available in print and on the Internet. Genealogical information on the Internet is exploding with new information posted every day. It can be overwhelming so be sure to focus on one genealogy problem at a time. Keep your pedigree chart and family unit charts close at hand. They are your road maps and will keep you on the right path to finding information about your family.

You are not alone in this pursuit. Seek out a genealogical society in your county or state. At the society's meetings you will learn from interesting speakers and will be able to talk to people whose eyes won't glaze over when they hear the "G" word. Look for genealogy forums and message boards on the Internet. RootsWeb (www.rootsweb.ancestry.com) has both message boards and mailing lists. A message board is an open forum in which anyone can participate. Click on the Message Boards tab. There are surname, locality, and topical boards. You can search for specific content or for a specific board. You can type in a surname for which you are searching and find messages, and answers, from people researching that same name. Perhaps you want to know more about research in Lithuania. You can find a message board on that locality. Maybe you would like more information about searching military records. There is a message board on that topic as well. Mailing lists on RootsWeb are similar to message boards but you must subscribe. When joining a list you enter your e-mail address. Then every time someone posts a query or an answer to a query, it will be sent to your e-mail address. Cyndi's List has links to mailing lists at www.cyndislist.com/mailing-lists.

Along the ancestor-hunting trail you may find new family members. My interest in genealogy, as I mentioned in the introduction to this book, began with Fred Williams. He was the grandfather my mother-in-law, Mary, never met. When I excitedly phoned her after finding Fred on the 1870 census living with his grandparents, Mary became excited as well. In fact, she became an avid genealogist. She began writing for marriage certificates, death records, and birth certificates. These were the days before the computer played such an active part in genealogical research. Through her research of Fred's ancestry, she found a grandson of the "other" Fred (Frederick) Williams. Fred's father, Warren Williams, had an earlier family in Massachusetts. His first marriage resulted in a son, Frederick. A divorce record has never been found for that first marriage, and evidence suggests there never was one. So, the granddaughter of Fred met the grandson of Frederick and along the way they met the granddaughter of Fred's (Fred the second's) sister. The three, in turn, met many other Williams family members on their path to finding the first Williams in their line who came to America. My mother-in-law, who was raised an only child, discovered a large family with whom she enjoyed sharing genealogy until her untimely death in 1992. Genealogy is not just names and dates. It is people and relationships and the joy of family.

Happy hunting and enjoy the trip!

NOTES

1. Board for Certification of Genealogists. *The BCG Genealogical Standards Manual* (Orem, UT: Ancestry Publishing, 2000), 1.
2. Elizabeth Shown Mills, *Evidence Explained: Citing History Sources from Artifacts to Cyberspace* (Baltimore: Genealogical Publishing, 2007).
3. This information, which I included in my book, came from *A History of Norway* by Karen Larsen (New York: Princeton University Press, 1950).

index

f denotes figures